THE POWER OF PRAYER

THE POWER OF PRAYER

*

Illustrated in the Wonderful Displays of Divine Grace at the Fulton Street and Other Meetings in New York and Elsewhere, in 1857 and 1858

*

SAMUEL I. PRIME

THE BANNER OF TRUTH TRUST

THE BANNER OF TRUTH TRUST
3 Murrayfield Road, Edinburgh EH12 6EL
PO Box 621, Carlisle, Pennsylvania 17013, USA

*

© The Banner of Truth Trust 1991
First published 1859
First Banner of Truth edition 1991
ISBN 0 85151 602 5

*

Typeset in 10½/12pt Linotron Plantin
At The Spartan Press Ltd, Lymington, Hants
Printed and bound in Great Britain by
The Bath Press Ltd,
Avon

Contents

PUBLISHERS' PREFACE................................... xi
PREFACE xiii

CHAPTER 1

The Work proposed – The Commercial Revulsion – No extraordinary Means – Prayer, and Prayer only – The Story – The Future... 1

CHAPTER 2

How the Revival began, and where – A lone Man on his Knees – The first Prayer – Who was he? – What has he done? – The first Thought of a Daily Prayer-meeting – The first Meeting – Increasing Interest – Christ loved and honored – Other Meetings established – Effect on the Public Mind – Faith in Special Cases – Preaching – The Work extending – The Religious and Secular Press – It spreads over the whole Land 5

CHAPTER 3

Features of the Work – Ways and Means – Enthusiasm – Catholicity of Feeling and Action – The Reformed Dutch Church – Union, a Type – Influence of Laymen – The Ministry aided and encouraged 30

CHAPTER 4

Preparation – Means following certain Results – Remarkable

[v]

Coincidences – Revivals at Sea – Convention at Pittsburg – Day of Fasting and Prayer – Convention at Cincinnati – Visitation of Families – General Influence of the Revival on the Church 35

CHAPTER 5

One Prayer-Meeting – The House and Rooms – The Business in Hand – Requests for Prayer – News abroad – The President – From Philadelphia – The Son and Mother – An Answer – Three Sisters – Six Children........................ 40

CHAPTER 6

An Infidel Lawyer's Conviction and Conversion............ 49

CHAPTER 7

Surprising Grace – A Successful Merchant – The Magdalens – The Saviour Waiting – A young Sailor – Danger of Delay... 61

CHAPTER 8

Remarkable Answers to Prayer – The Four Great Revivals – Power of Prayer – 'My Husband Saved' – Twenty Special Cases Selected – A Brother-in-law – A Drunkard Saved... 68

CHAPTER 9

Prayer-meeting at 'Hell Corner' – An Invitation on the Mississippi – A Daughter converted and driven out of her Father's House – The whole Family converted – Hungry Children ask a Blessing – An only Son – The Camp-meeting Convert.. 76

CHAPTER 10

Christ found at Home – The Man who found Peace in the Street 84

The New York Revival of 1858

CHAPTER 11

How a Revival began – Among the Mountains – Astonishing Answers – A Telegram to a Dying Man – A young Man's Testimony – The Prodigal – A repentant Student converted in a Car – A Brother saved – Another Conversion in a Car – Revivals multiplied by the Fulton street Prayer-meeting ... 91

CHAPTER 12

Individual Responsibility – Personal Efforts – Souls seeking Souls – A ten Years' pursuit of an Infidel and the Result – A Pledge Signed Twenty-six Times – Two Widows – An anxious Mother – A Brother-in-law – The Prodigal Son – A City Islander – The Happy Wife – Father and Daughter .. 100

CHAPTER 13

The Work among the Children – Randall's Island – The Romanist's Child, Mary – A dying Sunday School Scholar – Prayers for a Child – Conversions in a Public School – Columbus, Toledo and Geneva – Father and Children – Sabbath School Class and Teacher – The little Girl whose Heart would Sing 109

CHAPTER 14

The Revival of Religion among Men of Business – Laws of Trade – Conscience – A Hardware Merchant and his Customer – A Merchant and his Clerk – The Salesman and his Assistant – Conscience Awakened – Test of the Revival ... 119

CHAPTER 15

A Man of Pleasure – Goes to the Prayer-meeting – Is sorry for it – Thinks more of it – Reflects – His Mother's Prayers – Her Bible – He returns from Newport – In the Prayer-meeting again – Deep distress of Mind – Despair – Begs others to pray for him – Peace – Joy – Praise 126

CHAPTER 16

A Pastor's Sketch – An anxious Inquirer – Complains of a want of Feeling – Encouraged to Pray – Relapses and Returns – Instructed in the Nature of Faith – Relief not the thing to seek – Christ's Ability to save – A Glimmer of Light – The Sun of Righteousness 134

CHAPTER 17

A Roman Catholic Experience – Out of Employment – Reads in the 'Herald' of the Prayer-meetings – Attends – Is astonished – Power of Prayer – Contrasted with the Mass – His Deep Convictions – Fascinated – Reveals his State – Light Breaks in – His Wife follows him to Christ 142

CHAPTER 18

The Work among the Seamen – Many Languages spoken – Prayers better than Rum – An Irish Catholic – An aged Mariner – A sinking Vessel saved in the midst of prayer – 'The North Carolina' – 'The Wabash' – A Swedish Sailor at the Wheel – The awful Scene on 'The Austria', and singular coincidence – Six Sea Captains converted – Another Captain saved – His remarkable Experience 148

CHAPTER 19

Influence of the Revival on Crime and Criminals – Orville Gardner – A fast Man – Labors among the Poor – The City Missionaries – Grace and Grace only – A Mother and two Children – Father and Son – The Widow's Joy – Relatives and Friends 172

The New York Revival of 1858

CHAPTER 20

Wonderful Answers to Prayer – Two Children of a Widow – A Servant Girl – Nine Men in the Market – Seven praying Wives – Never Give Up – A German Boy – The Prayer-Meeting among the Indians – Answers to Prayer in Natchez 181

CHAPTER 21

Prayer-meeting at Aunt Betsy's – Power of Prayer remarkably Illustrated – A Visit to the Sing-Sing Prison – The Contrast – Luther and Melanchthon – Examples of Prevailing Prayer – The Church awaking – Understanding the Subject – A Mother's Faith – A Revival predicted 189

CHAPTER 22

Means of Grace – Preaching the Word – Revival Tracts – Private Efforts – Call to Prayer by Rev J. C. Ryle – Rev Dr Guthrie of Edinburgh, on Perseverance in Prayer – Rev Dr J. W. Alexander's Tracts: 'The Revival and its Lessons', – 'Pray for the Spirit' – Power of the Press 201

CHAPTER 23

Prayers for our Children sure to be Answered – Rev H. W. Smuller's Thoughts – The Promises of God – The Vials with Prayers of the Saints – Visions of John – Experience of Daniel – Long Delay – The Old Ladies' Meeting – Mrs F and her Soldier Boy – Have Faith in God 215

CHAPTER 24

The Book of Requests – Written with Tears – Desire – Affection – Conviction of Sin – Sorrow – Faith – Conversa-

[ix]

tions with the Drawer – The Converted gathered into the Kingdom 228

CHAPTER 25

A Year of Prayer – Review of the Meetings – Anniversary of Fulton street Meeting – Extraordinary Case of Awakening at that Meeting – Murder and Suicide prevented – The Sinner saved 235

CHAPTER 26

Prayer Shown to be Efficacious 244

INDEX 261

Preface to the Present Reprint

For the churches of the English-speaking world, at least, the revival period of 1857–59 warrants the title of 'the event of the century'. Beginning quietly and unexpectedly, it profoundly affected both sides of the Atlantic – restoring conviction of sin, recovering heart-felt praise, filling churches, transforming public morality and raising a new generation of Christian workers and missionaries.

Nowhere was the suddenness of the change more marked than in the city of New York and it was with reference to New York that the literature published at the time was most extensive. Along with the present volume, it included: *The Noon Prayer Meeting*, T. W. Chambers (Board of Publication of the Protestant Dutch Church, New York, 1858); *The New York Pulpit in the Revival of 1858, A Memorial Volume of Sermons* (Sheldon, Blakeman and Company, New York, 1858); *The Revival and Its Lessons*, J. W. Alexander (Anson D. F. Randolph, New York, 1859); and *Narratives of Remarkable Conversions and Revival Incidents* (Derby and Jackson, New York, 1859).

Of these titles, Dr Prime's *The Power of Prayer* (Sheldon, Blakeman and Company, New York, 1859) appears to have had the most extensive circulation. Written hurriedly in the midst of the events which it describes, it lacks the perspective which the passing of time would have brought and tells us little of what was happening elsewhere. Nor does the author give attention to the theology of revival – a subject that had already caused considerable controversy and upon which Ebenezer Porter's *Letters on the Religious Revivals which Prevailed about the Beginning of the Present Century* (Congregational Board of Publication, Boston, 1858) is a more valuable work. But Prime, with the emotion of a witness beholding present and marvellous events, concentrates on the *first* lesson in any true revival. He knows no explanation for the mighty change apart from the hand of God. To quote J. W. Alexander who was also a witness: 'The work of grace, in which we rejoice, was not the result of any human project, concerted arrangement, or prescribed plan. It was not an excitement foreseen, predicted, and made to order . . . No man pretends ever to have seen the like.' Had widespread, organized prayer been the precursor of the revival, prayer might have been treated as Alexander and other writers say, 'The foregoing season was one of remarkable aridity and dearth; so that multitudes of young Christians had never seen what is called a revival.' It was the grace of God which restored the *power* of prayer.

Samuel Irenaeus Prime was born in 1812 and studied at William's College and Princeton Theological Seminary before becoming a minister in the Presbyterian Church in 1834. The ill-health which accompanied his pastoral labours led him to concentrate upon a written ministry and from 1840 until his death in 1885 he was the Editor of the influential *New York Observer*. *The Power of Prayer* was his most popular book, attaining, it is said, a circulation of more than 175,000 copies, with reprints in Europe, Africa and Asia.

For the 'rediscovery' of this volume we are indebted to Dr Martyn Lloyd-Jones and its republication fulfils a desire he often expressed before his death in March 1981.

THE PUBLISHERS, JUNE 1991

Preface

A few short weeks ago, the Publisher solicited my aid in preparing this volume for the press. The idea was exciting. The work would be one of love and faith. To gather into a book the wonderful facts which had transpired around us for a year past; to trace the rise and progress of the great religious movement that marks the age and the land in which we live; to record the remarkable answers to prayer which are daily mentioned to the praise of divine grace; to recount the striking cases of conversion at meetings, in church, at home, and in the street; to tell of prayer in shops, stores and markets; thrilling religious experiences among all classes of people – lawyers, merchants, seamen, children; great sinners converted; drunkards reclaimed; wives obtaining the conversion of their husbands; children seeking and finding the conversion of their parents, and parents praying for and asking others to pray for their children, and obtaining gracious answers; poor prodigals brought back in answer to prayer; specific individuals prayed for and all converted; and scores of astonishing, tender and delightful facts, to show the POWER OF PRAYER! – this was what the Publisher desired me to do, and my heart responded *yes*, before I had time to estimate the labor and care it would require to make a record in any measure commensurate with the greatness and glory of the theme. But so much impressed was I with the importance of the undertaking, and of its present and future value to the church, that I resolved, with dependence on the help of him who has all the glory of this revival, that I would not decline the work which was urged upon me.

The second, third and fourth chapters of this book, comprising the historical account of the prayer-meetings, were written by the Rev L. G. Bingham, who has been a constant attendant upon them from their inception. He has also prepared expressly for my use the reports of the incidents here recorded, and many of them, intensely interesting, thrilling and wonderful, have *never been published before*. Without the aid of Mr Bingham, this volume could not have been prepared, as many of the facts were obtained by his private interviews with the persons, whose extraordinary religious experiences are here portrayed.

I am under great obligations to my friends, Rev Dr Plumer and the Rev Dr Murray, for the powerful and graphic chapters which they have contributed to these pages. The facts they have embodied, and the call to prayer which they utter, must produce a deep impression on every devout reader.

Never was my own mind so filled with AWE, as it has been while grouping these facts into consecutive pages and chapters. Never was the connection between prayer and the answer, the relation of the Asker to the Giver, so revealed to me as in the prosecution of this work. Here I find it confirmed by scores of facts and examples, not in history, sacred or secular; not traditionary or second-hand, but facts of present occurrence, in the midst of this noisy, busy, restless, worldly city; facts beyond all doubt or cavil, that the Lord will give his praying people whatsoever they ask in faith! We raise no question about miracles. We know what things are agreeable to God's will, and what submission requires. Here is the written proof that God will answer prayer, and no religious man can enter into the spirit of these prayer-meetings, or read the accounts here presented, without being overshadowed with the conviction that it is a solemn as well as a blessed privilege to pray; that God is willing to give his Spirit to them who ask him; and that believing PRAYER IS SURE to be ANSWERED.

It must be that these pages will be greatly useful in stimulating the people of God to prayer. It must be that this volume will be a monument to the glory of him who converts our children and neighbors, and revives our churches with the sun and rain of his grace. It must be that pastors will rehearse these facts in the hearing of multitudes, who will rejoice in the Lord, and give thanks for such manifestations of his power.

The most of these facts are given in the form of reports of the daily meetings. This secures for the volume more of the interest of the actual meeting than would attach to a separate narrative. We give them as they were given by the lips of those who saw or heard what the Lord has done in answer to prayer.

I am well aware that the volume is far from being as complete and perfect as it should be. To make it more so, let all those who read it send me other facts to illustrate the power of prayer, other exhibitions of the grace of God in the conversion of sinners, and they will be added to these records or embodied in a future history of this work of the Spirit, which we trust has only just begun.

With no other desire than to honor God, and encourage his people to pray, we send out this book, with the fervent prayer that others may find at least as much enjoyment in its perusal as the author has found in compiling it for the press.

NEW YORK, *November 27th*, 1858.

Chapter 1

The Work proposed – The Commercial Revulsion – No extraordinary Means – Prayer, and Prayer only – The Story – The Future.

The pen of an angel might well be employed to record the wonderful works of God in the city of New York, during the years 1857–8.

The history will be a memorial of divine grace. In all future time it will proclaim the readiness of the Lord God Almighty to hear and answer prayer; of the Holy Spirit, to descend and convert sinners; of Jesus Christ, to forgive and save.

TO GOD THE FATHER, GOD THE SON, AND GOD THE HOLY GHOST, BE ALL THE PRAISE!

The autumn of 1857 was signalized by a sudden and fearful convulsion in the commercial world. That calamity was so speedily followed by the reports of revivals of religion and remarkable displays of divine grace, that it has been a widely received opinion, that the two events stand related to one another, as cause and effect. In the day of adversity, men consider. When the hand of God is suddenly laid upon city and country, the sources of prosperity dried up, fortunes taking to themselves wings; houses, venerable for years, integrity, and success, tumbling into ruins; and names, never tarnished by suspicion, becoming less than nothing in general bankruptcy, it is natural to believe that men will look away from themselves, and say, 'Verily there is a God, who reigns.' As in the time of an earthquake, or wreck at sea, men's hearts failing them for fear, they will cry to him who rides upon the whirlwind, so it was believed that the financial storm had driven men to pray. And it doubtless did. Never was a commercial crisis so inexplicable under the laws of trade. It was acknowledged to be a judgment. The justice of God was confessed in arresting men in recklessness, extravagance and folly. Thousands were thrown out of business, and, in their want of something else to do, assembled in meetings for prayer. *But these meetings had been already established.* The Spirit of God had been manifest in the midst of them. Before the commercial revulsion, the city and the country had been absorbed in the pursuit of pleasure and gain. Men were making haste to be rich, and to enjoy their riches. Recklessness of expenditure, extravagance in living, display in furniture, equipage, and dress, had attained a height unexampled in the previous social history of our country, and utterly inconsistent with the simplicity and virtue of our fathers. These signs of prosperity had filled the minds of good men with apprehension and alarm before the panic seized the heart of the world. Christians who had kept free from the spirit of speculation and the mania for making money had trembled for the future of a people so absorbed in the material, as to be oblivious of the spiritual and eternal. These pious people had been gathering in meetings for prayer, before the convulsion began. Now, indeed, the meetings received large accessions of numbers in attendance, and a new infusion of life from above. More meetings were established, and larger numbers attended. The prayer-meeting became one of the institutions of the city. Christians in distant parts of the country heard of them. They prayed for the prayer-meetings. When they

The New York Revival of 1858

visited the city, the prayer-meeting was the place to which they resorted. The museum or theatre had no such attractions. Returning, they set up similar meetings at home. The Spirit followed, and the same displays of grace were seen in other cities, and in the country, that were so marvellous in New York. So the work spread, until the year has become remarkable in the history of the church.

This revival is to be remembered through all coming ages as simply an answer to prayer.

We must look behind all means, and acknowledge that this is the Lord's doing. He had said that he would be inquired of by the house of Israel, and when they called, the Lord answered and heard. This is to be the standing testimony which the revival will bear forever in the history of religion. It is this fact which is to make this volume a memorial of the truth and goodness of God in after years. The design of its preparation is to exhibit the faithfulness of God to his promises, and his willingness to give his Holy Spirit to them that ask him. It is to encourage and stimulate Christians in all places, everywhere, to seek the same glorious gifts of grace for themselves and perishing sinners around them. Pastors will read it, and communicate its wondrous records to their flocks. Thousands of the humble people of God, who know the way to the mercy seat, will here find their faith strengthened when they come to pray. In tens of thousands of meetings for prayer, the delightful stories in this book will be rehearsed amid the joyful tears of the people of God, while they will pray that such great things may be seen and done among them also.

Thus the revival is to be extended and perpetuated. Wherever the gospel is preached – this is to be told as a triumph of its love and power. Other trophies of the victorious grace of God are to be brought in, and their records too are to be made and published to the glory of

THE POWER OF PRAYER

Zion's King, and the work is to go on from conquering to conquest, until the earth is filled with the knowledge of the Lord as the waters fill the sea. This volume may be but the precursor of another at the close of 1859, in which the history of the great American revival will be continued.

We will now proceed to give an authentic account of the rise and progress of the work of grace in the city of New York. In the recital of the facts, the foregoing statements will be more than confirmed, and a record will be made, which will compel the reader to give glory to God. The object and tendency of the history are to illustrate the POWER of PRAYER. Every page of this book is a proof that the believer has power with God.

Chapter 2

How the Revival began, and where – A lone Man on his Knees – The first Prayer – Who was he? – What has he done? – The first Thought of a Daily Prayer-meeting – The first Meeting – Increasing Interest – Christ loved and honored – Other Meetings established – Effect on the Public Mind – Faith in Special Cases – Preaching – The Work extending – The Religious and Secular Press – It spreads over the whole Land.

In the upper lecture-room of the 'Old North Dutch Church', in Fulton Street, New York, a solitary man was kneeling upon the floor, engaged in earnest, importunate prayer. He was a man who lived very much in the lives of others; lived almost wholly for others. He had no wife or children – but there were thousands with their husbands and fathers, without God and hope in the world; and these thousands were going to the gates of eternal death. He had surveyed all the lower wards of the city as a lay-missionary of the Old Church, and he longed to do something for their salvation. He knew he could do many things – he could take tracts in his hand, any and every day, and distribute them. He could preach the gospel from door to door. All this he had done. To reach these perishing thousands, he needed a thousand lives. Could not something more effectual be done? So, day after day, and many times a day, this man was on his knees, and his constant prayer was 'Lord, *what* wilt thou have me to *do*?' The oftener he prays, the more earnest he becomes. He pleads with God to show him *what* to do, and *how* to do it.

A vast responsibility had been thrown upon him, of *caring* for the spiritual welfare of the neglected thousands in these lower wards. He had been appointed to this work without being trammelled by any specific instructions by the authorities of the church, being left to act at his own discretion in much of his labor. The prayer was continually in his mind and in his heart, 'Lord, *what – what* wilt thou have me to *do*?' He prayed for some way to be opened to bring the claims of religion to bear upon the hearts and minds of these perishing multitudes. The more he prayed the more encouraged he was in the joyful expectation that God would show him the way, through which hundreds and thousands might be influenced on the subject of religion. But though he prayed and believed, he had not the remotest idea of the methods of God's grace which were about to be employed. The more he prayed, however, the more confident he became that God would show him *what* he would have him do.

He had been earnestly seeking God's blessing and aid and guidance in the work which was before him. He had earnestly sought to be directed and instructed; and that he might be willing to follow the teachings of God's Spirit, whatever they might be. He rose from his knees – inspired with courage and hope, derived from above.

Shall we describe this man? His age is not far from forty years. He is tall, well made, with a remarkably pleasant, benevolent face; affectionate in his disposition and manner, possessed of indomitable energy and perseverance, having good musical attainments; gifted in prayer and exhortation to a remarkable degree; modest in his demeanor, ardent in his piety, sound in his judgment; having good common sense, a thorough knowledge of human nature, and those traits of character that make him a welcome guest in any house. He is intelligent, and

The New York Revival of 1858

eminently fitted for the position which he has been called to occupy, which up to the present moment he has so worthily filled.

Mr Jeremiah Calvin Lamphier was born in Coxsackie, New York. He became a resident of this city about twenty years ago, engaged in mercantile pursuits, united with the Tabernacle Church on profession of his faith in 1842, and was for eight or nine years a member of Rev Dr James W. Alexander's church. He joined the North Dutch Church in 1857, and in July 1st of the same year entered upon his work as the missionary of that church, under the direction of its consistory.

He began his labors without any plan of instructions, and was left to do all the good he could, very much in his own way, the consistory always aiding him as much as was in their power.

We have looked into this man's journal, which no human eye but our own has read, save the author's. The very first page is characteristic of the man. We copy the opening lines:

NEW YORK, *July 1st*, 1857.

'Be not weary in well doing.' – 2 Thess. 3: 13.

'I can do all things through Christ, which strengtheneth me.' – Phil. 4: 13.

'Read the fourth chapter 2d Timothy. Think I feel something of the responsibility of the work in which I have engaged. Felt a nearness to God in prayer, and my entire dependence on him from whom cometh all my strength.'

So began this man his labors, in the most neglected portion of the city of New York, the lower wards. And now for the first idea of a noonday prayer-meeting. He says:

'Going my rounds in the performance of my duty one day, as I was walking along the streets, the idea was suggested to my mind that an hour of prayer, from twelve to

THE POWER OF PRAYER

one o'clock, would be beneficial to *business men*, who usually in great numbers take that hour for rest and refreshment. The idea was to have singing, prayer, exhortation, relation of religious experience, as the case might be; that none should be required to stay the whole hour; that all should come and go as their engagements should allow or require, or their inclinations dictate. Arrangements were made, and at twelve o'clock noon, on the 23d day of September, 1857, the door of the third storey lecture-room was thrown open. At half-past twelve the step of a solitary individual was heard upon the stairs. Shortly after another, and another; then another, and last of all, another, until six made up the whole company! We had a good meeting. *The Lord was with us to bless us.*'

It will be seen that our missionary sat out the first half of the first noonday prayer-meeting alone, or rather he prayed, through the first half hour alone.

Thus, the noonday businessmen's prayer-meeting was inaugurated! It was to have new phases of interest. The old, long, cold, formal routine was to be broken up. Everything was to be arranged for the short stay of those who came. All the exercises were to be brief, pointed, and to the purpose, touching the case in hand. This idea grew out of the pressing necessity of men's engagements. They could come in and stay five minutes, or the whole hour, as they pleased. Staying five minutes, they might have an opportunity to take part, for no one was to occupy more than five minutes in remarks, or prayer.

The second meeting was held a week afterwards, on Wednesday, September 30th, when twenty persons were present. It was a precious meeting. There was much prayer, and the hearts of those present were melted within them. The next meeting was held October 7th. Speaking of this meeting, the private journal says:

'Prepared for the prayer-meeting to-day, at noon.

The New York Revival of 1858

Called to invite a number of persons to be present. Spoke to men as I met them in the street, as my custom is, if I can get their attention. *I prayed that the Lord would incline many to come to the place of prayer.* Went to the meeting at noon. Present between thirty and forty. "Bless the Lord! oh my soul, and all that is within me, bless his holy name."'

This meeting was of so animated and encouraging a character, that a meeting was appointed for the NEXT DAY, at which a large number attended; and from this day dates the businessmen's union daily prayer-meeting. The meetings were moved down to the middle lecture-room, as being more commodious. Of the meeting of the 8th of October, it is said, in this same journal:

'Attended the prayer-meeting at noon. A larger number present, and there was a spirit of reconsecration to the service of Christ, and a manifest desire to live near his cross.'

This meeting, as we learn from other sources, was one of uncommon fervency in prayer, of deep humility and self-abasement, and great desire that God would glorify himself in the outpouring of his Spirit upon them. We are not much surprised to find the following mention of the next meeting, Oct. 9th:

'Called on a number to invite them to attend the noon-day prayer-meeting. Went to the meeting at noon. A large number present. The meeting increases in interest – increases also in numbers. We had a precious time. *It was the very gate of heaven.*'

Passing on now to Oct. 13th, we find a rapid advancement in the intensity of religious feeling, as the following extract will show; this being, in every sense, a faithful and the only record which is preserved of these meetings.

'Attended the noon-day prayer-meeting, a large number present, and God's Spirit was manifestly in our midst.'

And of the next day, Oct. 14th, it is said:

THE POWER OF PRAYER

'Attended the noon-day prayer-meeting. Over one hundred present, many of them not professors of religion, but under conviction of sin, and seeking an interest in Christ; inquiring what they shall do to be saved. God grant that they find Christ precious to their souls.'

It is added: 'This is a cloudy, rainy day.'

Of the few following meetings, we find such notices as these:

'A large attendance; a good spirit pervaded the place; a great desire to be humble before God in view of past sins. I feel that God's Spirit is moving in the hearts of the people.'

And now, Oct. 23d, one month from the date of the first noon-day prayer-meeting, we have this remarkable passage:

'Called on some of the editors of the religious papers *to have them notice* the interest that is *daily* manifested in our meetings.'

Thus the great revival had actually commenced and had been in progress for some time, before any public mention had been made of it, so noiseless had been its footsteps. The religious interest at the Fulton street prayer-meeting, as it was now commonly called, had gone on increasing more and more, till its influence began to be powerfully felt abroad in different and distant portions of the city. During the first month of these meetings, many city pastors, and many laymen, belonging to the churches of New York and Brooklyn, had been into one or more of these meetings, and had been warmed by the holy fire already kindled. And as the sparks from the burning building are borne to kindle other fires, so these carried the fire to their own churches.

We come now to another portion of great interest in this work of prayer. Not only in the Fulton street meeting was prayer made, but morning prayer-meetings began to be established in different churches. The Broome street

The New York Revival of 1858

church was one of the first to open a morning prayer-meeting. Other churches followed, both in New York and Brooklyn, without any preconcert or any knowledge of each other's movements. Some time before any other was heard of, and nearly simultaneously with the Fulton street meeting, if not before, there was instituted a daily morning prayer-meeting in the Plymouth Church, Brooklyn. In a quiet and unostentatious way, others were commenced, earlier or later. In the second month of the Fulton street meetings, several morning daily prayer-meetings were in existence.

The fear of imitation held back some from moving in the matter. But more commonly there was no thought of this. The place of prayer was a most delightful resort, and the places of prayer multiplied, because men were moved to prayer. They wished to pray. They felt impelled, by some unseen power, to pray. They felt the pressure of the call to prayer. So a place of prayer was no sooner opened, than Christians flocked to it, to pour out their supplications together. Christians of both sexes, of all ages, of different denominations, without the slightest regard to denominational distinctions, came together, on one common platform of brotherhood in Christ, and in the bonds of Christian union sent up their united petitions to the throne of the heavenly giver.

The question was never asked, 'To what church does he belong?' But the question was, 'Does he belong to Christ?'

The early dawn of the revival was marked by love to Christ, love for all his people, love of *prayer*, and love of personal effort. Never in any former revival, since the days of the first Christians, was the name of Christ so *honored*, never so *often mentioned*, never so *precious* to the believer. Never was such ardent love to him expressed. Never was there so much devotedness to his service. The whole atmosphere was love. It is not strange, then, that

THE POWER OF PRAYER

those who so loved him, should love his image wherever and in whomsoever they saw it. It was a moral necessity. The union of Christians was felt. It needed no professions.

Hence there was no room for sectarian jealousies. It was felt that all Christians had a right to pray; all were commanded to pray; all ought to pray. And if all wished to pray, and pray together, who should hinder?

This union of Christians in prayer struck the unbelieving world with amazement. It was felt that this was prayer. This love of Christians for one another, and this love of Christ, this love of prayer and love of souls, this union of all in prayer, whose names were lost sight of, disarmed all opposition, so that not a man opened his mouth in opposition.

On the contrary, the conviction was conveyed to all minds that this truly is the work of God. The impenitent felt that Christians loved them; that their love of souls made them earnest. The truth now commended itself to every man's conscience in the sight of God. They felt that this was not the work of man, but the work of God. They were awed by a sense of the divine presence in the prayer-meeting, and felt that this was holy ground. Christians were very much humbled. Impenitent men saw and felt *this*. They felt that it was *awful* to trifle with the place of *prayer*; sacrilegious to doubt the spirit, the sincerity, the efficiency, or the *power of prayer*. It began to be felt that Christians obtained *answers* to prayer; that if they united to pray for any particular man's conversion, that man was sure to be converted. What made them *sure*? What made them say that 'they thought this man and that man would soon become Christians?' Because they had become the *subjects* of *prayer*. And men *prayed* in the prayer-meeting, as if they *expected* God would hear and *answer prayer*.

The New York Revival of 1858

All these convictions, combined, made almost all classes of men approachable on the subject of religion. It was not difficult to get access to their hearts. God thus prepared the way for their conviction and conversion.

We have been speaking of the beginning of the second month of union noon-day prayer-meetings. Concerning them, we find such words as the following in Mr Lamphier's journal:

'Attended the noon-day prayer-meeting. A good attendance and a good spirit prevails, for God is manifest in this movement. A blessed spirit pervades the place. Had conversations with awakened sinners. A young man arose in the meeting, and gave in his testimony to the benefit – under God – of coming to the prayer-meeting.'

It is very interesting to look, at this stage of the revival, at the character of the preaching which began to prevail, and the kind of subjects which were presented. The Holy Spirit seems to lead the minds of ministers to those portions of his word which he designs to make the fire and the hammer to break the flinty heart in pieces. He leads in this, as well as everything else which he uses as means of salvation.

Let us for a moment look at some of those passages of Scripture which were the subjects of discourses during the period of which we have been speaking, and see how remarkable they are. They are the foundation of sermons, by a great number of preachers, selected without any preconcert, and distinctly show how the minds of these ambassadors of the Lord Jesus were led. These are the texts of sermons which have never been published, but delivered during this period in the Old Dutch Church:

1 Corinthians 1: 30, 31: 'But of him are ye in Christ Jesus, who of God is made unto us wisdom, and righteousness, and sanctification, and redemption; that according as it is written, he that glorieth, let him glory in the Lord.'

1 Corinthians 10: 16: 'I speak as to wise men; judge ye what I say.'

Psalm 30: 6, 7: 'And in my prosperity I said, I shall never be moved. Lord! by thy favor thou didst make my mountain to stand strong. Thou didst hide thy face, and I was troubled.'

Psalm 17: 5: 'Hold up my goings in thy paths, that my footsteps slip not.'

Jeremiah 8: 22: 'Is there no balm in Gilead? Is there no physician there?'

Hebrews 10: 34: 'Knowing in yourselves that ye have in heaven a better and an enduring substance.'

Matthew 16: 19: 'And I will give unto thee the keys of the kingdom of heaven.'

Ephesians 4: 30: 'And grieve not the Holy Spirit of God, whereby ye are sealed unto the day of redemption.'

Titus 3: 8: '. . . to maintain good works. These things are good and profitable unto men.'

Malachi 3: 16, 17: 'Then they that feared the Lord spake often one to another; and the Lord hearkened and heard it, and a book of remembrance was written before him for them that feared the Lord and thought upon his name. And they shall be mine, saith the Lord of hosts, in that day when I make up my jewels, and I will spare them as a man spareth his own son that serveth him.'

Psalm 4: 7, 8: 'Thou hast put gladness in my heart more than in the time when their corn and their wine increased.'

1 Samuel 16: 17: 'For the Lord seeth not as man seeth: for man looketh on the outward appearance, but the Lord looketh on the heart.'

2 Corinthians 5: 20: 'Now, then, we are ambassadors for Christ. As though God did beseech you by us, we pray you in Christ's stead, be ye reconciled to God.'

Romans 8: 1: 'There is therefore no condemnation to

The New York Revival of 1858

them which are in Christ Jesus, who walk not after the flesh but after the Spirit.'

Psalm 84: 11: 'For the Lord is a sun and shield. The Lord will give grace and glory, and no good thing will he withhold from them that walk uprightly.'

Mark 3: 3: 'And he said unto the man that had the withered hand, Stand forth.'

Ephesians 5: 25: 'Christ also loved the church, and gave himself for it.'

1 Timothy 1: 11: 'According to the glorious gospel of the grace of God.'

Job 23: 3: 'Oh! that I knew where I might find him.'

Luke 19: 10: 'For the Son of man hath come to seek and to save that which was lost.'

John 10: 14: 'I am the Good Shepherd, and know my sheep, and am known of mine.'

We have taken these passages, in course, as they were recorded by a gentleman who heard the sermons preached. Being taken without arrangement, they indicate the class of truths which were felt to be appropriate to the state of things. There is something *specially noteworthy* in these passages, and anyone who will read them and reflect upon them will see the bearing they have. Doubtless there was much *prayer* connected with the preparation and preaching of these discourses. What a world of love must have been in these sermons! With what untold anxieties did these preachers strive to win sinners to Christ! We ask the reader to ponder upon these passages as a *type* of the revival, and observe that in view of that boundless love which characterizes these meetings for prayer, all those sermons were prepared and preached. The great beginning of the revival was love, and love must have been the burden of these appeals.

Before the close of the second month of the daily prayer-meeting, the two lower lecture-rooms had been thrown open, and both were filled immediately. Yet so gradually and unostentatiously had all this wide-spread religious interest arisen, that one meeting for prayer scarcely had any knowledge of what was doing in any other. The religious interest was now rapidly on the increase and was extending itself to all parts of the country. Many men of business from abroad, coming to New York on business, would enter into the noonday prayer-meetings and become deeply impressed, and go to their respective homes to tell what the Lord was doing in New York.

When we come to the history of the third month of prayer, what a change we find rapidly taking place, not only in the city, but all over the land. It was everywhere a revival of *prayer*. It was not prayer-meetings in imitation of the Fulton street meetings. Those that say so, or think so, greatly err. God was preparing his glorious way over the nation. It was the desire to *pray*. The same Power that moved to *prayer* in Fulton street, moved to prayer elsewhere. The same characteristics that marked the Fulton street meeting, marked all similar meetings. The Spirit of the Lord was poured out upon these assemblages, and it was this that made the places of prayer all over the land places of great solemnity and earnest inquiry. Men did not doubt – could not doubt – that God was moving in answer to prayer. It was this solemn conviction that silenced all opposition – that awakened the careless and stupid – that encouraged and gladened the hearts of Christians – causing a general turning to the Lord.

Such a display of love and mercy, on the part of the ever blessed Spirit, was never made before. The religious press, all over the country, heralded the glad news of what the Lord was doing in some places; thus preparing the way for what he was about to do in others. Thousands on thousands of closets bore witness to strong crying and

The New York Revival of 1858

tears before God in prayer all over the land. Thousands of waiting hearts, hearing that Jesus was passing by, begged that he would tarry long enough to look on them.

On the very first days of the present year [1858], the secular press in this city began to notice and publish the facts of this great movement to prayer. With scarcely an exception, this was done in the most respectful and approving terms. Most of the secular daily journals of this city spread abroad the intelligence of what was doing. The people demanded it, and the publication of it was a sort of necessity. The revival columns were read with the most eager interest over the whole country, and many thousands were influenced by them, who never looked into a religious paper. God's hand was in all this.

We give a few brief extracts from Mr Lamphier's private journal, to indicate the means which were used.

'A large attendance at the noonday prayer-meeting. We distributed the tract entitled "Three Words", and each one was to give it to some friend, and *ask God's special blessing upon it*'. Everything was done in prayer.

'Attended the noonday prayer-meeting. It was fully attended. The tract given out to-day was entitled "One Honest Effort". It was to be *prayed over*, and then given away – asking God to bless it on its mission, to the salvation of souls. Distributed tracts, called on several young men, and conversed with them in regard to their souls' salvation.'

'At the noonday prayer-meeting a young man, one out of a great number, told what the Lord had done for his soul, by attending the noon-day meetings, which sent a thrill through every Christian heart, and which will be remembered with joy.'

JAN. 5, 1858

'Called to converse with some of the editors of the *daily*

papers in regard to having some of the incidents, which occur from day to day in the prayer-meetings, inserted in them.'

This was, probably, the beginning of the notices of the secular press of the transactions of these meetings.

At the end of the fourth month, the Fulton street prayer-meeting occupied the three lecture-rooms in the consistory building, and all were filled to their utmost capacity. So were all other places filled in the cities of New York, Brooklyn, Jersey City, Newark, and their vicinity.

But the spread of the meetings requires a more special mention, in order that we may trace the hand of God in this revival. The three lecture-rooms at the Old Dutch Church had become filled to overflowing, one after the other, until no sitting room or standing room was left. And scores, and perhaps hundreds, had to go away, unable even to get into the halls. How noticeable is one fact, and it *must* be noticed in order that we may see that 'the excellency of the power is of God'. There had been no eloquent preaching, no energetic and enthusiastic appeals; no attempts to rouse up religious interest. All had been still, solemn, and awful. The simple fact, the great fact was, the people were moved to *prayer*. The people demanded a place to *pray*.

So noiseless was this work of grace, that one portion of the community did not know what any other portion were doing in the matter. Instead of devising plans, and executing them, to stir up the community, the whole community, as one man, seemed to be already roused. The daily prayer-meeting was not the means of the feeling, but the mere expression of it. Never, since the days of Pentecost, was such a state of the general Christian heart and mind; and never, since the world was made, was there such an important epoch. The more we go into the facts of it, the more is the mind filled with adoring wonder

The New York Revival of 1858

and amazement at the stupendous importance and extent of it. Every movement in it seemed to be following, not leading; not creating, but following the developments of a plan already marked out, the end by no means seen from the beginning, and no part of the plan seen, only as it was unfolded, from day to day, by him who devised it all.

Who would have foreseen the connection of the meeting of six men for prayer in that upper room, in which was one Presbyterian, one Baptist, one Congregationalist, and one Reformed Dutch, with the events which were to follow? When was there ever such a meeting before? made up of such elements? met for such a purpose? at such an hour? and gathered up without the shadow of any human contrivance as to any of the results which followed that haste with which God makes haste – '*slowly*' – and by which a whole Christian nation was to be shaken from centre to circumference? To this meeting in the upper room no one knew who was coming, or whether any one would come. And yet we find there the very elements of that deeply-affecting *Christian union*, which was the golden chain by which millions of Christian hearts were to be bound together, as they had never been in all time; by which the true unity of the church of Christ was to be manifested. Whose hand was in this but the hand of God? And this first meeting was a union of different denominations, as represented, there to *pray* – a union in the blessed work of prayer. Oh, who can fail to see that in this God is to be acknowledged and exalted! His hand has done it, and his name shall have all the glory!

We shall see in the sequel how rapid was the progress of the work from the point where we now are.

But God had a work to do, and his Holy Spirit was preparing the way. Going back to that first noonday prayer-meeting, and looking *forward*, we cannot see what it was that was to be done. But from our present standpoint, looking backward over the history of the past, we can plainly see what it was.

This revival is to be the precursor of greater and more wonderful things, which are yet to be revealed in the redeeming providence of God. What these are, we cannot tell. 'But coming events cast their shadows before.' As this is a law in the kingdoms of nature, providence, and grace, so we may unhesitatingly conclude that however eventful may be the interests of the present times, we shall 'see greater things than these'.

The time was to be hastened when larger views were to be taken, nobler aims indulged, more far-reaching plans laid, more costly sacrifices made, more lofty designs executed.

The religious press caught the spirit of the day and the occasion, and spoke out as one voice, in the tone of the prevailing and coming interest, and much more – in the beams of the light which was now breaking upon the world. Going back to this period, one paper says:

'*We are doing no more than we should always do, and can easily do, consistently with the performance of every duty.* Have a few weak prayers brought such a blessing, and shall we desist from praying? So long as the promise stands, "Ask, and it shall be given you", so long as we know that our God "fainteth not, neither is weary", so long as the "fields are white to the harvest" of immortal souls, shall we cease calling upon God?'

Another says:

'Shall the work cease? Shall a revival of religion, in some respects the most remarkable the church has ever enjoyed, come to an end because it is no longer winter, but summer? – as though the grace of God were like some compounds, that can endure only one climate. No one can think that God chooses to have it so.

The church, or more truly, individual churches, have

The New York Revival of 1858

often made what might be called exhaustive efforts for the conversion of sinners. They have taxed to the utmost for a few weeks both soul and body of every earnest man they could enlist. Such efforts *must be* relaxed. Flesh and blood cannot sustain them. But the present revival has had no such history. The church is still fresh, and may labor on indefinitely just as she has been laboring, and that without sinning against any law of mental or physical health. This revival has not overtaxed us; it has only toned us up. It has brought religion into alliance with our ordinary engagements; it has given *to our social character a completeness and balance which it never had before*. So far as it has gone it is an advance toward soundness and strength, and to fall back from it is not to rest after labor, but to be palsied.'

And another:

'The awakening is not only progressing in unabated power throughout the country as a whole, and not only extending into new regions, where it has hitherto been less felt, but in this city, if we are not deceived, the real earnestness of the churches for a continuance of the work, is manifesting itself in more deliberate and far-reaching plans for carrying forward permanent labors of the kind so signally blessed.

We must shake off old habits of mind, and arouse ourselves earnestly to the unprecedented demands of the time. God never called any former generation of men on this earth, as we are now called.'

There was preparation all over the city, and all over the land. God had made it. And men began to see it, and to look upward.

Early in February it was felt that these retreating hundreds, who came to the place of prayer in Fulton street, and could not get in, must be accommodated elsewhere. The old John street Methodist Church, only one square removed, was thrown open for noon prayer-meetings by our Methodist brethren, and the whole body of the church was immediately filled every day, at noon, with business men, who would come, and did come to pray. The galleries, too, were occupied, all round the church, chiefly by ladies. No denominational element seemed to be prominent one above another. No one could have told, who had come in a stranger, from the character of the meeting, whether it was held in a Methodist, Baptist, Presbyterian, or Congregationalist church, or that of any other denomination. It was found at once that the audience-room was insufficient, and the basement lecture-room was opened and immediately filled. It was estimated that two thousand persons attended upon these services daily.

There were now five regular noonday services – three in the Fulton street, and two in the John street churches – and yet hundreds would go away, unable to get into any of them, so much were men moved to prayer. Answers to prayer came down speedily, and multitudes were now turning to God, and seeking him 'with all their heart'.

On the 17th of March, Burton's Old Theatre, in Chambers street, was opened by a number of merchants in that vicinity for a noonday prayer-meeting. This was thronged to excess after the first meeting. For half an hour before the time to commence the services, the old theatre would be crowded to its utmost capacity, in every nook and corner, with most solemn and deeply affected audiences. The streets, and all means of access, were blocked up before the hour of prayer commenced, and hundreds would stand in the street during the hour. This continued to be the case until the building was required by the United States courts, when the further use of it for prayer-meetings ceased.

Immediately a store (No. 69 Broadway, second storey) was procured and comfortably fitted up for the purpose of prayer-meetings. The room was 25 by 100 feet, and this, from day to day, was filled, and the exercises were solemn beyond description.

After a time the Broadway meeting was removed to No. 175 of the same street. Here it was sustained by Christians in that part of the city of all denominations.

We shall never forget being present at one of those meetings, when it was conducted in the usual manner by the Right Rev Bishop McIlvaine, of Ohio. We shall never forget the earnestness of his opening prayer, when he kneeled down on the floor and led the devotions, so humble, so urgent, so importunate, so believing, so imbued with the revival spirit. We shall never forget his short, eloquent closing address, full of deep emotion, full of brotherly kindness, full of thankfulness and joy. It described the work of grace as it lay in his own mind – it recognized the hand of God in its inception and every step of its progress – it rejoiced at the spirit of grace and supplication which had been poured out on 'all Christians'. That address will long live in the memories of those who heard it.

Meetings for daily prayer were held as follows:

MORNING.

Seventh Avenue Reformed Dutch Church, 6 A.M.
Broome and Elizabeth Baptist Church, 7¾ A.M.
Church of the Puritans, 8 A.M.
Church of the Puritans (ladies), 10¾ A.M.
Hope Chapel, 8 A.M.
Fourteenth Street Presbyterian Church, 8 A.M.
MacDougal Street, 9½ A.M.
Home Chapel, Twenty-ninth street, 8 A.M.

NOON.

John Street Methodist Episcopal Church.
Fulton Street Reformed Dutch Church.

Mission Chapel, 106 Centre Street.
Duane Street Methodist Episcopal Church.
27 Greenwich Street.
Broome Street Reformed Dutch Church (corner of Greene).
Spring Street Hall (colored).
Twelfth Street, near Avenue C (workingmen).
Fourteenth Street Presbyterian Church, and others, in rotation.

AFTERNOON.

69 Broadway (merchants), 3½ P.M.
John Street Methodist Episcopal Church, 3½ P.M.
Mercer Street Presbyterian Church, 4 P.M.
North Presbyterian Church, 4 P.M.
Fiftieth Street Presbyterian Church, 4 P.M.
Central Methodist Episcopal Church, Seventh Avenue, 4 P.M.
Sullivan Street Congregational Church (colored), 5 P.M.
Stuyvesant Institute, 5 P.M.

And besides these, other meetings were established in almost every part of New York and the surrounding cities. The great features of all these meetings were union, and prayer, and corresponding effort.

A careful inquiry in regard to the facts, convinces us that not less than one hundred and fifty meetings for prayer in this city and Brooklyn were held daily at the time of which we are now writing – *all*, without one single exception, partaking of the same general character.

In February, Philadelphia established a noonday prayer-meeting, commenced, at first, in a church in Fourth Street, but soon removed to Jaynes' Hall. Soon the entire accessible places were filled – floor, platform, galleries, boxes, aisles, and office. Never was there, scarcely on the face of the earth, such meetings as those in

Jaynes' Hall. The death of Rev Dudley A. Tyng, of the Episcopal Church, a prominent leader in these meetings, gave an impetus to the work. And here again we find Bishop McIlvaine lending his influence, by his presence and his prayers and preaching.

The work spread, from Jaynes' Hall, all over the city. Prayer-meetings were established in numerous places – public halls – concert-rooms – engine and hose company's houses, and in tents, till the whole city seemed pervaded with the spirit of prayer.

Prayer-meetings almost simultaneously were established in all parts of the land, both in city and country – Boston, Baltimore, Washington, Richmond, Charleston, Savannah, Mobile, New Orleans, Vicksburg, Memphis, St Louis, Pittsburgh, Cincinnati, Chicago, and other cities, shared in this glorious work. The whole land received the 'spiritual rain'. The fervor of this awakened religious interest had become intense at the end of the fourth month of the meetings, and towards the close of the first month of the current year, the newspapers, both secular and religious, in all parts of the country, speak of an 'unwonted revival of religion' in all quarters, far and near. Everywhere men were crowding to the meetings, and the spirit with which they are impressed and which invites them to so general attention to the subject of religion, seems to animate the whole land. The northern, middle, western and southern States were moved as by one common mighty influence. The spirit of the revival spread everywhere, and seemed to permeate every nook and corner of the great republic. The subjects of the revival included all classes – the high and the low – the rich and the poor – the learned and the ignorant. The most hopeless and forbidding were brought under its almighty power. From the highest to the lowest and most degraded in society, the trophies of God's power and grace were

THE POWER OF PRAYER

made. Persons of the most vicious and abandoned character, supposed to be beneath and beyond the reach of all religious influence, by having lost all susceptibility, were brought to humble themselves like little children at the foot of the cross. Christians were themselves astonished and overwhelmed at those displays of divine mercy. They felt that God was saying to them, anew, and by a providential revelation – 'Before they call, I will answer, and while they are yet speaking, I will hear.' 'Open thy mouth wide, and I will fill it.' Christians became emboldened to ask great things and expect great things. Never before, in modern times certainly, was there such asking in prayer – such believing in prayer; and never such *answers* to prayer.

The spectacle of such universal confidence in God was without a parallel. It appeared in all prayers. It appeared in all addresses. It appeared in all conversations. It spread from heart to heart. There was humility, and yet there was a cheerful, holy boldness in the spirit and temper of the religious mind, and duty was attempted with the expectation of success. It seemed to be upon all hearts as if written with the pen of a diamond – 'My soul! wait thou *only* upon God, for my *expectation* is from *him*.'

Is it wonderful, then, that we should find that this state of heart and mind, in all praying places and praying circles – this earnest asking – this humble confiding – this far-reaching faith and confident expectation, should be followed by such a work of grace as the modern Christian world has never seen?

Christians began to feel that they had entered upon a new era of faith and prayer; and is it wonderful that this new joy and hope spread with vast rapidity over the land – that it rolled, like a wave, over the whole country? The numbers converted were beyond all precedent. The great revival in the times of Wesley, Whitefield, Edwards, and

The New York Revival of 1858

the Tennents, was marked by powerful *preaching*. The present by believing, earnest *praying*.

In New England, the present great revival commenced almost simultaneously in many cities, villages, and townships. Since the former 'great awakening', as it was commonly denominated, and just referred to, nothing had borne any comparison to the present religious interest. *This* 'great awakening' surpassed the *former* in all its aspects. It entered into all the frame-work of society, and permeated everywhere the masses. Christians gathered for prayer, and asked for large measures of the Holy Spirit to be poured out upon them; and the Spirit was sent down in copious effusions in answer to prayer. The prayer-meeting would be established in lecture-rooms and vestries, and all at once it would be found that scarcely could the largest churches contain the hundreds who would come up to the house of God to pray. Nothing was thought of or demanded but a place in which to pray. Conversions multiplied, so that there was, after a little, no attempt to compute their numbers. In some towns nearly all the population became, as was believed, true and faithful followers of Christ. The number of converted men and women constituted a new element of power. New voices were daily heard imploring the divine blessing on the work, and the moral transformation of those remaining impenitent. The day was breaking that should be gilded by the rays of a brighter sun than had ever shone upon the moral and religious world before. This was believed. It *is* believed now.

Over all the West and South, so far as the work extended, and it extended almost everywhere, the same spirit prevailed. It was the spirit of *prayer*. No confidence was felt in the mere use of means. Indeed, in no former revival was there ever such abnegation, on the part of Christians, of themselves; such distrust of all mere human agencies and instrumentalities, and such a looking away from all human ties, and such a looking away from all human aid and up to the 'heavenly hills', whence all help must come. Means must be used, and were used; not with any confidence in the use of them, or in those who used them. But with the most diligent and earnest use of means, the deepest possible conviction seemed to be, '*The power belongeth unto God.*' No wonder, then, that everywhere there was the universal acknowledgment of God's hand in the revival; and no matter what men did to promote it, to God was ascribed all the glory of it. It was everywhere felt that a proposal of any such meetings for *prayer* six months before, as were now held all over the land, even in the densest populations, with any expectation that it would be heeded, would have been considered a perfect absurdity. The appointment of such meetings for prayer *then* would have been a *failure*; *now* it was a *success*. The neglect of the place of prayer by the majority of church members, was felt to be a sore evil. It paralysed the energies of the pastor, and the more active, faithful members. They were drones. They were a weight which had to be carried. They were clogs in the way of progress. They neutralized the moral power of the church, and so weakened it that it was a constant effort for it to sustain itself. Every man who has been a pastor knows what we mean.

The changes which came suddenly over the church was most welcome. When the majority of the church became Nathanaels, it was soon felt that the church had just begun to find out her real power. It was a blessed spectacle presented to the world, a church alive, a church active, a church of prayer. It was a sublime spectacle, when this was seen to be the moral position, not of one church, but of a majority of churches; not in one place, but in every place, when all the land seemed to be moved by one common impulse. No wonder that Christians felt joyful in the Lord, when this new element of usefulness and power was found.

Chapter 3

Features of the Work – Ways and Means – Enthusiasm – Catholicity of Feeling and Action – The Reformed Dutch Church – Union, a Type – Influence of Laymen – The Ministry aided and encouraged.

The character of the work was as remarkable as its inception and extent. It had its peculiarities in feature as well as in power. It lacked almost everything that made up the leading features of the revivals of '30 and '32. There was no revival preaching. There were no revivalists; no revival machinery, such as was common to those days. The 'anxious seat', and the labor of peregrinating revival-makers were all unknown. In former times, a revival, even in New England, set in motion much that was stirring, and to many minds very objectionable. Now there was nothing of the kind.

There was no unrestrained excitement, no exuberant and intemperate zeal. There was nothing which required an effort to '*keep it up*', under the common idea that excitement was essential to the revival, and part and parcel of the same. The high wrought feeling of '32, which not unfrequently took forms which many could not but condemn, now is nowhere seen. This present revival is ever treated with respect, even by those who have no sympathetic interest in it. Opposition is disarmed. Ridicule is not attempted, and if it be, it is soon rebuked, and abandoned for very shame. There is no offence to good

The New York Revival of 1858

taste; nothing reprehensible in view of just propriety in this revival. This adds to its elements of power.

That there is enthusiasm – a well-regulated and joyful enthusiasm – we use the word in the best sense – we are most happy to admit. No right mind can contemplate great changes and great events for *good*, without enthusiasm. There is much of the moral sublime in this religious movement, when contemplated as confined to a single community. But contemplated as spreading over this great republic from Vermont to Florida, and from Maine to California, why should not enthusiasm be aroused? What mighty results are to be realized in the bearings of this work on the social, the political, the religious character of this nation? No human mind can compute them. No mind can think of them without being impressed with their overwhelming importance. As a nation, we were becoming rapidly demoralized by our worldliness, our ambition, our vanity, and our vices. The true, the great end for which, we believe, this nation was raised up, was being lost sight of. The very foundations were moving. We needed this 'great awakening' to bring us to our senses, to rouse up the national conscience, to arrest the national *decay*, and bring us back to a high tone of moral health. Nothing but the influence of a deep and all-pervading earnest piety can save this from the fate of all past republics. The tide of corruption must be rolled backward.

This was felt; everywhere felt. The place of prayer was *the* place to get the help we needed. Men rushed to the place of prayer with high resolves, and with weighty demands to ask great things of God. And men rejoiced with unbounded joy when they saw what God was doing. Why should not a holy enthusiasm be enkindled? It was kindled, and God be praised.

Another, and one of the most deeply interesting

characistics of this revival has been its catholicity. From its inception, this has been one of its distinguishing features. Unlike *all* former revivals, has it been in this respect. In the Old Dutch Church the revival began, but not in that communion only, or among the membership of that church only.

The Old North Dutch Church will ever be regarded as a sacred spot, on account of its being the birthplace of these prayer-meetings. But in that upper lecture-room, at that first noonday prayer-meeting, when only six were present, there were several denominations represented. This noble church had been mercifully preserved for this very purpose, it may be; not the head-quarters of a lawless band of British soldiery, as it once was, but the head-quarters of the first noonday prayer-meeting ever organized; made up of Christians of different branches of the church of Christ. The 'union prayer-meeting' became at once a feature as well as a fixture of this venerable and noble church edifice, and the 'union prayer-meeting' has been a feature all the country over.

We have sometimes thought that God had a design in keeping this one denomination from being mixed up in the questions, controversies and divisions of the day. The 'Reformed Dutch Church', as a denomination, is distinguished for purity and soundness of doctrine, above suspicion and above reproach. We do not know that the catholicity of this glorious work could have been inaugurated in connection with any other denomination of Christians, without exciting distrust or jealousy, or opposition. All were friendly to this peculiar church.

The 'union prayer-meeting' is now a *type*. It represents what has never been so well represented before in modern days, that among all Christians there are elements of coalescence and harmony; that there is a union deeper down, and which underlies all external 'unions'. Other-

The New York Revival of 1858

wise the 'union prayer' would be a misnomer – a name without a meaning. But now the name only suggests a meaning which fills all hearts with joy and gladness. The reality of this union is proved from the fact that in all our large towns and cities, the numbers attending upon the union prayer-meeting far surpassed the numbers attending any one church, or the same place. So it has been in New York. So it has been in Philadelphia, and all our large cities, thus proving that it *is* really what it professes to be, a union meeting. Thousands go without ever raising the question, whom they are to meet, or to what church organization do they belong. Neither do they care.

Another feature of this work is, that it has been conducted by laymen. It began with them. It continues with them. Clergymen share in the conduct, but no more than laymen, and as much as if they were laymen. They are often seen in these assemblies. But they assume no control. They voluntarily take their seats, mingle with the audience, and are in no way distinguishable from others, except it may be by something peculiar in their apparel, or manners. They oftener sit silent through the meeting than otherwise. Clergymen come to the place precisely for the same reason that others do – because it is the place of *prayer*. They say and feel as others say and feel, 'It is good for me to draw near to God.'

This lay conduct of the union prayer has been eminently successful, and very conducive to its catholic spirit.

We think we can see a wisdom above measure in so ordaining that this work should commence among laymen – and for the progress of which they should be so extensively enlisted. It has revealed a power which the church did not know it had within itself – a power which has been dead, or latent, and which even to the present hour is but little understood.

THE POWER OF PRAYER

In all former revivals a few – not the many – have done all the labor, and felt all the responsibility of the occasion. The minister would be weighed down under the burden of new cares which would come upon him, and he would struggle manfully to discharge all his duties. A few would be ready and willing to share with him the labors and responsibilities of the work. The great mass of Christians would stand still and see the salvation of God – not from obedience to the command – but from absolute inertia and want of life. Christians have felt what they have been made to feel – this, and no more. They have not felt the obligation 'to stir *themselves* up to take hold on God'. In all former revivals the hidden, aggregated power of a thoroughly awakened laity was not known. In *this* it has been more developed and manifested than ever before, and even now is only beginning to be fully understood. God has been working in such a way as to show more than ever the power of the *church* – not of the ministry only, but of the *church*. And he has done this in a way to arouse no unholy jealousies in any quarter. Never before, in these latter days, have ministers found such abundant help in the church; never have they preached and labored with such courage and hope.

Chapter 4

Preparation – Means following certain Results – Remarkable Coincidences – Revivals at Sea – Convention at Pittsburg – Day of Fasting and Prayer – Convention at Cincinnati – Visitation of Families – General Influence of the Revival on the Church.

We have said that many have been impressed with the idea, that it was the late financial revulsion – the severity of the times which followed – by which men were forced into an acknowledgment of their dependence upon a divine being, and their minds made ripe and susceptible to the operation of spiritual influences and the impression of religious truth.

But whether these causes were adequate to produce this result, we need not attempt to determine, for it will be seen, in looking back at the history of this work, that it had actually commenced before the financial revulsion took place. That the commercial distress which followed had its influence to arrest men's minds, and to make them feel their dependence upon God, we cannot doubt. But all speculations of this kind will fail to reach the *cause* of this wide-spread work of grace, and all inquiries into *causes* will resolve themselves into the sovereign grace of him who has promised to hear and answer prayer.

The first union prayer-meeting was held September 23, 1857, in Fulton street. It was not appointed to '*create* a revival'. This was not thought of. God had his own designs

[35]

in view. The union prayer-meetings all over our country have not been appointed to create religious feeling, but rather to give expression to, and increase the religious feeling already existing. The appointment of these meetings was to *meet* the *demand* of religious interest already existing, not to *create* that *demand*. There is a wide difference between the two things, which has a significant and emphatic meaning. The revival was nowhere attended nor preceded by any special measures intended and adapted to produce intense excitement on the subject of religion. All these union prayer-meetings have been the effects of a great first cause. *God poured out the Spirit of grace and supplication*, and to his name be all the glory. As nearly as possible was this awakened interest simultaneous over all this western world. Even ships at sea were overtaken in mid-ocean – knowing nothing of what was transpiring upon the land – by unusual religious anxiety, and came into port bringing the strange news of a revival on board, and of the conversion of some of the men. Who can doubt but the 'set time to favor Zion had come'? The popular voice spoke of the time of the union meetings, as they sprang up in various places, as the beginning of the revival in those places, when in fact it had begun before. The great feature of the revival everywhere was *prayer* – *prayer* by Christians *united* – *prayer* constant – each day sending up a cloud of prayer as a volume of incense before the throne of God – prayer that was divinely inspired and divinely answered. Such prayer has *power* – such prayer must always be heard – such prayer must *prevail*.

Among the indications of an awakened religious interest in the West was the calling of a convention on revivals at Pittsburgh late in last autumn. This convention continued in session for three days, for the purpose of considering the necessity of a general revival of religion in all the churches represented, and others as well; the means, the

The New York Revival of 1858

hindrances, the encouragements, the demand of the times, the indications of divine providence, and everything relating to this most momentous subject. It was a most solemn, anxious, melting, encouraging meeting. Much of the time of this convention was spent in prayer. There were not present less than two hundred ministers, besides many laymen, led in by the interest of the occasion. It was impossible that such a gathering should not be without a most timely and weighty influence. The 'obstacles in the way of revivals of religion' – 'the means of promoting them' – 'the encouragement to seek for them' – were discussed with signal ability and great solemnity. A committee was appointed, who drew up an address to the churches. It was prepared in the revival spirit, and was earnest and pungent in its appeals. It was timely and suggestive. It was recommended that this address be read from the pulpit by pastors on the Sabbath, so far as they were willing to accept it, and that the official members of the respective churches be called to meet in each church to discuss the same subjects as the convention had discussed, and to spend much time together in prayer; also, that a plan of personal visitation be adopted, according to which all the families of each parish should be visited by the pastor and some of his most experienced members; also, that he should preach on the subject of the importance of improving the present 'grievous visitation', and that he urge his people to *prayer*.

In conformity to this arrangement, on the first Sabbath in January of the current year, multitudes of ministers of the Presbyterian and other denominations delivered discourses on the necessity and practicability of revivals, and the first Thursday of the same month was observed as a day of humiliation, fasting and prayer. All these arrangements told upon the country with great power,

THE POWER OF PRAYER

and the awakening received an intelligent and mighty impulse.

Immediately after this convention at Pittsburgh, another was called at Cincinnati, having similar objects in view. It was largely attended, and was followed with similar results. The public mind was thoroughly roused, and the 'great revival' was the all-absorbing theme in hotels, stores, shops, taverns, railroad cars, and everywhere. The religious and secular press, especially in the rural districts, teemed with items of intelligence on this one great subject, the facts of the revival being the absorbing topic.

So far as this city was concerned, the organized systems of tract and Sunday school visitation had much to do with the beginning of the revival, with its spread, and with its continuance to the present hour. The latter part of last year a more thorough system was resolved upon of searching out and exploring the destitutions of this great city, and inducing the *neglected* and *neglecting* perishing thousands to attend upon the worship of God, and to send their children to the Sabbath school. It was determined to push this plan of visitation into the fashionable avenues as well as into the 'highways and hedges' of the city. The numbers were greatly increased of those who visited the '*house of prayer*'. All denominations nearly were benefited by this work, and many of them shared in the labor of it. In many Sunday schools the members were doubled, in all increased. In this way, thousands of persons – some from the 'brown stone fronts', and some from the garrets and cellars, swelled the numbers, who were seen on Sunday morning wending their way to the sanctuary. 'High life' and 'low life' were on the street together, and in the house of God together.

This system of visitation was adopted and carried out in New York and Brooklyn about the same time. It was an organized plan adopted by the churches to visit in their

The New York Revival of 1858

respective localities and search out every kind of destitution.

The effect of the revival upon cities, towns and country, is most manifest. That tide of worldliness which destroys the power of all religious feeling and action had rolled over the land. It had gone up to the flood, and threatened to sweep away the foundations. Men were hardly aware what a low, lax state of religious feeling prevailed. There was outward attention to religion, but the power, the vitality was gone. It was not seen so much on the Sabbath as in the week. The congregations did not forget the place where the sermon was to be preached, but they did forget the place where the prayer-meeting was to be held. It is believed that not one-fourth part of our members of the various churches made a practice of regularly attending the prayer-meeting. They might be, perhaps, sometimes in the place of prayer, when there was more than the usual amount of religious interest, and when any extra effort was made to get them there. But as a rule, they never went to the prayer-meeting. They left the burden of sustaining it to that quarter part of the membership who did attend. If any think that we under-rate the number of regular attendants on the prayer-meeting in proportion to those who did attend, taking our churches at large, we will say again, that an investigation into the facts, of which we have been observers for twenty years past, will convince them that we are *not far wrong*.

Chapter 5

One Prayer-Meeting – The House and Rooms – The Business in Hand – Requests for Prayer – News abroad – The President – From Philadelphia – The Son and Mother – An Answer – Three Sisters – Six Children.

We will now give a brief outline of one meeting, not an unusual one, but such as hundreds of our meetings have been. We might take any one, and it would be a sample of all the others. We do not mean that the exercises are always alike, and always equally interesting; they vary in some particulars, and the incidents of the meetings are always unlike, and give great effect to the spirit of the meeting.

There are three lecture-rooms at the rear of the North Dutch Church, as it is called, one above another, making first, second, and third storeys. All these are comfortably and closely seated; each has a pulpit or desk of its own. The entrances to these lecture-rooms are from Fulton and Ann streets; each room has a clock, and all the appliances of a meeting by itself.

We take our seat in the middle lecture-room fifteen minutes before twelve noon. A few ladies are seated in a row of seats in one corner; a few gentlemen are scattered here and there through the room; all is quiet and silent; no talking, no whispering; all has the air of deep solemnity.

At ten minutes before twelve, businessmen begin to come in rapidly. Ministers and laymen, all are seated

The New York Revival of 1858

promiscuously together, there is no distinction, except in respect to strangers; they are treated with attention and respect, and there are always some to see that they have comfortable seats.

Five minutes before twelve, the leader for the day passes in, and takes his seat in the desk. He is a business man; he has never led before, and a new one will come in his place tomorrow. All his movements are quick and rapid; he seems impressed with the importance of the moment, but seems of not the least importance himself. Two minutes to twelve, the room is packed to its utmost capacity. Many are standing in the hall, unable to get in.

At twelve noon, precisely to a minute, the chairman rises and gives out that beautiful hymn:

> Blow ye the trumpet, blow,
> The gladly solemn sound;
> Let all the nations know,
> To earth's remotest bound,
> The year of jubilee is come.
> Return, ye ransomed sinners, home.

The leader then calls on all to unite with him in prayer. His prayer is short, exactly to the point; he prays for the Holy Spirit, for the quickening of Christians, for the conversion of sinners here present at this very hour, for the spread of the revival, for the perishing thousands all around us.

Then he reads the seventeenth chapter of John. A word of comment while he stands with slips of paper in his hand. There is a little sea of up-turned, solemn faces. A deep stillness pervades the assembly. These are businessmen, and they address themselves to the great business before them. Oh, what a moment!

'I will read four or five of these requests, and will call on

THE POWER OF PRAYER

someone to follow immediately in prayer, remembering these cases.' He reads:

'A sister in Massachusetts desires prayers for a brother seventy years of age,' etc.

'A brother for a sister in Pennsylvania,' etc.

'A mother who has attended these meetings and thinks she has been benefited, desires prayer for a large family,' etc.

'I judge', said the leader, 'that this mother has lately found peace in believing.'

'A gospel minister sends a very urgent request for four brothers to be remembered in prayer, that they may be converted, and that they, too, may become preachers of the "glorious gospel of the blessed God"'.

'From Philadelphia, for a brother and sister who are *trying* to be earnest seekers after the grace of God.'

'Now,' says the leader, 'will someone lead in prayer?'

Prayer was offered by a clergyman. When this prayer was concluded, which was very short and in reference to the specific cases before the meeting, a gentleman arose in the back part of the room and begged the prayers of all present for himself and his sister. Prayer immediately followed.

Then all sang one verse of the hymn,

Jesus – my Saviour and my Lord.

A gentleman from St Louis now arose and addressed the meeting with great animation.

'We have heard of this meeting by the mouth of those who have been here with you. We have heard of you through the religious and secular papers, and we have heard from you by means of the telegraph. Who would have thought of this last as a channel of communication in regard to this great work of salvation? And yet, how did our hearts, away in St Louis, rejoice to be told by

The New York Revival of 1858

telegraph, of what the Lord was doing for you here in New York. Oh, what a bond of union was opened between us. I cannot tell how we are cheered and encouraged by what we hear from you every week. We look along the columns of our religious papers, and especially of those which come from your city, and you cannot tell how eagerly we gather up the revival intelligence which comes from this meeting, and how we are encouraged by it.

We rejoice at the high ground you have taken here, and as you elevate your standard, so other places will elevate theirs. The work of grace has been wonderful among us, and especially among the colored churches in St Louis. We have such churches, and they have colored educated pastors – able men, and sound and thoroughly orthodox preachers of the gospel – and they have their Sunday schools, and day schools, and their children are taught to read. It is against the law, that is true, but the law that forbids teaching a colored child to read, in St Louis, is a dead letter. We want to hear from you, to hear from this meeting, every week. We ask for a kindly remembrance in your prayers.'

Another speaker followed. He was a venerable, fine-looking gentleman. We know not who he was, but took him to be an old thrifty merchant. He spoke of our having had signal answers to prayer, and referred to some signal recent cases. He then spoke of the importance of praying for our rulers, our judges, and all in authority. He spoke especially of the gratifying fact, that when President Buchanan was at the Bedford Springs, he attended daily upon the prayer-meetings with most exemplary and respectful attention. And why should we not pray, said he, for Mr Buchanan? Why not send up our prayers to God that he may be a true Christian? When the righteous rule, the earth rejoices. When the wicked rule, the people mourn. As he was resuming his seat, the leader invited

THE POWER OF PRAYER

him to lead in prayer for the objects he had named. He rose again, and poured out a fervent prayer for President Buchanan by name, in a manner of the utmost respect for him, his character and office; but *for him*, as a sinner like ourselves, needing an interest in the atoning blood of Jesus Christ; for him as needing the wisdom that cometh from above to guide and assist him in his arduous duties, and under his great responsibilities; *for him*, whose evening days were coming, and who needed a well-grounded hope of heaven. There was a remarkable propriety in this prayer which touched a chord in every heart.

It is now twenty minutes to one P.M. How the moments fly! Time on swift, noiseless wings is passing.

The leader stands with slips of paper in his hand. These have been going up to the desk as the meeting progressed.

'I have several more of these to read,' says he. He reads:

'A lady requests prayer for a profane father and his numerous family.'

'A church in Dutchess County, that they may not be passed by in this day of salvation.'

'A church in Keene, N.H., where a few mercy-drops have fallen, asks prayer for the plentiful shower.'

'Prayer for a young lady.'

'Prayer for two brothers, sons of a deceased pastor of one of our Dutch Reformed churches.'

And last, but not least,

'Prayer is asked of the Fulton street prayer-meeting by a daughter of a missionary who died upon a foreign shore, for a brother, unconverted, that he may become a Christian, and if it be the will of God, that he may be prepared to take the place of his father in the ministerial office, and in the missionary work.'

An earnest prayer for these by the gentleman from St Louis. Then one verse of the hymn:

The New York Revival of 1858

All hail the power of Jesus' name,
Let angels prostrate fall.

Oh, what a power in that ever-precious name. All hearts here seem to feel it, as they sing with united hearts and voices.

Time passes on apace, and we seem to have much yet to do. Several rise to speak. A Philadelphian gets the floor, and tells, in a few brief words, of the wonderful work of grace going on still in that city; now truly a sister city; a city of brotherly love. All the prayer-meetings are filling up. God pours out his Spirit afresh. All are animated with new hope and zeal. We are expecting a great refreshing from on high. Then he made some brief and impressive statements of the state of things in the prayer-meetings at Jaynes' Hall, the hose-houses, the big tent; the conversion of the firemen; the combination and earnestness of the ministry; the preaching of the gospel in unwonted places; the crowds that flock together to hear; the activity of the Young Men's Christian Association; and of the encouragement we all have from the accounts we receive from New York. '*Pari passu*,' said the speaker, 'we go along with you.'

A leading hardware merchant made some observations of a very earnest character, in regard to the kind of action to be adopted by the 50,000 professors of religion in this city, fitted to reach the 1,000,000 in this city, resident, or who come here to do business from the surroundings, or from abroad. The great point is, for each one to take one individual or a family under his special supervision, and endeavour to lead them to Christ.

Very brief prayer follows for all the objects.

A verse was sung, and a man arose and said:
When a person presents a request for prayer, and that prayer is answered, he felt it to be a duty to communicate

[45]

THE POWER OF PRAYER

the fact for the encouragement of the meeting. He said that he presented a request here some six weeks ago, that God would bless his efforts to establish a prayer-meeting at a place in the country, where he was about to spend a season. 'The first week we had about twenty in attendance, second week about thirty, third week about forty, and last week about one hundred. The meetings have all been very solemn and interesting. There was much deep emotion in the audience. Many were affected to tears, and the Holy Spirit was evidently operating on the hearts of the unconverted.'

One said he felt timid on this matter of so many requests being sent here for prayer. 'I am afraid of this,' said he; 'I am afraid of spiritual pride. I am afraid the Spirit of God will leave us. I have my misgivings about all this. Every request read here is a dagger to my heart.'

Another arose and said, 'Oh, do not discourage these requests for prayer. Where would my son have been had it not been for your prayers? I have followed him around the globe with mine. He lately came home from sea unconverted. I brought his case right here. I said, "Men of Israel, help." I wanted you to help me pray for him. I knew you would not do anything for him *but* pray. God must do all the work. He must bow that stubborn will, and humble that proud heart. Oh! what cause of thankfulness and joy I have, that God hears and answers prayer. That son is today a new creature in Christ Jesus, as I humbly trust, and to him be all the glory. Do not feel tried with the coming of these requests for prayer. Oh! no! no! Let us rejoice that they *do* come. But let them pray who send them to this prayer-meeting. Let the language of all the hearts in this assembly be, "The power belongeth unto God." "Turn us, O Lord, as the streams of the South." Let us pray for all who ask us to pray, believing, trusting, hoping, and humbling ourselves low before God.'

The New York Revival of 1858

A clergyman said he was accosted in the street by a stranger a short time since. He was concerned for his salvation, and had been for some time. He had been to the Fulton street and the John street meetings a great many times, but could obtain no peace. He said at the Fulton street meetings he would watch to see who took an active part, and then the next day he would get a seat beside them, hoping they would say something to him. But all in vain. No man seemed to care for him. 'One day a request was put in by a mother for a son. It struck me that that was from my mother. After meeting I got sight of that request. And sure enough, it was from my mother, in her own handwriting. She cared for me.'

A youth sent in a request to be prayed for some time ago; and again to-day a request that we would give thanks to God that he had found Christ precious to his soul. The leader said he knew this young man, and hoped he would be here himself to tell what the Lord had done for him. After a little time he came in and arose and said that he had requested an interest in the prayers of this meeting; and O, what a change! How was his darkness turned into light, and his sorrow to joy. He called upon all to praise God for the great change. This young man in his boyhood had been a member of a class in the Sunday school connected with this church, and his teacher, who had not seen him for years, was here to meet him to-day.

A gentleman said he met a teller of one of our city banks, who felt greatly concerned for the salvation of those three sisters unconverted. He presented a request at one of our Fulton street prayer-meetings, on behalf of those three sisters, from the brother, asking us to pray for their immediate conversion. 'And now I am here to say that those three sisters are rejoicing in the pardoning love of Jesus, and are rejoicing with that joy which is unspeakable and full of glory.'

[47]

THE POWER OF PRAYER

A praying mother died a short time since, leaving six unconverted children. The last of those six children was converted a short time ago. 'I am', said the speaker, 'one of those six children; and I am *that last one!*'

The time was up; what a brief hour, a heavenly place; the minutes had fled on the wings of prayer and praise, and the precious season was over.

This is but a sketch of one of the many meetings in Fulton street and other places in this city.

Chapter 6

An Infidel Lawyer's Conviction and Conversion

The narrative that follows is one of the most remarkable and interesting among the records of the revival. It was drawn up by the gentleman who is the subject of it, and being in the form of a diary, shows the gradual progress of the work of grace in his soul:

It is past six o'clock – clients and office-companions have all left for their quiet homes – I only am left alone. In that corner stands my cot, on which I shall presently rest for the night, to renew on the morrow the same dull routine that I have passed to-day and many days before.

Alone! alone! how shall I occupy or kill the time now intervening before it is ten, my usual resting hour?

I will go out and read the papers – no, I will go over to the saloon – there I shall meet someone with whom to converse about the news of the day – Congress, the State Legislature, Kansas, politics, perhaps the great revival – what interest have I in that? I have examined the subject of religion, the Bible, the divinity of Christ. I reject the whole; it is not sustained by legitimate testimony; it is all foolishness; many beautiful sayings are found in the Bible; the benevolence of Christ is above all praise; the writers of the Old Testament had some faint idea of the existence of a spiritual God; it was obscure, imperfect. Once I believed the Bible was a revelation from God – enjoyed religion –

THE POWER OF PRAYER

did not doubt its reality – was more happy then than now. Those exercised by it now appear to enjoy themselves. I will do nothing to mar their apparent happiness; it will all end in death to be sure, but still I would reverse the sentiment of Paul, 'If in this life only we have hope in Christ, we are of all men the most miserable.' For from observation and experience, I would say, if there be no immortality, no judgment, no heaven, no hell, no eternal *life* for the good; if all religious enjoyments end at death, the Christian's faith, and the Christian's hope are greatly to be preferred, as a means of present enjoyment.

There is that anonymous letter – I read it to-day for the first time in twenty years; it is rather a good letter – was doubtless well intended – I will read it again. 'My dear brother in Christ' – I wonder if you know how far I am from Christ now? That address was thought to be proper at its date ('March 17, 1838'). What is that on the desk? Notice of meeting – 'Greene street Methodist Episcopal Church, J. T. Peck, Pastor; religious services every evening this week at half past seven o'clock; come thou with us and we will do thee good.' Have a good mind to go – have not been in church for a long time – wonder if they will look cross, stiff as they did at Thirteenth street the last time I was there? It is half an hour yet – will read the letter – (did read it) – will go to church – it will be a good enough place for a couple of hours – then it will be time for retiring. Am in the church close by the door – hope I shall not intrude – will be very civil – they are singing, praying, singing, preaching; prayer-meeting announced – shall I go home? 'all are invited to stay' – that does not mean me surely – stay though – leaders in the altar – singing – praying – anxious ones invited to come to the altar – 'if there are any in the congregation who desire the prayers of Christians, let them manifest it by rising' – a pause – nobody rises – wonder why the whole congregation do not

[50]

rise – have a good mind to rise myself and rebuke them for their stupidity – thought everybody wanted the prayers of Christians, if they were sincere – ashamed of the poor sinners who will not stand up to signify their desire for prayers of Christians, gratuitously offered – singing, praying – several members walking through the aisles speaking to individuals – one comes where I am seated – 'Do you enjoy religion?' It is pleasant to be here if I do not disturb any one. 'Are you a member of any church?' – Episcopal. 'We are glad to see you here; will you not take a seat further up? it will look more sociable.' If it will oblige you I will go – went up – began to feel some interest in the proceedings – they – Christians – seemed to enjoy it. How much better they are employed here than they would be in some *rowdy meeting*, as some of them, doubtless, would have been, had they not been here. Collections go round – put five cents in the plate – save two shillings for another purpose – felt better on that account – went home – slept well.

It is again past six o'clock P.M. – again alone – what shall I do this evening? There is that Greene street church notice – wonder if M. forgot it – he ought to take it to some place where it may do good; shall I go again to-night – that anonymous letter again.

TROY, *March 17th*, 1838.
DEAR BROTHER IN CHRIST:
Let me adopt this method of conversing on the subject of religion; let me ask a few plain and pertinent questions in a Christian temper. Dear brother, are you enjoying your religion as you did some three or four years since? You will remember the time when you used to attend the regular prayer-meetings of this church (Dr Beman's), and I well remember – and think I was happy in those days, when you used to read Finney's Lectures on Revivals. I

well remember when you used to lead in prayer, and pray that sinners might be brought to a knowledge of Jesus Christ; you used to attend the little social circles of prayer, and I think my heart has been revived and refreshed in those little meetings that savored of Heaven.

You will remember the time when you used to take a great interest in the Ida Hill Sunday School, and many persons through your influence were induced to attend. Oh! dear brother, your voice is now silent on the subject of the salvation of sinners; you have deserted the prayer-meetings, and you no more assist us in this struggle to save souls. Dear brother, stop and think; pause, I beseech you, and see the influence that you are exerting in the cause of Christ; ask yourself, am I doing *all* that I can for God? are you living as *you promised* God you would when you hoped you gave yourself up to his service? Are you leading a life of prayer? Do you feel anxious that sinners should be saved, and do you warn sinners to flee from the wrath to come? Oh! enter into the work of Christ, and pray with us that sinners may be saved; look at your past life and repent, and join with this church, and help us to save souls. We must soon die; let us work while the day lasts, for the night cometh wherein no man can work; we need your help; when professors of religion are cold and stupid, God will not work. Look to it, that you do not oppose God or stand in his way; look to it, lest you may be a stumbling-block to sinners, and that the Lord will lead you to reflect and repent, and do your duty, shall be the earnest prayer of a brother in Christ.

Good advice: well, yes – think I will go to church this evening. If I thought M. had left that notice here for me, I would not go. There is a package of them; he doubtless left them by mistake, or forgetfulness; I will go to meeting – what for? The Bible is no revelation, Christ is no God, God

The New York Revival of 1858

is sovereign, and will do with me just as he pleases, in time and eternity. Why should I care? why fret about that which I cannot help? hell cannot be much worse than earth. I had nothing to do with bringing myself into this world; if I had been consulted about it I would not have come. At all events, when I get into hell, I shall be rid of one difficulty that torments men here – the fear of death. If I am to live there eternally, I shall have a constitution fitted for eternal duration and be rid of fear of death, which troubles most men most; I do not care anything about it – I have many a time wished myself dead. Pity it is I ever had any existence. If my soul is immortal, it has existed somewhere before this state of existence. I am not conscious of it, and doubt if I will be conscious of any existence after death. Have seen animals die; oxen, horses, sheep; have seen men die. After death, what's the difference between them? They rot and decay alike, alike they are forgotten; what is there about animal man, differing from animal beast? Nothing – nothing. Is my soul immortal? will it eternally endure? It may be so – what then? It will be a merely spiritual existence, mingling with, and lost in the great mass of immaterial existences – no individuality – no consciousness – it will be as it was before my present state. I will go to church again to-night – what will *they* say – *I* can never be renewed – I shall never again enjoy any religious emotion – how can I? I like to see others enjoy it. There is my best friend L——, his whole soul is wrapped up in it – he seems to enjoy it – appears to be happy amidst trials and conflicts enough to drive a man crazy; his circumstances in this life are almost as bad as mine, yet he is always happy – I always miserable. I once did enjoy something of it; the letter reminds me of it – was happier then than now. I was sincere in my devotions then, and believed others were. How did I lose it? (Let darkness – deep, black, lasting darkness cover the story of

[53]

my declension. God knows it, and he only has the right to disclose it. He has pardoned me, man cannot; man would not if he could; none have grace enough for that.)

In church again; occupy the same seat. Few are present; it is early. Again requested to seat myself nearer to the altar, it will oblige him, the same kind member; it is done; services as before; inquirers kneeling at the altar, the pastor by the side of one of them, (a man, advanced in years) on his knees in prayer. The Spirit of God is in that prayer; it presented my case. God help me to take it to myself. I was very mellow for a little season; wondered how any person there (where all were to me strangers) should know my history on religious subjects. Went home unsatisfied; restless, sorry, glad, uneasy; thankful that I went to church. Reminiscences of former times crowded upon me; those happier days, when religion, feeble in it as I was, gave joy to my soul, which many years of subsequent, established, and sincere infidelity could not wholly obliterate: those days, I shall enjoy them no more! Others do, and may continue to rejoice and glory in religious services; they are not for me: believe, cannot; hope, I may not: how can I answer my own scepticism, my own infidel arguments, my own reading of the Bible? I always believe in God; *my* God, but not the Christian's God; what would S——, and G——, and M——, and H——, and B——, and others say? they who have so often complimented the conclusiveness of my infidel arguments, to hear me now attempt to refute them myself, and argue for Christianity? No matter for them, what would Christ say? How could I speak to him? of him? Christians *now* are more happy than I; the future world alike to all, all nothing – nothing – nothing.

Days passed, weeks passed; the subject was continually upon my mind. I came to that day, that night of agony – of agony unspeakable; how shall I speak of it? how write? I

The New York Revival of 1858

cannot; it must not be written. Well can I remember, but cannot speak, cannot write, can scarcely think again one tithe of *that* which came, pressed on, departed in quick succession from my mind. Was it a dream? As those days and weeks passed by, daily the meetings in Greene Street sanctuary were by me attended. Associates joked, ridiculed me for it. M——, a newcomer into our office, was a religious man; he had left those notices of meetings at Greene Street purposely for me (thus I learned). I was glad of it; thought I was not entirely abandoned to infidelity; this thought was strengthened by the members of the church, who, with kindness, several of them expressed pleasure at seeing me in their meetings. Asked myself often if there was a possibility for me to become a Christian; no, it cannot be. B——, my other office associate, was, if possible, more infidel than myself. It was, perhaps, vanity in me that led me to see the weakness of his infidel arguments; thought I could present them much more forcibly than could he. He, like myself, was a very wicked man. I could always refute him with the Christian's argument. I told M—— that he ought to get B—— converted: it would do him good, for he did not know enough to be an infidel; he did not understand the Scriptures well enough to maintain an infidel argument. M—— replied, 'That is just what he says of you; he thinks it would be the best thing that could happen to you to get religion.' I thought it was impossible for me, and told him so; but if B—— would put himself in the way of religious services, he would soon be converted. I, attending the church, was often moved to distress, doubt, anxiety, despair. One evening, the pastor came to the door of the pew I occupied; I was the only person in it. 'Please move along,' said he, 'and let me sit beside you.' I did so, and he sat beside me. 'I should like to know the state of your mind,' said he. I replied, 'I like to attend your meetings; hope I am not in the way of any person?'

[55]

THE POWER OF PRAYER

'Do you enjoy religion?'

'No, not as I once did.'

'Do you belong to any church?'

'No – yes; I am an Episcopalian; was educated in that church, but for several years have seldom attended it; am not now a Christian, and suppose I never shall be; still, I like to be here; it is a pleasure to me; and if I do not intrude, shall continue to come.'

'Come, and welcome; we shall be glad to see you here, and hope it will do your soul good.'

'Thank you, sir.' Invited to go to the altar: inquirers were there; had a mind to go, but did not. Meeting closed – went home – was alone in my room: old memories revived: distress: anguish: pray I cannot – try – no: it is of no use for me to try; whatever joy there may be in religion for others, there is none for me. The Bible: it speaks not for me. Jesus Christ; He is repudiated, rejected, slain – yes, crucified, but not for me; there was a time it might have been for me; that time is passed; now, it cannot be for me; for me? no, no, never; sins of a lifetime: how long? how many? all concentrated – real, deep, dark, damning: O memory! my soul sinks under their crushing weight! Sins: against myself, man, God – against God; sins terrible in aggregate, more terrible in detail; they enlarge, magnify all, all in a moment; nothing else but sin – no, nothing. Oh, God! how they cluster around me! The room is dark – darker the gloom upon my soul; in bed – alone – sleep: there is none for me; agony, agony. Is it a dream that comes over me: reality? yes, reality. Jesus at a distance – Satan near (so it seemed); pray, pray; a voice seemed to say: try, try to pray; no! God appears: still at a distance stands the Saviour, his face fearfully solemn – no signs of anger in it. I think he would, but cannot, save me; his countenance alters not. Satan suggests: there is no hope, no hope for me; I feel it – know it; my soul sinks in

[56]

The New York Revival of 1858

despair. I look at the Saviour: he seems to smile on me, and say, 'How foolish you are: I have saved others as bad as you. Doubt not my power: when you are in earnest, then look to me.' 'What, me?' 'Yes, you; my office is to save the worst. You have thought and said hard things of me, and now, in all your trouble, you look towards me, but do not trust me: you have not faith in my power to do you good.' Is it possible that I can be saved from this crushing load of sin? Thoughts innumerable, troublesome thoughts, press heavily upon my mind and memory; hours pass – try to be penitent, to believe, to pray: cannot; exhausted – try to dispel these gloomy thoughts – will not go at my bidding. Why am I troubled in this way? it is all nonsense; I cannot be in my right mind – must be crazy: horrible thought! I will go to sleep – shall feel better in the morning; eyes closed – cannot sleep – get up and look out of the window; why, it is daylight, and I have not slept a wink all night. What shall I do? I am not sick; my pulse is quick, but not much quicker than usual. I will go to meeting to-night – yes, to the altar: how absurd! how foolish! Lie down again, mentally saying, Blessed Jesus, let me sleep; Satan, begone, I am resolved to go!

Again awake – two hours have passed. Blessed Jesus, I thank thee; canst thou indeed save *me*? comforting thought, is it *possible*? Jesus, have mercy on me; Lord Jesus, have mercy on me, even me. Feel strangely, something no language can describe what it is; Jesus is near, Satan stands back; there is hope, faint, faint hope; get behind me, Satan. 'Whosoever *will* let him come unto me.' I will, blessed Saviour, help me; am helped, I feel it; will believe in Jesus, *my Saviour*; help me to say so, Jesus; Father in heaven, have mercy on my soul, for the sake of Jesus; Spirit of the living God, direct me, help me. Oh, help me, even *me*.

[57]

THE POWER OF PRAYER

The hour of business has arrived: I am unfit for it, am not happy, hope I shall be: afraid not; in doubt, in hope, and fear, the day passes to near its close. I will go to the meeting this evening, will not go to the altar, that is not necessary; will confess my sins to God, whilst they are praying; will they pray for me? they would not if they knew my moral position; if they only knew how bad I am, they would not have me in their house. I will give it up: God knows just how bad I am; He has pardoned some very wicked men . . . I will go to the altar, why should I hesitate, others have there been blessed, why may not I? They will pray for me – if they do not, God may forgive me: He has pardoned others – the thief upon the cross, denying, swearing Peter . . . Friend L—— is experienced in these matters – I will see him and tell him all; he knows me – all my circumstances; he will not believe a word I say – will think it pretence; not a being of my acquaintance but would do the same. None of them will believe that I can repent and be saved; cannot blame them – would not believe it myself, I only hope it may be possible. I will go and see L——: it will not do any good – he will say I am drunk or crazy; have drunk no liquor in months: he will scold me: I will see him, nevertheless – I want his advice.

On the way to L——'s – wonder if he is at home – I hope he will not be there; what will he say? I will turn back – won't make a fool of myself – these feelings will all be gone in a little while – shall then be ashamed I ever had them; turn back, turned round, people in the street will think me crazy – can't help it – God help me – words of prayer, do I mean them? Try mentally to pray – enter L——'s room – none there but him: – how do you do? 'Why, C——, what is the matter with you?' Don't know. 'Are these tears of penitence? it would rejoice my heart to think so.' No answer. 'Come, let us kneel down and pray.' He prayed,

[58]

prayed for me. 'You pray for yourself.' 'God have mercy,' I heard my own voice say. I had mercy – felt it – was relieved – told L—— all my feelings and resolutions. 'You have resolved right – you just do it.' Did resolve, and was happy; if tears were shed, they were grateful tears.

On the way from L——'s to the church; will tell the brethren what the Lord has done for my soul, will thank them for their prayers and kindness, will acknowledge God my Saviour before them, and pray for Divine assistance.

In the church, sermon is ended – brethren in the altar – singing – sinners invited to come to the altar; I rise to speak; cannot utter a word; altar, altar, altar, seems to sound in my ears; start for it; kneel; they are singing – praying; the heavens are brass over me – no God – no Saviour – time passes – sounds are heard – they become faint – fainter – cease – consciousness is suspended; I feel a pricking sensation about my head, hands, feet – all over me – similar to that I once felt when restored to consciousness from apparent death; I hear music – 'come to judgment' – a well-known voice in prayer (the voice of M.); 'Oh! my Saviour,' it says – I seem to see the Saviour on my right side – Jesus smiling upon me, his face radiant with love – my soul is filled with grateful joy – literally unspeakable and full of glory – standing up before the altar with my brethren as their shouts of thanksgiving ascend to heaven; I am too full to utter anything but thanks to my brethren, thanks to my God and Saviour.

As I look back upon that hour of agony and deliverance, with what thrilling emotions can I repeat the words of one of our hymns:

> Tongue can never express
> The sweet comfort and peace
> Of a soul in its earliest love.

From thence, hitherto I have, by God's grace, rejoiced

THE POWER OF PRAYER

with thankfulness in the blessed assurance of his willingness and ability to pardon and save to the uttermost all who come to him through Jesus Christ my Saviour.

> What I have felt and seen
> With confidence I tell,
> And publish to the sons of men
> The signs infallible.

I *know* that *my* Redeemer lives, for whose sake God has *pardoned* me, and I rejoice every day in believing that here and hereafter I shall be happy; that it may be so, my constant prayer to God shall ascend for grace and the aid of his Holy Spirit.

To this narrative, we are able to add that the writer has taken a decided stand on the Lord's side. At the Globe Hotel prayer-meeting, two months after the close of this sketch, though there were clergymen present, he was requested to lead, which he did, to the edification of those present, as with great modesty and humility he proceded with the exercises. He read some of those very portions of Scripture, after singing, which once he had been most ready to deny, and which most fully represent the office work of Christ. How marked and emphatic was that reading; how he seemed to enter into the meaning and spirit of the inspired penman. His whole manner and voice evinced the emotion of his soul. Then prayer followed – addressed directly to Christ, as a *divine* Saviour, acknowledging him as the Wonderful, Counsellor, Prince of Peace, head over all things to the church, name above every name, King of kings, and Lord of lords – acknowledging all the divine attributes of Christ, which some present had often heard him deny, dwelling upon the glories of the Saviour with unspeakable satisfaction, thankfulness, and joy.

Chapter 7

Surprising Grace – A Successful Merchant – The Magdalens – The Saviour Waiting – A Young Sailor – Danger of Delay.

The subject is a successful merchant of New York. His early life was spent in Nova Scotia, but at the age of fourteen he left the home of his childhood and the intervening years, to the age of manhood, were spent upon the sea. During this period of his wanderings, he was constantly followed with the deep solicitude and earnest prayers of a pious mother; and to the influence of these prayers, and the constant impression made by a knowledge of that solicitude on his mind, he now ascribes his preservation from almost innumerable temptations, and his recent conversion to God.

For several years he had been accustomed to attend, with his Christian companions, upon the public service of God's house; but not till the beginning of the present year had he experienced any deep and permanent convictions of sin, or felt any apprehension from his exposed condition as one under righteous condemnation. About this time the religious interest in New York and vicinity had become very deep, and but few could be found who were not more or less anxious with reference to the salvation of the soul. In the hidden depths of the heart, thousands then carried convictions of guilt, such as they had never experienced before, and some who had even despised religion felt strongly attracted to some of its simplest appointments.

THE POWER OF PRAYER

There were many, however, who, through the influence of pride, struggled hard and long to conceal their feelings. Their most intimate Christian friend was not permitted to know their state of mind, and yet, in secret, they were the subjects of an almost overwhelming sorrow.

Of this class was the subject of this sketch. For several weeks he had been in a state of deep spiritual distress, but avoiding as far as possible the stated means of grace, and excusing himself from all special religious appointments, he was endeavoring *secretly* to seek reconciliation with God. With this view he had spent quite a number of evenings in his counting-room, reading his Bible and offering prayer. Failing, however, to obtain the relief and comfort which his heart needed, and for which he had thus sought, his next resort was to 'union prayer-meetings', and to religious services with churches, where, as a stranger, he might feel willing to make himself known as an inquirer. The noon hours, as well as the evenings of several weeks, were spent in this wandering from meeting to meeting, and from church to church, without effecting any encouraging change in the state of his mind, and he was almost ready to sink into despair, when he was made to see that the real difficulty existing in the way of his salvation was nothing more or less than *pride*. It was this, he saw, that had made him resort to his place of business for prayer, rather than to his chamber. It was this, too, that had led him to give a preference to general appointments for religious worship among strangers, rather than to those services where he would have met and mingled with his friends.

But having now satisfied himself of his error and sin in thus shunning the cross, he purposed, in the fear of God, to embrace the earliest possible opportunity of denying himself, by openly avowing his wretched state of mind to the church and congregation with which he had usually met for worship.

The New York Revival of 1858

This secret purpose, with the circumstances leading to it, was made known on the Sabbath evening following, when, at the close of the sermon, he left his seat, and taking a position immediately in front of the pulpit, related in a most affecting manner the struggles of mind through which he had been passing, and the deep sorrow of heart under which, for many weeks, he had been suffering.

At the close of his statement, which, as may well be supposed, produced an indescribable impression, he remarked that he had never asked God's people to pray for him, and that he could not consistently do so until, from the lowest depths of humiliation, he had first prayed for himself. Then, in the presence of all the congregation, he fell upon his knees, and with a heart bursting with grief, and all helpless in its throbbing anguish, he poured out his prayer to God for mercy.

The very next day he was enabled to rejoice in a Saviour's love, and in the evening of that day, at a social meeting, he bore a feeling testimony to the amazing grace of God, as displayed in his conversion.

The following came through the matron of the *Magdalen* Asylum, where the person had taken refuge, and is certified to as being her own, and written of her own accord:

'To the Fulton street prayer-meeting. I desire the prayers of the church. I feel that I have been a very wicked girl, and that I have led a very bad life, and I feel my need of Christ. I want to be a Christian.'

Another:

'The prayers of this meeting are respectfully requested for G. B——, who has lived all his life in wickedness, and only a few days ago contemplated suicide and the great crime of murder, in the hope of ending his misery.'

THE POWER OF PRAYER

On reading these requests, the leader remarked, that if the persons making them were present (and one we know was present), he wished to say to them, that the Lord Jesus laid down his life for just such sinners as they – that he came to seek and to save them that are lost – he came, not to call the righteous, but *sinners* to repentance.

Then arose one in the meeting, after having made several unsuccessful attempts to get the floor, and said: 'I came to hear – not to say a word. But when, on coming into the room, I saw hanging on the wall this passage, "Him that cometh unto me, I will in no wise cast out," and when I hear these requests read, and feel that there are some poor sinners in this room that need just such an assurance as that, I cannot hold my peace.' Then he told of another place and another scene. He was from the West – and in the West he accosted a little girl, not supposing she was a Christian:

'"Do you love the Bible?" said I to her.

"Yes, sir, I love the Bible."

"Is there any one portion of it, or one passage in it, which you love better than the rest?"

"Yes, sir, there is, though I love all the Bible; if I may be permitted, I love this more than any other: "Him that cometh unto me, I will in no wise cast out."'

'There she rested,' said the speaker, 'and there every sinner may rest his hopes for eternity. I feel impelled to speak, because I believe and feel that the destiny of souls hangs upon the hour. Look, sinners, at the passage on the wall. There is a whole sermon in it. No matter what a sinner you have been, "Him that cometh unto me, I will in no wise cast out". I am as sure as I feel of my own existence, that there is some sinner who needs just such an assurance as this to rest upon, and I must urge you to cast yourself upon it and be saved.' Many wept.

Instantly a young lieutenant of the navy, from the U.S.

The New York Revival of 1858

ship-of-war 'Sabine', arose close beside the leader, and said: 'I wish to add another passage to that on the wall. It is this: "Though your sins be as scarlet, they shall be as white as snow, and though they be red like crimson, they shall be as wool." What does my impenitent friend need more than these to assure him of God's readiness to pardon?'

Two stanzas of that beautiful hymn were sung:

> One there is above all others,
> Well deserves the name of Friend.

Then prayer followed – and prayer has been the great feature of these services; while the whole assembly appeared to be impressed with the presence of God.

A young sailor arose. He was evidently a Scotchman by birth. He was deeply impressed, as all could see by his voice and manner, that this was a critical moment, the turning point to some awakened souls.

'Will you take a sailor's advice,' said he, 'a stranger sailor; you who are now deciding that at some future time you will be a Christian? Will you take a sailor's advice, and not delay your choice another hour, but come now and be on the Lord's side? You cannot possibly magnify the danger of delay. You cannot believe it to be half as great as it is.' And then he spoke of some of his dreadful experiences of the effects of procrastination. He related the following as coming under his own observation.

'I remember', said he, 'when in Panama, one of my brother sailors was taken very sick. I had previously, on many occasions, urged him to take Jesus as his guide, counsellor, and friend. But his answer had ever been, "Time enough yet." That fearful putting off, that delivering himself up to the power of Satan, who was constantly whispering in his ear, "Time enough yet," reached its fearful crisis at last. As he lay sick upon his mattress, his

THE POWER OF PRAYER

writhings and contortions denoted the fever and pain that were within. But the fever of his soul was causing much more anguish than all his bodily ailments.

I said to him, "You need a Saviour now." "Oh," said he, "I have put off seeking Jesus too long." I earnestly begged him to look at the cross of Christ, and there learn what Jesus had done and suffered, that a poor sinner like him might not perish, but have everlasting life. But he replied, with choking sobs, "Too late, too late!" "Oh!" he cried, "no rest for me. I am going to some place, I know not where. Oh! I know not where!" His head fell back upon the pillow. I cried, "Ned! are you dying?" But all I heard was, through the gurgling in his throat, "No rest;" and my dying shipmate was gone.'

Another touching incident he related as intimately connected with his own conversion, bearing upon the danger of delay. It was at his own home. He had a very pious, God-fearing mother, who had never neglected any opportunity which offered, to impress upon his young mind the urgent need of seeking a Saviour in his youthful days. But he had constantly neglected to pay more than a passing attention to his mother's admonitions, until one Sabbath morning she invited a young girl, a neighbor's daughter, to accompany them to the house of prayer. 'She replied, in a light and trifling manner, "Oh, no, I cannot go till next Sunday. I shall have a new bonnet then; my old one is too shabby." Alas! that next Sabbath never came to her. On Monday she was taken quite sick. On Wednesday she died. My mother told me, with streaming eyes, as she came home from watching at her bedside, "Emma is gone; and gone, I fear, without conversion." This was so sudden, so unexpected, that it woke within my heart the cry, "What must I do to be saved?" And, blessed be God, that cry was not made in vain. Jesus had mercy on my soul. He has been ever since that time the Rock of

Salvation. Oh! come to him, all you who need the saving grace of a dying, risen Saviour! Will you take a sailor's counsel? Will you come? God is calling you! Come now.'

There were not many dry eyes in the room at the close of this touching, tender, earnest appeal. It came from a warm heart, and it found its way to every heart.

Chapter 8

Remarkable Answers to Prayer – The Four Great Revivals – Power of Prayer – 'My Husband Saved' – Twenty Special Cases Selected – A Brother-in-law – A Drunkard Saved.

We are now, said a venerable clergyman of the Reformed Dutch Church, in the fourth great revival under the gospel dispensation. The first commenced in Pentecostal times, and continued several centuries. The second commenced in the time of Martin Luther, and was long continued in the church. The third was in the days of Edwards, and Whitefield, and the Tennants. The fourth is that which now pervades our country, and is spreading to all other lands.

The great fact and truth established by the first great revival was the supreme divinity of our Lord and Saviour Jesus Christ. It began with the dispensation of the Spirit on the day of Pentecost. It went on through the days of the Apostles. This was the great rejoicing truth and fact of the period. It filled all hearts with gladness. It was the great truth on which the faith and the fate of a perishing world depended. It was necessary that this truth should be established and felt as a foundation on which the world would build its hopes.

The great truth illustrated and established by the great revival in the time of Luther and the Reformers was the doctrine of justification by faith in Christ. This cardinal doctrine was the platform on which they stood, in their

The New York Revival of 1858

opposition to the errors of the Church of Rome. It was necessary that the world should be set right on this subject. And it *was* set right. It was this that aroused the true church with amazing power, so that kings and dynasties sunk feebly down before her, as she marched on in her glorious triumphs.

The first truth illustrated and established in the third great revival in the time of Edwards, and Whitefield, and the Tennents was the doctrine of instantaneous conversion and regeneration by the Holy Spirit. It was necessary that this great doctrine should be enforced and stamped indelibly upon the convictions and heart of the world, so that it should remain an undisputed fact, received and acknowledged by all.

And now the great truth illustrated and established by this great revival of the present time, the fourth great revival, is the cardinal doctrine of Christian union; oneness of the church; a real unity; a oneness of all her members in Christ, the Head.

It is this great truth that is in this revival, and by this revival impressed upon the world. It is this that arms the church with its energy and power, by which she overcomes and goes on to victory and triumph. This is the truth which is to live in the convictions of men, till Christ has subdued all things to himself.

After reading requests, and earnest prayer, a highly respected Presbyterian clergyman arose and said:

'We should remember that all these great revivals were bestowed in answer to prayer. I wonder if my brethren ever think of the *power* of prayer; of the *power* they have to *prevail* over the divine mind. If you ask me *how* this is, I cannot tell you *how*. But just see what the Bible reveals and teaches on this subject. It seems as if God had disclosed the fact that he cannot withstand the prayers of his people. Just see what he says about this. Look at the case of Moses on the Mount. God complained to Moses, as if he had said: these people whom I have brought out of Egypt with a high hand and outstretched arm have made themselves a golden calf; and they bow down and worship it, and they forsake and forget me, who scooped out the waters of the sea for them to pass over; who wrought miracles for their deliverance in the land of bondage. Now my wrath is waxed hot against them. Now, Moses, let me alone that I may destroy them. I will make of you a great nation. I will cut them off utterly. But if you fall down and pray, I know I cannot do it. Don't ask me to spare them, and I will make of you a great people.

What did Moses do? Why, he fell on his knees. "Oh! my Father, what will become of thy great name?" he said. "What will the heathen say, and they of Egypt? Why, they will say that you just brought them out here into the wilderness to destroy them, and could not or would not save them. That be far from thee, Lord." And what did God do? Why, he seemed not to be able to withstand the prayer of his servant, and rebellious Israel was saved.

Take other examples. At the prayer of one man the rain was stayed; not a drop of water or dew upon the earth for the space of three years and six months. And then at the prayer of one man the heavens gave rain.

Take another example. They of the Amalekites, and Moab, and Mount Seir, combined against the Jews to destroy them with a great army. But they awoke in the morning, and 180,000 of them were dead corpses. What was the matter? Why, one man had gone out against them armed with prayer.

So when God poured out his Spirit in these great revivals, it was in answer to prayer. Oh! when will the church learn that God hears and answers prayer, that prayer with God *prevails?*'

'As I was leaving the prayer-meeting,' said another of

The New York Revival of 1858

the speakers, 'when I had gone a little distance, a lady came rushing up to me and exclaimed: "Oh! my brother, my brother; oh! is not my husband to be saved? I have put in a request that he might be prayed for, three times; and three times this request has been read; and in each case no allusion has been made to my case in the prayers which followed. My husband has not been prayed for. What does it mean?"

'Well, I said to her,' said the speaker, "Suppose you keep on praying for him. I will pray for him. I will speak to others to pray for him. We will carry his case to other places of prayer."

The heart of this wife was very much encouraged. When I met her again, I inquired, "Is your husband converted yet?"

"Oh! no, he is not converted; but I believe he will be. My husband is certainly to be a Christian. I feel assured he will be."

In a few days I met her again. I asked her, "Is that husband of yours a Christian yet?"

"Oh, I am afraid not. I have been praying and hoping, and believing. I am so distressed with anxiety for him, that I have had to give up all attention to all household duties. I cannot oversee my house. My hope is in God, and I will trust in *him*, for vain is the help of man."

A few days after, I met this same wife again.

"Is your husband converted yet?" Her countenance lighted with a spiritual, serene, and holy joy.

"Oh yes, I hope my husband is converted. He came home from his business; he ran to me, threw his arms round my neck, and, in weeping rapture, exclaimed, 'Oh! I have found the Saviour! I have given myself up to him, and on the very next Sabbath I am to unite myself to the people of God. I am with you now for time and eternity.'

"I asked him where he was," said the wife, "when he

THE POWER OF PRAYER

experienced the change. He answered, 'In the Fulton street prayer-meeting.' And this was the first knowledge I had that he ever attended the Fulton street prayer-meetings at all. So, while I was praying, he was going to the place of prayer, where the Lord met him in his mercy."

'Were I to name him,' continued the speaker, 'you would all know him, for he is a marked and eminent man in this city.'

The tears were flowing freely all around the room.

'Now, just mark one thing,' said the same voice, 'how God, by the Spirit, supported the faith of this humble, feeble believer; and how, at the same time, he broke her off from all human reliance, that the excellency of the power might be of God, and not of man.'

A melting, hallowed influence fell upon the prayer-meeting.

Then how beautifully came in these lines, which were sung with deep emotion:

> One there is above all others,
> Well deserves the name of friend;
> His is love beyond a brother's,
> Costly, free, and knows no end.

A colored woman, devoted to her Saviour, in her humble, earnest way, determined to select twenty of her acquaintances, and pray earnestly for their salvation. She was a member of the Broome street church, known intimately to Miss Maynard, since called to heaven, who was well known by many who attend this Fulton street prayer-meeting. This colored woman kept her resolution, selected the twenty, prayed without ceasing for their conversion, and subsequently had the blessed satisfaction of believing that they all had embraced the Saviour.

The New York Revival of 1858

A Montreal clergyman, whose son was in Yale College, and unconverted, prayed earnestly for God's saving grace to descend upon him, and quite recently had evidence that his prayers were heard and answered in the conversion of that son.

A pastor who was settled seven hundred miles from New York, who visited this meeting one year ago, was much impressed; considered the Fulton street prayer-meeting as the mother of an awakened religious feeling all over the land, and his attendance here had made him wise to win souls to Christ. He had been greatly blessed in his ministry, had labored with uncommon zeal, fervor, and success. He had improved the golden hour for gathering in the harvest of souls.

A friend, in rising, said it gave him great pleasure to inform the meeting that a brother called at his place of business on that very morning, and with an unusually happy face, exclaimed, 'My son, for whom I have prayed so long, is at last under conviction of sin. His sister has prayed earnestly for him that he might be brought to Christ. For three months he has been suffering from a sense of his unworthiness, but never told his nearest and dearest friends. Yesterday he met an acquaintance who urged him to visit the theatre in the evening, in his company. He promised to go. After they separated, he thought, "I had resolved to go to the prayer-meeting this evening; I do not know about going to the theatre. This may be the last opportunity I may ever have of attending such a prayer-meeting; I must not lose it – I will not." He resolved not to go to the theatre, but to go to the prayer-meeting. He did so, and was so convinced of his sins, and of his need of a Saviour, that he rose in that same prayer-meeting, and related the experience he had passed through, in terms so touching that there was scarcely a dry eye in the house.

THE POWER OF PRAYER

That son', said the gentleman speaking, 'is now in this room for the first time.'

On a late occasion, when many requests had been read, and the chairman had made an earnest appeal for prayer for the objects thus presented, a gentleman arose in the audience and said:

'Mr Chairman, bear with me a moment before prayer, while I add to these requests one for my brother-in-law, and state some facts. He was in this room for the first time last night, at a night prayer-meeting. He is in this business men's daily prayer-meeting now, and in this meeting for the first time to-day. The Holy Spirit met him in his mercy last night. He came here entirely careless and thoughtless, by my persuasion. And this morning he sent for me, before he left his room, to come and pray with him. He has just returned from Newport, where he had spent the summer as regardless of religion as the hundreds with whom he was daily associated. I found him in great distress of mind. I found him on his knees, praying and shedding a flood of tears. I talked to him, prayed with him, and heard him pray. And now I ask you to pray that he may be converted this very hour – before we leave the room.'

Then followed fervent, earnest prayer. What solemnity settled upon the minds of all. What a sense of the divine presence.

The next day this same case was again remembered. The man was present again, affected to tears through the whole meeting. On the next day he, of his own accord, and without any solicitation, put in the following request.

'The brother-in-law, for whom prayers have been offered in this room, desires to add his testimony to the efficacy of prayer. He humbly trusts, through the merits of a dying Saviour, that he has been hopefully converted; and he earnestly requests the continued prayers of this meeting that his faith may be strengthened in the Lord.'

The New York Revival of 1858

In a subsequent chapter, the record of this case is given in detail.

A man arose, greatly agitated respecting his soul and its destiny. Well he might be, he said. He had been a man of such a course of life, that he had much to repent of. He had been a great transgressor – profane – idle – dissolute – intemperate – a hater of religion and all its duties and requirements – a disbeliever in much that is called religion. He had lived a hardened, ungodly life, till he chanced to stray into one of the Fulton street meetings.

He came up to the upper lecture-room in great trepidation of mind. He wanted to find, he said, some place where there was a temperance pledge. He wanted to sign it. He would prefer to go to the rooms of the American Temperance Union, and sign there. He wanted to begin, he said, at the beginning – and the first thing was to quit the abomination of strong drink. This was the beginning, he said, of 'Let the wicked forsake his way', and then he hoped he should be able to forsake everything else that was wicked. He appeared to be in great haste. He said he was 'in a hurry to be a Christian'. This seemed to be according to the Scriptures, and yet he seemed to be wholly taught of the Holy Spirit.

We saw him a few days after this. He had been faithful in coming to all the meetings. He had been faithful to his pledge of total abstinence. He was very jealous of himself. His great fear was that some 'old evil companion' would get power over him – would get him to drink just one drop; then all would be gone, soul, body – all, said he, will go to hell together. He said his continual prayer was, 'Lord! hold thou me up and I shall be safe.' 'I cry to God continually,' said he, 'for I feel that God must help me or I shall fall. No man can realize the power of this appetite who has not felt it. I must be a Christian to be safe.'

[75]

Chapter 9

Prayer-meeting at 'Hell Corner' – An Invitation on the Mississippi – A Daughter converted and driven out of her Father's House – The whole Family converted – Hungry Children ask a Blessing – An only Son – The Camp-meeting Convert.

'There is a locality', said a strange gentleman in the Fulton street prayer-meeting, 'in New Hampshire, concerning which I wish to state a few facts of recent occurrence, which go to prove that the Holy Spirit can work with means or without them, according to his sovereign will and pleasure. In the locality of which I speak, there are about twenty families living isolated, and cut off from all association with the surrounding neighborhoods. They have no communication with anybody beyond themselves. These families are distinguished for their profanity, wickedness, gambling, and almost every vice. They have no respect for religious institutions. They are shut out from all means of grace. They are a reckless, hardened set of people. On a late occasion one of these men was at a neighbor's house, and while there indulged in the most horrid oaths. The woman of the house said to him:

"If you don't stop swearing so, I am afraid the house will fall down over our heads."

"Well, I should think", said the man, "that you are getting very pious, from what you say."

"Well, I should think it time for some of us to be getting religious."

[76]

The New York Revival of 1858

"If you feel that way, suppose we have a prayer-meeting in your house," said the man.

"Yes, we will have a prayer-meeting; we will have a prayer-meeting," chimed in many voices.

And a prayer-meeting was agreed upon, and the time was fixed. They got a man to lead the meeting – the only man living in the neighborhood who had ever been a professor of religion. He was a notorious backslider, and of course answered their purposes all the better for that; for all this was meant as a burlesque upon prayer-meetings.

The time came for the meeting, and all assembled. The backslider undertook to lead the meeting, but broke down in his prayer and could not go on. They undertook to sing, and could not make out anything at that. They determined not to give it up so. They appointed another prayer-meeting, on the next Sabbath, at 5 o'clock P.M. They sent to a deacon of a church living three miles off, saying that there was to be a prayer-meeting at Hell Corner – the common name by which the place was known – on next Sabbath afternoon, and wanted him to come down and conduct it. The good deacon did not dare to go. He thought it was either a hoax or a plan to mob him. He however spoke to a neighbor about it and asked:

"Had I better go?"

"Go, by all means, and I will go with you," said the neighbor.

So on the next Sabbath afternoon they went to the prayer-meeting at Hell Corner. All were assembled, preparing to give solemn and serious attention to the services.

"I had not been there but a few minutes," said the deacon, "before I felt that the Spirit of the Lord was there." Four or five of these hardened, wretched men were struck under conviction at this first meeting. Anoth-

[77]

er meeting was held, and more were converted. 'These prayer-meetings are continued,' said the speaker, 'and many of those who were convicted have since become converted, and have become praying men and women. The work is going on with amazing power. At the last meeting heard from, more than one hundred were present. Here was a case where God's Spirit went before the desires of the people in the region that was blessed. God heard the prayers of his children in other places, or it pleased him in his sovereign mercy to pour out his Holy Spirit upon this wicked community, and turn sinners from the error of their ways unto himself.'

A gentleman said at the prayer-meeting at the Globe Hotel, that six months ago, as he was standing on the west bank of the Mississippi River, a handbill was put into his hand, inviting him to attend a prayer-meeting in the city of New York. It was the Fulton street prayer-meeting. 'You can scarcely imagine the influence of such a little event as that upon the feelings, decisions, course, conduct and eternal well-being of an individual. I was invited when one thousand miles away to attend a noonday prayer-meeting of business men – I, a business man, in this great city of business, where time is money – surely there must be something in the religion of these men of business that amounts to something like a reality.' He said that on coming to the city, he complied with that invitation, which he had still in his pocket and intended to keep, and he should always have reason to be thankful that he ever attended one of those meetings. He had been on further East, to the cities east of us, and he everywhere found the daily prayer-meeting.

He then went on to speak of revivals in places at the West. He spoke of one in particular of great interest. In a neighborhood where there was a large population but no church, the people built a large school-house, and when it

The New York Revival of 1858

was finished, they resolved to hold in it union meetings for prayer. They were commenced and were largely attended. And when all who came could not get in, they would crowd around the windows to hear. The Lord poured out his Spirit in great power and many were converted.

Living in the neighborhood of that school-house was a very wealthy, proud, infidel, irreligious man. Some of his family were inclined to go to the prayer-meeting. He called his family together, and told them that if any of his family went to that prayer-meeting and 'got religion', as he called it, they were to be disinherited and banished from the house. His wife was included with the children. She had been, and so had his oldest daughter, which put him in a rage. The daughter continued to go to the prayer-meetings and soon found peace in believing in Jesus. When an opportunity was given for those who had a hope in Christ to make it known – she meekly arose and spoke of the 'great change' in her heart, and her humble hopes of salvation through a crucified Saviour.

There were those standing at the window outside who immediately went and told the father of this young lady of the professions she had made. When she went home that night, she met her father standing in the doorway with a heavy quarto Bible in his arms.

'Maria,' said he, 'I have been told that you have publicly professed to-night that you have got religion. Is that so?'

'Father,' said the girl, 'I love you, and I think I love the Saviour too.'

He opened his Bible to a blank leaf, and pointing with his finger, he said:

'Maria, whose name is that?'

'It is my name, sir.'

'Did I not tell you that I would disinherit you if you got religion?'

'Yes, sir.'

THE POWER OF PRAYER

'Well, I must do it. You cannot come into my house.' And tearing the leaf out of the Bible, 'There,' said he 'do I blot out your name from among my children. You can go.'

She went to the house of a pious widow lady in the neighborhood, and heard no more from her father for three weeks. One morning she saw her father's carriage driving up to the door. She ran out and said to the driver, 'What is the matter, James?'

'Your father is very sick, and thinks he is going to die; and he is afraid he shall go to hell for his wickedness, and for the grievous wrong he has done you in disinheriting you and turning you from his house. He wants you to jump into the carriage and come home as quickly as possible.'

She found her father sick, sure enough, on going home; but she soon saw that he was only sin sick. She talked with him; she prayed with him; she endeavored to lead him to Christ. In three days the father, mother, two brothers, and a sister, were all rejoicing in hope, making the whole family, all made heirs of God, and joint heirs with Christ, to the heavenly inheritance. How faithful God is to those who put their trust in him.

The disinherited was made the honored means, in the hands of the Holy Spirit, of unspeakable blessings to all her father's household, by going straight forward in her heavenly Master's service. What a glorious crown of rejoicing will be hers in the great and trying day, when the Lord comes to reckon up his jewels!

At another prayer-meeting, one of the speakers said it had been noticed that something was the matter with four little children, from the same family, in one of our public schools. One of the teachers inquired what the matter was, and she ascertained that these lovely little children were suffering for lack of food; that all they had to eat for days was a crust of bread and water. They had come to school

The New York Revival of 1858

with no better. They were German children, and their parents were unable to obtain food for them.

This teacher, who had ascertained the facts, went to the head teacher and communicated them to him. He sent home immediately, and had a good dinner prepared for them. He then took them to his own house. On arriving there, the youngest refused to go in. He said he did not know what kind of a house it was, and he did not like to go into a house without his mother knowing and approving of it. Finally, after very much persuasion, they got them all into the house. They took them to the parlor; there was an abundant meal set out. They seated them at the table; they urged them to eat: they could not persuade them to touch a mouthful. Finally it was resolved to leave these little children alone; perhaps they would eat then. The lady of the house paused at the door, and looking through the crack, what was her surprise to see the oldest little boy put up his two little hands together, and say grace – asking for God's blessing, and thanking him for his mercies. 'May we not all learn a lesson', said the speaker, 'from these little children, who, though they were starving, refused to eat till they had first acknowledged God's hand in the food provided?'

When these facts were related, there were not many dry eyes in the assembly.

An only son, unconverted, was prayed for in his presence. He became very angry, and so much incensed, that he resolved to sell his farm and go West, away from his relatives, who were praying for his salvation. They continued to pray, and he finally sold his farm, and was going to start for Albany, on his way to the West. He passed the prayer-meeting, on his way to the cars, and having some time to wait for the train, thought he would just go in to pass the time away, and see what was going on. He went in, and was hopefully converted before he left the meeting.

THE POWER OF PRAYER

A gentleman arose in the back part of the room. He said he was from the mountainous lumbering regions of Pennsylvania. 'We hear of your meetings through the medium of the religious papers. We love to know what the Lord is doing among you. All through the mountains of Pennsylvania the Lord has been pouring out his Spirit, and among these thoughtless, wicked men, as they are in our country, he has brought many to repentance. For forty-nine years, I lived the life of an impenitent man. It is not more than three months since I commenced a religious life. I went to a Methodist camp-meeting in our neighborhood. I did not go to it at the beginning. I thought I had so much to do that I would not go. I went toward the close of it. As soon as my pious wife saw me come upon the ground, she said, "You must come into the praying circle." I went with great reluctance. It pleased the Lord to awaken me at that meeting. But it closed, and I found no relief. I went on from day to day in great anxiety about my soul. I heard of another meeting, and I went more than a hundred miles to attend it. I sought but I did not find. I was made the subject of prayer. It came to the last day of the meeting, and I was afraid I should have to go away without any change of heart. When near the time of closing the meeting, it was proposed to spend a little time in the tent for prayer. Some said it was unseasonable. Some said they had a little season that might thus be occupied; and I was invited to read a portion of Scripture and pray. It took me by surprise. I opened the Bible to the chapter about the talents. I read. I was tempted to hide my talent as did the slothful servant. I resolved I would not do it. And I kneeled down to pray. The Lord met me in that prayer. He led me to make a complete surrender. The burden was gone. The anxiety was taken away. I felt that my sins were forgiven. I find peace and joy in believing. I am always happy, and happy to be in such a meeting as

The New York Revival of 1858

this especially. I feel it my privilege and duty to bear testimony for Christ. I love him much. I have had much to be forgiven. I have been greatly blessed since I first loved the Saviour. I intend to bear my cross and do my duty everywhere, at all times, and on all occasions.

The Lord is doing a great work among the mountains. Whole neighborhoods are turning to the Lord. The preaching of the gospel wins its way to the hearts of sinners, and many are coming out on the Lord's side.'

The speaker's manner was earnest, hearty, having great simplicity and deep feeling, which found its way to every heart. Then a stanza of the beautiful hymn:

> There is a fountain filled with blood
> Drawn from Emmanuel's veins;
> And sinners plunged beneath that flood,
> Lose all their guilty stains

was sung with deep emotion, in which all seemed to join in delightful harmony. Two or three prayers followed, and all those were earnestly and cordially remembered who had sent in their petitions to the throne of grace.

Chapter 10

Christ found at Home – The Man who found Peace in the Street.

A young man of fashion, of wealth and education, of high social position in one of the fashionable avenues in this great city, found out in the progress of this revival that he was a sinner, that he had a soul to be saved or lost. He felt himself on the verge of ruin, and the brink of eternal despair. He was bowed down under the load of his sins as a grievous burden. He sought relief and found it not. The requirements of the law stared him in the face, and he felt justly condemned. His heart was filled with sorrow. His countenance bore the marks of woe. Day after day he went about with his head bowed down like a bulrush, and day after day the burden became more and more insupportable. What should he do? Whither should he fly? He had at home a young wife whom he loved as he did his own life, and more than his own life. She was like him, devoted to the pleasures of the world, knew not what religion was – cared not. He had a sister living with him. They had been all well mated in the love of fashionable folly – the gaieties and worldly amusements commonly enjoyed by persons in their position in life. The wife and sister looked on this husband and brother with mute astonishment at the great change that had come over him.

One day, in one of our meetings, that burdened young man found his burden removed, faith in Christ sprang up

[84]

The New York Revival of 1858

in his soul, found his repentings kindled together, felt in himself the hope that maketh not ashamed, realized a Saviour precious to his soul. He believed that God, for Christ's sake, had forgiven his sins. He determined that he would never be ashamed of Christ. He would acknowledge and honor him everywhere.

The opportunity – the time and place soon came. He was returning to his home in the evening. 'Now,' said he, 'I must honor and obey God in my family. I must set up family worship.'

'Oh, no,' said the tempter, 'not yet. Don't be in a hurry. Take time. Get a little stronger, and then you can go on better.'

'I must begin to-night. I do not know what my wife and sister will say; but it is a duty, and I am resolved to do it, and trust God for the rest. I must pray in my family.'

'Not to-night,' said the tempter; 'you don't know how to pray. You have never prayed much. You are unacquainted with the language of prayer. Wait and learn how first.'

'No, no, I *must* pray to-night, I will pray to-night. Get thee behind me, Satan.'

He passed into his dwelling, and into his library, and there, before God, his heavenly Father, and in the name of the Lord Jesus, he poured out his heart and asked for strength and grace from on high to assist him in his duty.

When he met his wife that evening, she saw at once that a great change had taken place in him, and she saw it with awe, but said nothing. At length he said:

'My dear wife, would you have any objections to our having family worship?'

After a moment's surprise and hesitation she said with true politeness:

'Certainly not, if it is your pleasure.'

'Bring me a Bible then, please, and draw up under the gas-light, and let us read and pray.'

THE POWER OF PRAYER

He read a chapter, and then kneeled down, but his wife and sister sat upright in their seats, and he felt that he was alone on his knees. He lifted up his eyes to God, and cried out in the bitterness of his soul, 'God be merciful to me a sinner.' And gathering strength, he went on in his prayer, pouring out his most earnest cries and supplication that God would have mercy on his beloved wife and sister. So earnest, so importunate was that prayer that God would show his converting grace and power on the spot, that the heart of his wife was melted and overcome, and she slipped from her seat upon her knees beside him, and putting her arms around his neck, ere she was aware, she burst out into one agonizing cry to the Lord Jesus for mercy on her soul; and then the sister knelt down by his other side, and she, too, put her arms around him, and burst into a flood of tears.

He continued to pray; he devoted himself and those with him to God. He confessed and bewailed his and their manner of life hitherto; he pleaded the promises of God to all those that seek him, and with unspeakable joy he made mention of the amazing grace of God in the pardon of his sins, and he besought that they all might find and obtain together peace and forgiveness through a crucified Saviour.

The submission was complete; the surrender was fully made; repentance and faith sprang up together in the hearts of all the three, and as they rose from their knees, it was to acknowledge each to the other what new determinations and resolutions and consecration they each had made during the progress of *that first prayer in the family*, in *that parlor*, of all they were and all they would be, or should be to Christ.

Since that first prayer in the parlor, God has been daily acknowledged in the same place by the same circle.

The New York Revival of 1858

Then out from that circle they go from day to day in their walks of usefulness, and on their errands of mercy in this great city, seeking out the perishing, ten thousand times happier than they ever were before. Now they scatter blessings all around them; and long as eternity endures will they remember that first prayer-meeting in the parlor.

At another time was related the story of a man who has often, of late, been seen at the Globe Hotel and Fulton street prayer-meetings. A few weeks ago, this man was seen walking back and forth on the sidewalk of the Old North Dutch Church, while the prayer-meeting was going on. He was dressed in a blue striped shirt, and pantaloons of the same material, with an old green pea-jacket hanging on his arm. His countenance bore the marks of a decidedly 'hard case'. He appeared like one who had been destroying himself by intemperance – nothing left of him but the dilapidated remnants of a man, although he appeared clean and sober. He was evidently agitated with inward contending emotions. A great struggle was going on in his own bosom. He paused in his walking, and coming up the steps to the second storey lecture-room, he inquired of the lay missionary of the church, who is always at the door to see that strangers get comfortable seats, if they would allow such a miserable looking object as he was to come into the meeting.

'Certainly we will,' said the missionary, 'and glad to have you come. Come and welcome,' and he showed him to a seat.

Daily for weeks that man was seen coming to the prayer-meeting. He began at once to leave off drinking. He became interested in the subject of religion. After four weeks of total abstinence, he voluntarily signed the pledge, promising to 'taste not – touch not – handle not'. He kept his pledge. He was often without food. His

[87]

lodging-place was some hole about Washington market. He who feeds the ravens seemed to take care of him, and so to provide that he should not absolutely perish with hunger. Several times he found little packages of bread, or meat and bread, done up, in the streets, as he was walking up and down. In other instances, small sums of money were given him. None was given him at the prayer-meeting, lest he should be induced to come for the sake of the money he could pick up. Thus the Lord provided for him.

His convictions of sin grew more deep and pungent; his countenance betokened increased anxiety; he would loiter after the prayer-meeting, evidently hoping some one would speak to him on the subject of religion. A few evenings after, at the Globe Hotel, he was urged to an immediate acceptance of Christ. He went down to his place in Washington market to lodge. He could not sleep. His distress increased. He had been told to come to Christ. But how should he come? The language of his heart was, 'Oh! that I might find him.' He arose and walked the streets to see if he would not feel better. But no relief came. Sin was a heavy burden on his soul. The language of his heart was,

> Oh! that my load of sin was gone,
> Oh! that I could at last submit.

He kept on his walking – he knew not – he cared not whither. At length he paused at a lamp-post. He put his hand upon the post, and bent down his head upon his hand, and poured out his soul to God in prayer. The tears of penitence flowed apace. The fountains were broken up. He begged God for Christ's sake to have mercy on him. All at once, Christ appeared unspeakably precious to his soul. The burden of sin was gone. He rejoiced in his Saviour with exceeding joy.

The New York Revival of 1858

How long he remained in this position he does not know. He took no note of time. He walked the streets the remainder of the night, his whole soul filled with joy. He longed to meet some one to whom he could tell what the Lord had done for him. He went to various places, but could find no one whom he knew. He went to the Battery, and seated himself on the grass. He took out his New Testament, and began to read, and as he read he could not restrain his tears. At length, a gentleman, who had been standing near, observing him, said:

'My friend, what little book are you reading?'

'I am reading the New Testament.'

'Where did you get your Testament?'

'I got it at the Fulton street prayer-meeting.'

'Do you attend the Fulton street prayer-meeting?'

'I do.'

'Do they do you any good?'

'Well, I hope they have done me good. I hope I have found Christ very precious to my soul.'

And then, in his simple and artless manner, he narrated how he had found Christ at the lamp-post the preceding night, and how his whole soul had become filled with joy.

'Well,' said the listener, deeply affected, 'I have heard of these Fulton street prayer-meetings, and I believe they are doing a world of good. Now I will tell you what I want. I want you to come to my store at ten o'clock to-morrow morning.' He gave his name and number in Broad street, and they parted.

Meantime he sought the kind missionary at the Old Dutch Church. He ran up into the upper lecture-room, where he found him and two or three brethren with him. His whole face was beaming with inward peace. In a few brief words he told the story of the lamp-post and the great change.

THE POWER OF PRAYER

'Oh! blessed be God,' said the missionary, and in a moment all were on their knees.

'Now let us all pray in turn,' said he, and he lifted up his voice to God in thanksgiving and praise for his unspeakable mercy to his *dear brother* in Christ, in thus meeting him in his pardoning mercy and renewing grace. One after another followed in prayer, and last the voice of this new creature in Christ Jesus.

Punctual to the minute, at ten next morning, our brother in Christ was at the store in Broad street, and there he found a new suit of clothes provided for him, throughout, and a place had been found where he could have constant employment at fair wages. He is at present at all our evening meetings and his face shines as the face of an angel.

A few weeks afterwards, as we were sitting in the upper lecture-room of the Fulton street Church, this man came running up the steps to the room. The meeting had been closed for some time, and two or three were lingering in the room. Oh! how happy and radiant was his face. He was passing, he said, and could not go by without coming up and telling us how changed was everything in regard to him. A little time ago he was the slave of sin and Satan and intoxicating drink. Now he feels emancipated from the wretchedness and thralldom in which he then was. A little time ago he had no home, no friends, no visible means of living. Now he is well clad, has a good home, and constant employment. He is employed by a member of the Baptist church, residing in Brooklyn.

It is pleasant to hear from such cases as this, after some time has elapsed to test the genuine character of their conversion. Thus far all the evidence goes to show that these are fruits of the grace of God, and will endure to his praise.

Chapter 11

How a Revival began – Among the Mountains – Astonishing Answers – A Telegram to a Dying Man – A young Man's Testimony – The Prodigal – A repentant Student converted in a Car – A Brother saved – Another Conversion in a Car – Revivals multiplied by the Fulton street Prayer-meeting.

'I will tell you', said a speaker in one of our Fulton street meetings, 'how the revivals began in Kalamazoo, Mich., last winter. We heard of the wonderful work of grace in this city and in other parts of the land. We thought we ought to share in it and not stand idly by. Still we had no such feeling as was here. We appointed a daily prayer-meeting however. Episcopalians, Baptists, Methodists, Presbyterians, and Congregationalists, all united. We appointed our first union prayer-meeting in much fear and trembling. We did not know how it would work. We did not know that anybody would come. We did not know how the measure would be regarded. We came together. At our very first meeting, someone put in such a request as this: "A praying wife requests the prayers of this meeting for her unconverted husband, that he may be converted and be made an humble disciple of the Lord Jesus." All at once a stout, burly man arose and said, "I am that man. I have a pious, praying wife, and this request must be for me. I want you to pray for me." As soon as he sat down in the midst of sobs and tears, another man arose and said, "I am that man; I have a praying wife. She prays for me. And

THE POWER OF PRAYER

now she asked you to pray for me. I am sure I am that man, and I want you to pray for me."

Three, four or five more arose and said, "We want you to pray for us too." The power of God was upon the little assembly. The Lord appeared for us and that right early. We had hardly begun and he was in the midst of us in great and wonderful grace. Thus the revival began. We number from 400 to 500 conversions.'

'Let me tell you', said a speaker, 'of an instance of the power of prayer. The owner of a line of omnibuses kept a rum-shop or drinking saloon, made money, and wasted his spiritual good in all manner of ways, useless, irreligious. His wife went to these prayer-meetings. She became a truly converted woman. He forbade her going to the prayer-meetings, but she would go. She kept on going, though he got angry and said she must not. Finally he told her she must leave him or quit going to the prayer-meetings. He told her something like this, "Now if you will go up in the chamber and pray with me, you may pray as much as you please, but you must not go to the prayer-meetings." She said she did not know how to pray for him or with him, for she had only just begun to pray for herself. So they went into the chamber and he was very much surprised to hear her pray. That day everything went wrong. The next morning they went into the chamber to pray. "I thought I would let her pray it out, and by keeping her from the prayer-meetings I should break the charm." So they kneeled down together, and she prayed such a prayer as took a deep hold of his heart; as they rose from their knees, he kissed her, and went away. His heart was softened, subdued, and he came humbly at the feet of Jesus, a converted man. We rejoice over scores such as he. He abandoned his liquor selling at once. He witnesses a good confession.'

Another said: 'I dwell in the shadow of the Catskill

The New York Revival of 1858

mountains. We have a great work of grace among us. We have added to our church over one hundred, a great many conversions among our children and youths. Our ministers have left us for a little rest from labor, but we have resolved to carry our prayer-meetings through the hot weather, to meet our ministers on their return.'

'A father', said one of the speakers, 'had three sons in distant and different parts of the country, all unconverted. He brought them to the meeting as subjects of prayer. They were prayed for as only those who believe can pray. What has been the consequence? Three letters have been received from these three sons, who have not communicated with each other, each giving an account of his own conversion.' Another father requested prayer for a son at sea. He was away in the Pacific. His case was made the subject of earnest prayer. He has just returned to port. He was converted in mid-ocean, and just about the time he was made the subject of prayer. 'I thought', said the father, 'I would put down the date of that prayer-meeting, and the date of that prayer. I have no reason to doubt that the prayers of God's people were answered. It is wonderful. Away at that distance, God called up his attention to religion, convinced him of his guilt, led him to Christ, and the very first thing he had to tell me on landing was, what the Lord had done for his soul. He knew nothing of our prayer-meetings. He did not know that he had been made the subject of special prayer, and yet the Lord has made him the subject of special grace.'

One of the most affecting objects of prayer was this. A father brought into one of our meetings a sealed letter to a son in South America, and laid it upon the desk, and requested the prayers of Christians, that the Spirit and blessing of God might go with that letter, and make it the means of the conversion of that distant and much-loved

THE POWER OF PRAYER

son. The letter was an earnest entreaty that he might become reconciled to God.

Thousands and thousands of instances, doubtless, have transpired within the last few months, of wonderful and speedy answers to prayer. *'Only believe!' 'Only believe!'* This is the voice of God's providence, and grace, and Spirit.

'Some of you', continued one of the speakers, 'have read of the conversion of a British soldier in India by means of the telegraph. He was lying near to death. He had neglected and reviled religion all his life, but now he was dying, and no Christian friend near to tell him how he might be saved. He bethought himself of a Christian living at the distance of one hundred and sixty miles. He sent him a telegraphic message, as follows: "I am dying. What shall I do to be saved?" Instantly, the message went back to him: "Believe on the Lord Jesus Christ, and thou shalt be saved." And so the messages kept passing from the dying man, until the physical powers of the soldier sank away, and he died with the words of hope and joy upon his lips. Who knows that we may not live to see the same glorious message pass over the world on these wires, and the prayer of the inventor be answered – the joyful responses of nations to nations be heard – and millions on millions be heard singing the "everlasting song" of salvation to our God?'

'I wish to bear my testimony,' said a young man, 'and tell what the Lord has done for me. Fifteen years ago I came from a neighboring village into this city. I had pious parents, who prayed constantly for me all these fifteen years. Yet in all that time I did not know that I had a single serious impression. I don't remember that I ever had any anxiety on the subject of religion till last January, when I heard a sermon upon this passage: "Cut it down; why cumbereth it the ground?" I heard it as every word of it

The New York Revival of 1858

addressed to me. I did not suppose that there was another one in the house that it applied to. I was the unfruitful fig tree. I was plunged into the deepest anxiety, and knew not what to do. I had a wife, and I did not know how she would regard my state of feeling. At length I found that she had been awakened by the same sermon. We went to our pastor and told him all our hearts, and in a little while were permitted to hope for pardon and peace through our Lord Jesus Christ. I have been often at these meetings, and have wished often to speak, but never could get courage to do so. There may be some young man who hears me, whom I may persuade to come to Jesus – some one for whom a father and mother are praying, or have prayed in times past. I have exchanged the theatre for the church, and the drinking-saloon for the prayer-meeting. I earnestly entreat you to do the same.'

'I have a letter of eight pages,' said another speaker, 'giving an account of a young man's conversion. He was the son of a pious widow; he deserted his mother; went off to a great distance, became very wicked, has been made the subject of special prayer, has been overtaken by the Holy Spirit, been renewed in the temper of his mind, is a new creature – his letter is so affecting, I could hardly read it.'

'I attended the last Saturday night prayer-meeting in the College,' said one, rising. 'It was very full and very solemn. God has converted many of the students during the term now at its close. There came into this meeting a student who had been graduated two years before. Of course here were now in college two classes, with whose members he was acquainted. He had been noticed for shining talents, scholarship and irreligion. Here were students over whom he had exerted a very pernicious influence. He had been converted. He came to tell his fellow students the story of the "great change". As he went on in his experience, every cheek was bathed in tears. He had come expressly to confess his penitence for his former course. He had studied a profession two years. Now he abandons it to lay all at the feet of Jesus, and preach the everlasting gospel.'

'As our city missionary', said a speaker, 'was getting into a Sixth Avenue railroad car, in his quiet, unobtrusive way, he said to the conductor:

"Will you take a tract?"

"Certainly, I will, and be thankful for it."

"Are you a Christian?"

"I hope I am."

"Where did you become a Christian?"

"In this railroad car."

"How was that?"

"Why, you see I could not go to the prayer-meetings. I had to stand here all day. I felt very much concerned about my soul. I was bowed down with sorrow. I did not know what to do; and so I just gave myself up to God, right here in the car. I cried to him for mercy, and mercy came quick. Oh! what joy I had, and none knew anything about it. God can forgive sins in the railroad car as well as anywhere else. I am thankful for the tracts, sir. It was these that first convicted me of sin, and it was these that led me to Christ."'

'I passed through this city a few days ago,' said a speaker, 'and I sent up a request that you would pray for an unconverted brother. I sent it up to that desk, and when it was read, I got up and stated that I had sent up that request, for an unconverted brother, the only remaining one of a large family of brothers, out of the ark of safety. I told you I was going to see him. I had come from the west and was going east, a thousand miles in all to see him. I felt very anxious about him, as the only remaining one out of Christ, and alienated from us on account of some difficul-

The New York Revival of 1858

ties about the division of property. He would not write to us. I got into the cars praying. I rode on praying; I stopped and came here praying; I asked you to pray, and then I went on praying; and when I met him, oh! an answer had come to our prayers. He threw his arms around my neck, and said, "Oh! my brother! my brother! God has had mercy on my soul. Let me kiss you; let me fold you close to my heart."

And now I am on my way back to the west; but I felt as if I could not go through New York without coming to this meeting, and telling you the story of my brother's conversion, and asking you to join with me in thanksgiving to God, that he has answered our poor requests, when we had so little confidence in him.'

It was said by one speaker, that a profane and wicked young man was going on his journey from Springfield, Mass., to Albany. When going up some of the inclined planes, he thought to himself how easily his life might be taken away – how suddenly some accident might cut short his probation; and how surely his soul would be lost if he should die as he was. These thoughts recurred to him again and again. He felt he was a sinner, lost and undone. The more the thought of his life was pressed upon him, the more unhappy he felt. Conviction and alarm followed in this train of thought, till he was led to inquire within himself, 'What shall I do? How shall I escape destruction and ruin? Who will help me, when I deserve no help? I cannot help myself! I have no one here to speak to: none to pray for me!' All at once a voice seemed to say within him – 'Come unto me and be saved. I am able to save to the uttermost. Put your trust in me and you shall be saved. Follow me and you shall be my disciple. Now are you willing to do it? Will you do it?' The young man answered, 'I will.' And peace and light and joy broke forth in his heart at once. And long before he finished his journey – all

THE POWER OF PRAYER

unknown to his fellow passengers – he had entered upon that path that leadeth up to eternal life. The whole work of conviction and conversion had been wrought in a railroad car. All his plans, character, and prospects for time and eternity were changed. He went into the car a swearing, profane child of the devil. He went out of the car a new creature in Christ Jesus. Old things had passed away; all things had become new. And he has since witnessed a good profession. Who but the Holy Spirit had anything to do with the conversion of this young man?

A young man from Iowa was on his way to this city. In the cars he made the acquaintance of a man from Ohio. As they journeyed on, they spoke of coming to New York. The Ohio man said:

'Have you heard of the meetings in New York?'

'What meetings?' said the man from Iowa.

'The Fulton street prayer-meetings.'

'No, I had not heard of them: what about them?'

'They are held every day, at 12 noon, in the Old Dutch Church, Fulton street, by business men, and God pours down his Holy Spirit upon them in great power, and many are converted. Will you go with me to them when we get to New York?'

'Certainly I will.'

'And true to his word, he did,' said the speaker, 'and I am the Ohio man that was with him. The second day he came here, he put in his own request to be prayed for, and soon he was converted in these meetings, and in eight days from the time he came, he was on his way back to his home in one of the southern counties of Iowa, a converted young man. He lived in a village of nine hundred inhabitants, with no church, no minister, no means of grace. What did he do? Why, the first thing he did was to open a prayer-meeting in his own room. In a little time he had to move his meeting to a school, because his room would not contain those who came to his daily prayer-meeting. Then they had to get another room, because the school-house was too small. God poured out his Spirit, and that noonday prayer-meeting resulted in the organization of two churches. Just see what a little personal faithfulness can do, when accompanied with the blessing of God. Who can tell where such a line of influence shall end, or how many may in the end, through this one young man's conversion, be brought into the kingdom of Christ?'

Another speaker said: 'Last Sabbath I spent in a small village in Pennsylvania, where I had the satisfaction of seeing one hundred make a public profession of religion. They were mostly young people. The place had enjoyed a revival of religion since some time last winter. It commenced somewhat in this manner: Several gentlemen were on their way to New York city. When they approached the city, some boy was passing through the cars, distributing a handbill, which told of this noonday prayer-meeting. They took the handbill, and looked at it, and seeing what it was, they called the boy back to inquire more about it.

'"Come back here, and tell us more about this prayer-meeting; what do you know about it?"

'The poor boy knew nothing more than what the handbill said. They resolved that they would come to this prayer-meeting and see for themselves. They came; they caught the spirit of the meeting, and when they went home they set up a prayer-meeting in their place. It was very much owned and blessed of God, and of the fruits of the revival which followed these, one hundred were added to the church: others will follow at the next communion. Here was a daily prayer-meeting, planted by this simple instrumentality, in a distant town, and here were the fruits of the effort.'

Chapter 12

Individual Responsibility – Personal Efforts – Souls seeking Souls – A ten Years' pursuit of an Infidel and the Result – A Pledge Signed Twenty-six Times – Two Widows – An anxious Mother – A Brother-in-law – The Prodigal Son – A City Islander – The Happy Wife – Father and Daughter.

Among the members of our churches, there has been a sad want of a sense of individual obligation, and proper appreciation of the value of personal effort.

The present revival has wrought a revolution in men's minds in this respect. A power has been developed which was almost unknown to the modern church. It was the power of personal fidelity to souls, the power of individual personal effort for their salvation; the power of prayer and effort when concentrated upon one specific object; the power of love, when an individual feels that it centres in him – when it follows him with unceasing anxiety and importunity, and never forgets or leaves or despairs of its object till it is securely housed in the ark of safety. The hiding of the Saviour's power is in the personal fidelity of every one and each of his disciples. This the revival has abundantly proved. 'Go ye into all the world and preach the gospel to every creature' has commonly been regarded as the great commission to the *preachers* of the gospel. Now it was felt to be a commission which is given to every Christian, and that he is bound to carry the gospel message to every individual mind and heart – 'every creature' – in highways and by-ways, in garrets and cellars, in parlors and counting-rooms, in cottages and palaces, wherever there is a 'creature' who is impenitent, to him, to her, we are to preach the gospel – blessed tidings of good – as if we felt the high import of our mission and the glorious work we are to perform. We are to preach it as the great remedy for the woes of the perishing world; every one is to preach it to every one till there is no need of preaching it, 'for all shall know the Lord from the least to the greatest'.

In this revival men have been astonished at the success with which they can 'preach the gospel'. They have been astonished at the efficacy of lay labor and individual effort. Impenitent men have been found ready to hear and ready to obey the gospel call. This very discovery has roused up the individual faithfulness of Christians, and they have felt the value of personal effort as they never felt it before since the days of the first Christians. Men have been surprised at the success of a little labor, and this has encouraged more labor. One man has gone prayerfully and affectionately to another, and urged the importance of the hour, the space given him for repentance, and the necessity of improving it to make his peace with God. When he goes to him a second time he finds him in great anxiety of mind. He asks now, What must I do? What *can* I do to be saved? He finds that sleep has departed from the man. His days are restless, and night brings him no repose. What is the matter with the man? Why, nothing, except that from his knees a man has gone and spoken to him at an unexpected moment, with unexpected earnestness – with unwonted emotion, and with irresistible tenderness and love, has besought him to attend the gospel message, as a sinner needing an interest in Christ. This is all; all that the Christian has done. But this is not all. It has pleased God to clothe that message with amazing power – the power of the Holy Spirit. And it will be so evident that the work is all of God, that the Christian is humbled, while, at the same time, he is encouraged. 'Even so, Father, for so it seemeth good in thy sight.'

It is felt, too, that the Christian must preach, and keep preaching – that he must take hold of the sinner, and never let go till he is brought into the kingdom of Christ. Not that *he* can bring him in, but God can bring him in through the faithful believer's instrumentality.

Shall we illustrate what we mean? We have given, in chapter 6 of this volume, the case of the converted infidel lawyer. There is a record of personal fidelity about that case which is known to us but which cannot be told. Suffice it to say, that one individual – an unlettered man – a comparatively poor man – followed him up for more than ten years with a never-failing kindness, costing money and time, to win him to happiness and holiness and heaven – the records of which never will be revealed till the great day when the secrets of all hearts shall be revealed. This untiring benefactor – this unwearied friend, was one of the six – *the original six* – who attended the first noonday business men's prayer-meeting in Fulton street. He took hold never to let go till he had brought the poor lost sinner to the feet of Jesus. It was a ten years' effort, but it succeeded at last! It was an unremitting effort, but glorious in its results. How few in these days make such an effort as this! So earnest, so affectionate, so self-denying, so long protracted, so eager of pursuit, and so patient in expectation and hope.

We will speak of another case by way of illustration. A man endeavored to secure the signature of an impenitent friend and neighbor to the temperance pledge. He succeeded, and it was signed with flowing tears. It was broken within forty-eight hours. What did this poor man's benefactor do? Did he say, 'He's gone below and past redemption, and I will give him up?' No! He

The New York Revival of 1858

persuaded him to sign a second time, and within a week it was broken again. Was he discouraged? Oh, no! He had taken hold never to let go, and he induced this poor unstable man to sign the pledge again, and again, until he had signed it twenty-six times, and the twenty-sixth time he kept his pledge, and has always kept it from that time onward. And what is more, he has become a Christian, and is now a burning and shining light in the church and in the world.

This is what we mean by individual responsibility followed out till the object is gained.

If all the church would act on this plan, how long before the world would be converted? A revival, once begun, when would it cease?

We have a large class of examples on the point before us, to encourage the feeblest to do what they can, as all the success of effort belongs to God. 'Paul may plant, and Apollos may water, but God must give the increase.'

'I came here a few days ago, after many hours of wearisome travel on purpose to ask you to pray for one who was very dear to me, and for whose salvation I have long been deeply concerned. It had been many months since I had seen him, but my confidence was strong in God that he would hear and answer the united prayers of his people offered in this hallowed place. And now I return to tell you what great things the Lord has done for his soul. I have learned, to my inexpressible joy, that he whom I love has given his heart to Christ. Let us rejoice and give thanks to him who loves to hear the prayers of his children.'

At a recent meeting, the leader presented two letters, from an extreme eastern and an extreme western State, both from widows. The one from the West requested prayer on behalf of three adult sons, whose father had been pious and his influence exemplary, but who were

[103]

THE POWER OF PRAYER

indisposed to give heed to a mother's counsels. That from the East was in behalf of a son early deprived of a father's care, and who manifested the same disregard of his mother's wishes and prayers. This was so peculiarly affecting that the leader was not able to get through the reading. All sympathized in his emotion, and there was hardly a dry eye in the room. After two or three attempts to proceed, he requested a friend near the desk to finish the reading. It is as follows:

'I read weekly of the wonderful works the Lord is doing in your midst, converting sinners in answer to the prayers of his people. I have an only son, given to God in infancy, left fatherless in early childhood, but who has been a subject of prayer ever since his birth up to the present time. He is now thirty-five years old. I have not seen him for the last ten years. His home is in Oregon. Our communications by letter have been frequent, and he is very kind, and has proved the kindness of his heart by liberal presents. But he does not love religion. In a recent letter he entreats me not to write him any more religious letters. He has endured them for the last twenty-five years – read them, not because he loved their subject, but because they were his mother's letters, but earnestly desires me not to allude to the subject again, as it will do him no good. I need not say all a mother's soul was stirred within me. I wrote him in reply as faithfully as I could, for the last time on that subject, on condition he would promise to acquit me at the judgment bar as having done all a mother's duty for the salvation of his soul. I have not heard from him since, but have felt to agonize with God in prayer for his speedy conversion, till within a short time, I have not had that intensity of feeling, and fear the Spirit is saying, "He is joined to his idols, let him alone." I have asked the Lord what he would have me to do, and my mind is inclined to send a request to the Fulton street

The New York Revival of 1858

prayer-meeting that special prayer might be made for the speedy conversion of his precious and immortal soul. It has long been my prayer, "O God, convert my son!" I feel, like the mother of Augustine, that I cannot, *cannot* give him up – cannot leave any effort possible to be made for his salvation unattempted. This request is, therefore, submitted to the Fulton street prayer meeting.

AN ANXIOUS MOTHER

When the reading was finished, the leader desired someone to pray, but no one seemed willing to trust his feelings. One or two, on being called on, declined on this account. Finally, one brother made a brief, earnest petition in behalf of the son on whom was laid the awful responsibility imposed by the importunate mother's faithfulness. It was a most solemn moment. All seemed to feel that words could only detract from the impression that had been made on every mind. The meeting soon closed.

It is not always that we may see the fruit of our labor and prayer while we live. Many a pious parent has prayed and wept, and the fruit has been gathered long after the laborer had gone to his rest in the heavens.

Sometimes a long-delayed blessing comes for ourselves while we are laboring for the good of others, as in the following case:

A written request was handed to the leader of the meeting, that prayer might be offered to the Throne of Grace for the conversion of the son of an aged clergyman. A pastor, well stricken in years, who had long been praying that his own son might be led to see the error of his ways and be brought to the feet of Jesus, rose and made earnest supplication to God that 'this son of an aged clergyman' might be brought to seek redemption through a dying and risen Saviour. His own son, unknown to him, sat in the same room, some distance behind him. This son had been walking through the street, and seeing a great crowd entering the door of the meeting, out of mere idle curiosity was induced to enter and take a seat. And there he heard his own father praying for the conversion of just such a son, and just such a sinner as he himself was. He left the meeting in great distress of mind – could not think of sleep, but walked the streets the whole night. Sometimes he would sit down on the steps of the house whose owner he knew was a Christian, and ponder within himself whether he had not better ring the bell, rouse up the family out of sleep, and beg them to pray for him. It was with difficulty that he could persuade himself that it was an unseasonable hour, and that even though he feared the 'wrath to come', he must wait till morning before any would pray for him.

At length morning came. He returned as a prodigal to his father's house, and, through God's grace and mercy, was enabled to humble himself before God, and give up his evil courses, and enlist in the service of Christ who suffered on the cross, that sinners like him might be saved. That same son of an aged clergyman is now daily employed in persuading sinners – such as he lately was – to come to Christ. That same son, who went into the prayer-meeting, attracted out of mere idle curiosity, is now seen daily in the prayer-meeting, ready to take his part in the work and duty of prayer. How changed from the night he walked the streets in agony of mind – now rejoicing with joy unspeakable and full of glory.

Take another striking case. A stranger said:

'I am from City Island. It has about four hundred inhabitants, and only about twenty of these are witnesses for Christ. I am here to ask you to pray for City Island. I am but very young in the Christian life. I came here some weeks ago and asked you to pray for this people. I felt so anxious for a revival that I got up here, though I had no religion then, and asked you to pray for City Island.

The New York Revival of 1858

I went home and the first thing I heard was, "When are you going to come out on the Lord's side? Some of us have been praying for you ever since you have been gone." It went like an arrow to my heart, that while I was here asking you to pray for them, they should be praying for me. How strange! I was bowed down with sorrow. At length the Lord turned my sorrow into joy. I have gone on rejoicing ever since. I believe God heard your prayer for City Island, and first of all had mercy on me. Religion is all my joy now. I love its duties. I love to stand up for Jesus. I come again to ask you to pray for City Island and pray also for me.'

What untold agony has a wife or a mother endured when the blessing has *waited*? And how God often leads his own dear children through trials, in order that they may see whether they walk by faith or by sight. This is illustrated by the following example:

A young man from this meeting went to visit his impenitent father in Massachusetts. He took passage on a Long Island Sound steamer. He took a state-room alone, and spent nearly all the night in prayer for his unconverted father. He was borne down with a heavy burden of anxiety. He made several attempts to sleep, but sleep fled from his eyes. How little his fellow-passengers knew what was going on in that state-room. What a place for prayer! and yet a window in heaven was opened upon that state-room. There was an ear that was attentive to that prayer.

When the son arrived at home the next evening, he took down the Bible, and said, 'Father, let us read a chapter in the Bible, and pray.' 'Certainly,' said the father; 'you read.' After reading, to the surprise of the son, the father led off in prayer – pouring forth such fervent prayer as he had scarcely ever heard. It was the first out-gushings of the new-born soul.

As they arose from their knees, the son said to the father, 'Father, how long since God gave you a heart to pray?'

THE POWER OF PRAYER

'I first began to pray last night. I was awakened, and cried to God for mercy, and he has had mercy upon me.'

That son had an unconverted sister in Boston. He went immediately on to see and tell her of the conversion of her father. He found her, and told her of the joyful news. He exhorted her to an immediate surrender of herself to God. All her Christian friends united in prayer for her. She yielded, and in twenty-four hours he was on his way to tell the father what the Lord had done for her soul.

Chapter 13

The Work among the Children – Randall's Island – The Romanist's Child, Mary – A dying Sunday School Scholar – Prayers for a Child – Conversions in a Public School – Columbus, Toledo and Geneva – Father and Children – Sabbath School Class and Teacher – The little Girl whose Heart would Sing.

Perhaps the most interesting field of contemplation and discovery in the history of this work would be among the children and youth of our city and country. They cannot attend the meetings, but they are remembered there. 'Yesterday', said a speaker, 'I went to Randall's Island, where I met 2,000 children and youth in one body. The ten Governors have 5,000 children under their care, and in all our institutions there are from 30,000 to 40,000, without hope and without God in the world. What are we doing for these? I see some here before me who will go out to-morrow (Sunday) among them. Who are the tenants of our jails and prisons, and various institutions belonging to the city? Three-quarters of all our criminals are under twenty-one years of age. Are we doing all we can to save the young – that very class who will rule or ruin us? I ask you to do what you can in the lanes and alleys, and among the haunts of the miserable, and criminal, and degraded, to bring them to know God, and Jesus Christ whom he has sent. Here is a great work, and but few, comparatively, are engaged in it. How few even know of the misery, and

[109]

THE POWER OF PRAYER

pauperism, and crime, which prevail in this great city. How many of us are doing what we can to carry the gospel to the perishing thousands in the midst of us, absolutely perishing at our very doors? Let us look this great matter in the face, and see what we can do to turn the tide of sin and ruin.'

'Many', said a speaker in the union prayer-meeting, 'think it is of no use to invite the children of Catholic parents to go into a Protestant Sunday school. There never was a greater mistake. They are often not only willing, but glad to have them go. And often their going is of unspeakable good to their parents. Let me give one illustration. Away in the west lived a Catholic family in which there was a little girl seven years old. She was induced to go to a Protestant Sunday school. The father became very anxious about his soul. His distress increased daily, and one night, at the midnight hour, he arose from his bed in agony. He begged his wife to pray for him, as he said he did not know how to pray for himself. She told him she 'could not pray – any better than he could'.

'What shall I do, then?'

'Perhaps', said she, 'our little Mary can pray.'

So the father went up to her chamber, where she was fast asleep and took her up from her bed in his arms, and bore her down stairs, and putting her gently down, he said to her with great earnestness, 'Mary, can you pray?'

'Oh, yes, father, I can pray.'

'Will you kneel down and pray for your poor father?'

'Yes, I will pray for you.'

So she kneeled, put up her little hands, and said – 'Our Father who art in heaven,' – going through with the Lord's Prayer. Then she prayed for her father in her own language, asking God to love him and have mercy upon him, and to pardon all his sins for Jesus Christ's sake.

When she had finished her prayer, her father said to her, 'Mary, can you read in your Bible?'

The New York Revival of 1858

'Oh yes, father, I can read. Shall I read to you in my Bible?'

'Yes, read to me.'

She began at the third chapter of the Gospel according to John. She read along till she came to that verse –

'As Moses lifted up the serpent in the wilderness, even so must the Son of Man be lifted up: that whosoever believeth in him should not perish, but have everlasting life.'

'Oh, Mary,' said he, 'is that there?'

'Yes, father, it is here. Jesus Christ said so.'

'Well, that is just what I need – what your poor father needs.'

'Yes, father, and hear the rest of it.'

'For God so loved the world that he gave his only begotten Son, that whosoever believeth in him might not perish but have everlasting life.'

'Oh, that is for me – for just such as me: "whosoever believeth in him" – I *can* believe in him – I *do* believe in him.'

And from that hour that father went on his way rejoicing in Christ Jesus with great joy.

A child from a poor family had an intemperate father, who often used to abuse his wife and children. This child had been to the Sunday school – had become pious. The physician told the father that his little girl would die. No! he did not believe it. Yes, she will – she must die in a few hours. The father flew to the bedside, would not part with her, he said.

'Yes, father, you must part with me, I am going to Jesus; promise me two things – one is that you won't abuse mother any more, and drink no more whisky.'

He promised in a solemn, steady manner. The little girl's face lighted up with joy.

'The other thing is, promise me that you will *pray*,' said the child.

THE POWER OF PRAYER

'I cannot pray; don't know how,' said the poor man.

'Father, kneel down, please. There, take the words after me, I will pray; I learned how to pray in Sunday school, and God has taught me how to pray too; my heart prays, you must let your heart pray; now, say the words.'

And she began in her simple language to pray to the Saviour of sinners. After a little he began to repeat after her; as he went on his heart was interested and he broke out into an earnest prayer for himself; bewailed his sins, confessed and promised to forsake them; entered into a covenant with God; light broke out upon him in his darkness; how long he prayed he did not know; he seemed to have forgotten his child in his prayer. When he came to himself he raised his head from the bed on which he had rested it; there lay the little speaker, a lovely smile was upon the face, her little hand was in that of the father, but she had gone to be among the angels.

'Oh,' said the speaker, 'you who are Sunday school teachers, take courage in your work. Gather in the children, gather them in; sow in their hearts the good seed; you know not whether shall prosper this or that, or whether all shall be alike good.'

'The prayers of this meeting', said another speaker, 'are requested for a son twelve years old, a Sunday school scholar, a child of much prayer, a very dutiful and promising boy.

Please allow a few statements. Three years ago this morning (July 13th), the mother of this boy went to her rest. The day preceding her death, she talked and prayed with him for the last time, exhorting him to be a devoted Christian, and if spared, to do all the good in his power, and prepare to meet her in heaven.

A few weeks ago, owing to an injury, this boy seemed to be dying. It was very sudden – without warning. His pulse was 120 a minute, and his respirations were five a

The New York Revival of 1858

minute. Before going out for a physician, though the case was so urgent, the father, fearing he would not find him alive when he returned, asked him a few questions, in order to know the state of his mind.

"Eddie," said he, "have you ever thought what you would like to do, if you should grow up to be a man?"

"Yes, father; I should like to be a missionary."

"Where would you like to go?"

"To any place among the heathen."

"Why should you wish to go to the heathen?"

"Christ said, Preach the gospel to every creature, and I think we ought to do it."

"If you could not go to the heathen, then what would you want to do?"

"I would wish to be a minister."

"At home?"

"Yes."

"If you were to die now, Eddie, where do you think you would go?"

He hesitated – paused in deep thought – then said:

"I don't know, father, but I hope, to heaven."

The boy has recovered from the very brink of the grave.

And now the father asks your prayers that this boy may become a Christian, if he is not, and, if he is one, that he may be fitted for usefulness in God's own time and way, and that his father and friends may be willing that he may be a minister – a missionary – or anything else, as "the Lord our God shall call" and appoint.'

At another meeting, a gentleman from Columbus, Ohio, made some very interesting statements in regard to the work in that city. The churches had shared in the great revival which is going on in various portions of the country. They had received large accessions by reason of the number of conversions. One of the most remarkable

THE POWER OF PRAYER

features of this work had been manifested in the public schools. In the public High School of Columbus, all the boys of the school had been converted, with two exceptions. The number could not be less than one hundred. The duties of the school had been carried on as usual, the scholars were from families of different denominations, and of no denomination, and yet, the work had been carried on in such a way as to excite no animosity, or jealousy, or opposition. It was a noiseless, but a solemn, thorough work; and all hearts rejoiced in it. There were no extraordinary means used. The teachers were pious, and God blessed their prayers and counsels to the salvation of these dear youth.

The public schools of Toledo had been blessed in a similar manner, and large numbers had been hopefully converted. A fervent prayer followed these statements for the conversion of all our schools.

A gentleman from Geneva said in this meeting that some months ago they established a union prayer-meeting, to be held daily, which is still maintained, and which has been blest in the conversion of about 400 souls. Among the number are many remarkable cases. One is as follows:

A young man became convinced of sin, and was in great distress of mind. He had a very wicked and ungodly father. One night he said to his father, 'Father, ought we not to have family worship?' The father looked at him in astonishment, as if in doubt whether his son could be in his right mind, but said nothing. The father, however, could not get the matter of family worship out of his mind, with all the efforts he could make. An arrow of conviction had been sent to his heart. The Holy Spirit was striving with him.

The father resolved to establish family worship, though he had no Christian hope. He began in fear and trembling,

The New York Revival of 1858

and much embarrassment; but he began. In five days from that beginning, that father, that son, and two daughters, were rejoicing in the hope and peace of believers in Jesus.

Another addressed us, and said he was there as a father, rejoicing over the conversion of three of his children. He had presented them here as the subjects of prayer, and he had two more who he wished might be prayed for – one of them was a daughter fifteen years old to-day. He talked with her last evening on the importance of a new life. This case was made the subject of fervent prayer.

We found a boy in the meeting; he was about fourteen or fifteen years of age. We noticed that he seemed to be very much agitated. He remained loitering behind when the meeting was over, as if he were anxious that some one should speak to him; seeing which, we said to him:

'Do you wish to become a Christian?'

'Very much I do.'

'Do you know what it is to become a Christian?'

'I must repent of sin, and believe in the Lord Jesus Christ.'

'Where did you learn that?'

'In the Sunday school.'

'Where did the Sunday school learn it?'

'From the word of God.'

'Will you repent and trust to the Lord Jesus Christ alone for salvation?'

'I will try to do it, sir.'

'Will you come here to-morrow to the prayer-meeting?'

'I mean to be here every day, sir.'

'Do you desire that this meeting shall pray for you to-morrow?'

'I do.'

'My class numbers nine boys,' said another, 'in age from fourteen to eighteen. Most of them had attended Sabbath school for a number of years, but as they grew up, were becoming restless under its restraints, and careless of its teachings. As much as possible, in teaching, I sought to apply the lessons to them individually, and talked much with them familiarly on the great truths of the Bible, the plan of salvation, of youth as the seed-time, the value of right habits, and sought to impress upon them the vast importance of *now*, and that the days and hours they were then wasting were the most precious of their whole lives. At times they would manifest some interest, but generally it was to them like a tale that was told. Often have I left the room with a heavy heart, almost feeling that it was all in vain, and then nerved to action again by the thought that the object of Sabbath schools was to benefit just such boys as those, and unless they were reached and blessed by religious instruction *now*, the chances were decidedly against their ever finding an entrance into the kingdom.

Conversing one day early in January with a Christian brother, I mentioned to him the circumstances of some recent acts of flagrant insubordination in my class, and the anxiety it gave me.

"Hold on, brother," said he, "the dawn will yet appear!"

These words were like the balm of Gilead. Striving to rest with child-like confidence in the great truth that salvation is of God, that Jesus Christ died to purchase it, that the Holy Spirit leads men to embrace it, that it is in accordance with God's purposes of mercy to save men, that he rejoices to do it, and that he only waits for men to get in a proper attitude for it, so that he may open the windows of heaven and pour out a blessing, that there be not room enough to receive it – I did hold on.

In a few weeks the revival commenced in good earnest, and while many of our older scholars were pressing into the kingdom, I watched over my own charges with deep solicitude, and sought personal interviews with them,

The New York Revival of 1858

feeling almost that God had committed the care of their souls to me.

At length the dawn *did* appear, and one after another they nearly all came, asking earnestly the great question, "What must I do to be saved?" The Spirit of God had commenced its work among them, and ere long five of them expressed hope in Christ, and went forth asking, with the Apostle Paul (our lessons of late had been of him), "Lord, what wilt thou have *me* to do?" Their voices were often heard in the converts' and boys' meetings, and were zealous and earnest in persuading their companions to seek the same Saviour whom they had found. Three have since united with the church, and (strange to me, though all plain with God) the most troublesome lad in the class is today the most cheerful, earnest, decided, growing young Christian that it has ever been my lot to meet.

Oh, it was then a pleasure to teach that class! How earnest they were – how they listened – what questions they asked! Often did the tear stand in the eye as the truth of God was spoken. Now could I praise God enough, and yet my faith was weak, and my labor too little. If I had been more faithful, and prayed and labored more earnestly, which I might have done, would not the same God who converted *some* souls to himself, have also made *all* of that class his own? But their increased attention, and evident knowledge of and interest in divine truth, are evidence that some seed is sown in the heart, which one day may spring up and bear fruit. "For as the rain cometh down, and the snow from heaven, and returneth not thither, but watereth the earth, and maketh it bring forth and bud, that it may give seed to the sower and bread to the eater: so shall my word be that goeth out of my mouth; it shall not return unto me void, but it shall accomplish that which I please, and it shall prosper in the thing whereto I sent it."'

THE POWER OF PRAYER

He also related an incident of a little girl whose heart God had lately touched by his Spirit. She was so happy that she was singing all about the house. Her mother one day took the little girl with her in her call upon a lady acquaintance, and as the lady was not pious, she charged her daughter not to sing while she was in the house. The lady introduced the subject of religion, and immediately the child commenced singing. She looked up, caught the eye of her mother, and stopped. But as the conversation went on, she commenced one of our beautiful hymns – singing it through. When she had finished it, she ran to her mother, kneeled down on her knees, and putting her face into her mother's lap, burst into tears. 'Oh, mother,' said she, 'I did not mean to disobey you. But I could not help singing – you may whip me – you may do anything to me. But it keeps singing in my heart all the time, and it *must come out*. I must sing.' 'That', said the chairman, 'is religion. We want something that must come out. We want something that will make us act.'

Chapter 14

The Revival of Religion among Men of Business – Laws of Trade – Conscience – A Hardware Merchant and his Customer – A Merchant and his Clerk – The Salesman and his Assistant – Conscience Awakened – Test of the Revival.

It has often been said that 'the laws of trade' are the ways and means by which men make money; that they are the 'tricks of trade', and cover all the practices by which shrewd men, who claim to be honest, seek to get the advantage of each other.

It was often made the subject of daily prayer, that none who came there to pray might go away to do business according to what was commonly denominated the 'laws of trade'. We remember that men of business prayed that they might be always enabled to do business on Christian principles, and go from the prayer-meeting to carry out the principles of the gospel into daily life. We have often heard men exhorted to do their business on Christian principles. There has been a great quickening of the consciences of men in regard to this matter. Much that was done in business was considered to be in direct contravention of the laws of Christ's house. Many have had great trials in their own minds in regard to their business. Some have felt that they must give up their pursuits or lose their souls; many have felt that if they carried the gospel into all their business relations they must *fail*, as they would stand no chance in the close and

THE POWER OF PRAYER

keen competition in trade if they were scrupulously honest.

An extensive hardware merchant made an earnest address in the Fulton street prayer-meeting on this very subject. He appealed to his brethren to set a holy example in this business, to have the same religion for 'down town' which they had for 'up town' – the same for the week-day that they have for the Sabbath – the same for the counting-room as for the communion-table. This address was four or five minutes in length, and was very effective. He was followed to his store by a well-known manufacturer with whom he had had dealings for many years, and of whom he had bought largely.

'You did not know', said the manufacturer, 'that I was in the meeting, and heard your remarks. But I was there. Now, sir, I have for the last five years been in the habit of charging you more for goods than other purchasers. I want you to take your books and charge back to me so much per cent on every bill of goods you have had of me for the five years last past.'

The merchant came into the prayer-meeting the next day and told what had transpired, and made another exhortation to the same effect – on doing business on Christian principles.

In a few days he told of another incident in his own business relations. 'I have received today', said he, 'the payment of a debt of several hundred dollars, which has been due for twenty-eight years. The man who paid me today was just as able to pay me twenty-five years ago as today; but I had given it up and never expected to receive it, and I cannot account for its being paid now, but upon the supposition that the revival has reached the man's conscience, and he could not rest without paying that honest debt.'

Another case was that of a recent convert. He was also a

The New York Revival of 1858

merchant of large business. When he came to Christ and gave up all to him – it was indeed *giving up all*. He believed Christ meant just what he said: 'Seek first the kingdom of God.' And he did seek it before his business and everything else; and in his business and everywhere. The kingdom of God was first with him; when he walked, when he talked; in his counting-room, in the prayer-meeting, at home – abroad. It was refreshing to look in his smiling, cheerful, happy face, and see the joy that was dwelling there. He had a pious confidential clerk, but not of the stamp of his employer, and that clerk thought he must give that employer a warning.

'They are saying, sir, that you are neglecting your business, and that it must suffer.'

'Who says it?' said the employer.

'All your neighbors along the street, sir.'

'Do any Christians say it?'

'Well, I hardly know whether they are Christians or not; I suppose not. But I thought I ought to let you know what was said. Besides, there is a good deal of money to be paid, and I do not know where it is coming from.'

'How much are you short?'

'About six hundred to-day, and other bills mature to-morrow and next day, and I felt anxious to know how they are to be met.'

'Do you believe our Saviour meant anything, when he said, "Seek first the kingdom of heaven?"'

'Certainly I do.'

'Well, what do you suppose he meant?'

'Oh, I do not know. I have never thought of it. Perhaps I should not be able to answer it if I should try. But I do not think that business is to be neglected.'

'I am very much astonished to hear you, a professor of religion, talk in this way. As for me, I believe he means just what he says, and I mean to do literally what he

[121]

requires. I do not neglect my business. I know what paper is maturing, and I do not give myself the least uneasiness about it. I use all proper diligence, and the rest I leave to God.'

When speaking of it, the merchant said, 'I knew where I could lay my hand on the money at once, though I did not tell my clerk of it. I went to the noonday prayer-meeting as usual. On coming home after one P.M., I asked my clerk about the means to meet my bills for today.

'Oh!' said he, 'we are all right. Mr B—— has been in, and has paid $1,800, and some other money has come in.'

'This $1,800 was a bad debt which I *never expected to be paid*,' said the merchant. 'So the Lord takes care of me, while I take care of the affairs of my own soul and the souls of others, and seek first the kingdom of heaven.'

This man is one of the new recruits into the great army. His hand, his heart, his mind, are ready for every good work, every good word, and no duty is left undone.

Said a salesman in one of our heavy wholesale houses to a young clerk – a young and *honest* disciple of Christ:

'You ought not to have said what you did to that buyer. I sold him the goods at a good price for *cash* – remember, *cash* – and now he will not take them.'

'He asked me about the goods, and I told him the truth, that they were *damaged*. I cannot tell a lie for all the goods there are in the store; and I will not,' said the young clerk.

'I am *sorry* – I am *very sorry*', said the salesman, 'to say that I must report you to the firm. But I feel it my duty to do it. I cannot be balked in this way, when I have done a good thing for the employers, to have it all upset by your squeamishness. I must go back to the counting-room, and report you.'

'Very well,' said the clerk, 'I will go with you, and go *now*. I shall tell them honestly the whole transaction, and we will see what they have to say to your fleecing a customer in this way.'

The New York Revival of 1858

The salesman's courage failed, for within a few weeks the leading member of that firm had been converted, and he was a little afraid he might be disposed to 'do his business on Christian principles', so he did not risk the appeal, and report.

This clerk was but a mere boy of nineteen. We are happy to know that many a pious young man has made up his mind to do honor to his Christian profession, and not compromise himself by following the 'laws of trade'.

Thus the power of the revival is felt in all departments of business. It infuses itself into the modes of doing business, and controls the public commercial conscience, compelling men to do right. We do not admit the charge of commercial dishonesty against the merchants of New York, more than against all and any others. We believe that for integrity and uprightness no men stand higher than the merchants of New York. This, we must say, as a matter of sober conviction, and strict open-handed justice. But while all this is freely claimed, we must admit in all candor and fairness that here was a field where the power of this revival was intensely needed. There never was that high tone of honor which could not be a higher tone. The length and breadth of a man's honor should not be measured by his punctuality in paying his notes – should not be measured by the fact that no paper of his ever went to protest, while a thousand impositions and abuses crept into his mode of doing business, some of which he might *know*, and in regard to some of which he might be in profound ignorance. Under the power of the revival it was not felt to be enough that the buyer should be so wide awake as not to have goods put upon him, which he did not want, and which he could not sell. It was not enough to say that 'buyers must take care of themselves', as had been often said before, with a thousand such maxims, that cover up knavery of the blackest dye.

THE POWER OF PRAYER

Hundreds of men in this city and in other cities have long been in the habit of suffering things to be done in their name, under the false assumption of necessity, that would never bear the light of eternity, and that would be condemned by every conscience properly enlightened by the Spirit and the word of God. When these white frauds, these little deceptions, these concealments of truth, no better than declarations of the false, were exposed in the light of the prayer-meeting, a discovery was made that startled hundreds from their self-confident security, and led them to repentance and reform. It was admitted and it was felt that doing business on Christian principles meant something; to arrest these evils, to strike at some commercial sins – meant to uphold the standard of true commercial honor, and to hold that standard so high that even the most rigid interpretation of the gospel would not condemn it. Of course there were evils to be remedied, or 'doing business on Christian principles' would be without a necessity – as urged upon business men at the Fulton street prayer-meeting. The business men who came here daily at noon to spend an hour in prayer, might be supposed to stand in the very foremost rank of the classes to which they belonged for commercial honesty; and yet they confessed there was room for the urgency of the exhortation to 'do their business upon Christian principles'.

What has been the effect of the revival in this regard? It has had powerful influence in the direction of correcting abuses all over the land. It has sunk down deep into the consciences of men, and instructed them in their duty. It has shed its light upon the hearts of men in all branches of trade, and made them feel what the laws of the gospel demand in all the business relations of life. Men have felt that they could not become Christians while they continued in unlawful employments, and any business is wrong in the sight of God which is injurious to the community. And many religious men have had their consciences so stimulated and enlightened that they could not continue in their business, and have been compelled to abandon it.

We hope to see the time come when every commercial and trade agency in the land, after summing up the various qualities and responsibilities of those whose names are on their books, shall be obliged to say, in order to add to perfect character and confidence, 'THIS MAN DOES BUSINESS ON CHRISTIAN PRINCIPLES.'

If this revival of religion exerts no permanent power on the conduct of men in their daily walk and conversation, making them more sober, godly, and heavenly-minded; if it does not reach the intercourse of man with his fellow man in the social and commercial relations of life, making merchants more honest, mechanics more truthful, tradesmen of every name more upright, conscientious and punctual in their engagements: if it does not elevate Christianity in the estimation of the world, so that a man's religion shall be an additional security for his integrity; if, in fine, it does not reach and pervade and purify the business principles of business men, it will have accomplished far less than we anticipated for the honor of Christ and the good of men.

Chapter 15

A Man of Pleasure – Goes to the Prayer-meeting – Is sorry for it – Thinks more of it – Reflects – his Mother's Prayers – Her Bible – He returns from Newport – In the Prayer-meeting again – Deep distress of Mind – Despair – Begs others to pray for him – Peace – Joy – Praise.

The record that I am about to give is drawn up by the Rev L. G. Bingham, who has been identified with the prayer-meetings in Fulton street from their commencement. He has furnished me with many cases that have fallen under his own observation, and in which he has been personally interested; but not one of them is a better illustration of the power of united prayer than this:

PART FIRST

'It is after midnight. The inmates of this house are wrapt in sleep. I went to the prayer-meeting to-night quite as thoughtless as ever. I never did think seriously, if I could help it. I must think *now* for I *cannot help it*. How came I to be so unwise as to consent to go to that prayer-meeting? I have before been invited and politely declined to patronize such a place and such an object. It is enough for me to patronize the church sometimes – not often. My life has been one that has admitted very little church going. I have had all I could do on Sunday to get ready for Monday. I have travelled all over the world and all round

The New York Revival of 1858

the globe, and ever have I made it a rule to let religion alone. A merry, gay life is the life for me. My wife, good soul, often wishes me to be a Christian. But, at my time of life, to think of turning saint – why it is all preposterous. To think that I, who surely may consider myself better than most Christians, should turn psalm-singer, and be held up as an example of early piety, is most ridiculous and absurd. Yet I am here – wide awake after hours of effort to get myself to sleep – and yet the later it grows the farther sleep flees from my eyes.

That was a wonderful prayer-meeting to-night – never saw anything like it – never heard such prayers in all my life. It was a medley of all sorts of Christians, and all to *pray*, how earnestly to pray. I wonder when I have prayed. I never pray – never *have* prayed – if those prayed to night – never. I should suppose that they thought to take heaven by storm. They expect to have the things they pray for, that is very evident. I never prayed in that way they did to-night, I am sure, yet if I were condemned to die, it may be I should beg for my life, much as they begged for me. I knew not one soul there, save the friend I went with, and yet they prayed for me, just as if they had known me all my days, and had known all my manner of life. Who told them? Not my friend, for he did not leave me a moment. Who told them? They confessed me to be just what I knew myself to be, a very wicked man.

Twenty-five years ago to-night my mother went to heaven, my beautiful, blessed mother, and I have been alone, tossed up and down upon the billows of life's tempestuous ocean!

Shall I ever go to heaven? She told me I must meet her in heaven. When she took my boy's hand in hers, and turned her gentle, loving eyes on me, and gazed earnestly and long into my face, and then lifted them to heaven; in

THE POWER OF PRAYER

that last prayer, she prayed that I might meet her in heaven. I wonder if I ever shall!

Will this night never wear away? If I see the light again, shall I ever see another such happy day as I have seen? I am not happy – I have not been since I went into *that* prayer-meeting. I am miserable. *What a wretch I have been* – a wretch.

My mother's prayers! oh! my sweet, blessed mother's prayers. Did ever a boy have such a mother as I had? For twenty-five years I have not heard her pray, till *to-night* I have heard *all her prayers over again*. They have had in fact a terrible resurrection. Oh! how she was wont to pray. She prayed as they pray to-night – so earnest, so importunate, so believing. I really believe *she expected* me to be a Christian. Shall I ever be a Christian? *She* was a Christian. Oh! how bright, and pure, and happy was her life. She was a cheerful, happy Christian. She was holy in all her ways. She was afraid to sin. She abhorred sin. Yet I have sinned, sinned without inducement, and sinned without end. Oh! what a sinner I have been. I did not know I was half so bad; I can see nothing right about me, but enough that is wrong. Shall I ever pursue the *right*? Will it ever be morning? Yes, it *will* be morning. Days will come and go, but what will days be to me, if I spend them as I have spent the past?

There is my mother's Bible: I have not opened it for years. Did she believe I could ever neglect her precious, very precious Bible so? She surely thought I should read it much and often. How often has she read it to me? How did she cause me to kneel by my little bed, and put my little hands up in the attitude of prayer? How has she kneeled by me, and over me, and I have felt her warm tears raining down upon my hands and face. Blessed mother! Did you pray in vain for your darling boy? It shall not be in vain! Oh! no! no! no! It *shall* not be in vain. I *will* pray for myself.

The New York Revival of 1858

If she were only here, to pray once more for me, how happy I should be. I pray? *I pray?* I know not *how* to pray. It will be a mockery. They *prayed* in the prayer-meeting to-night. My heart says that *was prayer*. Can I not ask them to pray *for* me? to pray *with* me? If they could pray for me, without asking – as they prayed to-night – how much more when they see me come, and make the special request that they will pray for *me*! Yes *me*.

They meet to-morrow noon to pray. That mid-day hour I will give to prayer. I will ask them to pray. Will it ever come? Oh, God! be merciful to me a sinner.'

PART SECOND

He had just returned from the gay scenes of Newport – one of the gayest of the gay. He loved the pleasures of this far-famed watering-place. He drank deeply of them – none more deeply. He had been but one week in the city. He had not a thought for his soul. The ball-room – the cotillion party – the card party – the opera – the theatre – the ride on the avenues – the race-course – the shooting gallery – these were his favorite places of resort. He was not what is regarded as an immoral man in the world's esteem. The world seldom knows the real character of the devotees of pleasure or mammon in a great city like this New York. A thousand coats of specious glazing over of the real character conceals what would almost anywhere else be known. Curious, eager, prying eyes would spy out the moral 'nakedness of the land'.

This young man passed for an amiable, social, gay, moral, charming fellow, full of hilarity, well read in the quaint fun of Dickens, and the like. He was shielded by the coat of mail of what he called strict morality. He paid all his notes. He never had a piece of paper go to *protest*. His pecuniary obligations were *met*.

THE POWER OF PRAYER

Who would dare to say he was not a moral man? He considered himself very moral. He despised those poor, immoral Christians who could not meet their obligations. Religion was, in his estimation, only a cloak for a vast amount of sin. The failures were principally among canting hypocrites, who made great pretensions to religion. He seldom went to a place of worship, and when he did, it was not out of any regard to principle, or because he wished to go, but to accompany some friends, or to please his wife, or for some such reason. He really considered himself much better than most of those church-going people. The prayer-meeting he considered altogether beneath his notice. He had often been invited to go, but with no little superciliousness he declined. He had his reasons for not going. He never gave them to others. He had, however, strayed into one of the Fulton street union prayer-meetings – held at night – he hardly knew how it came to pass, and an arrow had found its way 'between the joints of the harness'. He was a deeply wounded man.

PART THIRD

'Shall my mind ever have relief? How can I endure this anguish? Morning is come. I hear the family astir. But alas! it is no morning to me! The gladness is all gone out of my soul. I turn my despairing eyes every way for relief, but none comes. I *pray* – I am shut up – I cannot pray. It is not prayer. Oh! for one moment with my mother. Oh, for one of her prayers. But she prayed as they pray at the prayer-meeting. I have not heard anything like it for twenty-five years. I will go again to-day; I will ask them if they can pray for a wretch like me, who have never prayed in all my life, but as the Pharisee, thanking God that I am not like other men. I surely am not like other men, for who has been so hardened as I have been? Who has sinned

The New York Revival of 1858

against so much instruction as I have? – against so many precious prayers put up to heaven for me, by one of the most lovely, tender, pious, confiding trusting of mothers in her Heavenly Father's care and grace. She never doubted – she believed. She always prayed as if she did. So they do at this union prayer-meeting. I must go there to-day – I will go there. No power on earth or in hell shall stop me. I well know that there are powers of darkness that would hinder me. I sent for that Christian friend who invited me last night, to come and converse, and pray with me as soon as I was out of my bed, or as I thought he had risen.

Oh, if God will only have mercy on my poor soul? I have besought him to remove all the obstacles, and take them out of the way, and teach me by his Holy Spirit, how to come to Jesus as a Saviour. I have never thought much of Christ – never understood his office, work, and character. If he is the only Saviour, I *must* understand it. I have no ability of my own; no righteousness of my own. I am as an unclean thing, and my righteousness as filthy rags. I assent to the truth because it *is* true, and I *must*. It is of no use to hide the truth from myself. My Bible – my mother's Bible – and my conscience, teach me what I am, and what I have made myself. Oh, the bitter pangs of an accusing conscience! Oh! the unspeakable anguish of the heart that cannot speak one word for itself! I need a Saviour – mighty to save. I must seek him – I will. I am on the sea of existence, and I never can get off from it. I am afloat – no anchor, no rudder, no compass, no book of directions – for I have put them all far from me. What a thoughtless, guilty, suicidal creature I have been, dancing upon the edge of an awful precipice, my very "feet taking hold on hell". God of mercy, save! Saviour of the perishing, save, or I perish.

It is time. The noon-tide hour – the blessed hour of

prayer. Oh, that they would pray for me to-day. I shall ask them – I must. I shall say: Oh, pray for me, a poor, miserable, self-ruined wretch as I am.'

PART FOURTH

It is the hour of prayer. The soul-stirring hymn has been sung by animated voices. The holy word of God has been read. The fervent prayer has been offered. A solemn stillness pervades the lecture-room. Every part is crowded. There is a little sea of earnest, upturned faces. It is

THE UNION PRAYER-MEETING

A young, fine-looking gentleman rises in the back part of the room and begins to speak with evident and suppressed emotion:

'My brethren! I stand before you, a monument of God's amazing mercy and goodness. Yesterday you were asked to pray for me; today I come to join you in ascriptions of praise to him who saves sinners by his grace. I stand here to tell you that the Lord has put a new song into my mouth. I praise him with my whole heart for what he has done for me. Oh! such a blind, ruined, self-righteous sinner as I was but two days ago, when I came into the first prayer-meeting. I have been the world over. I have seen everything worthy of being seen, but I never saw such a prayer-meeting as this; and glory be to God, for ever bringing me in his mercy to this place of prayer, for here he met me. Here the bandages were stripped from my eyes, and I stood out before myself, naked, in my own deformity. Here I saw the inside of the whited sepulchre, full of all uncleanness. Oh, what a sinner I have been! But the blood of Christ cleanseth from all sin. Yes, forever blessed be his holy name, that I can feel that his blood

The New York Revival of 1858

avails for me. I will praise him, oh, I will praise him, while I have my being. All I have and all I am I consecrate to Jesus, my Saviour, my God. I love him with a love that is all unutterable. Oh! if I had words to tell it! But words are too poor to tell the love I feel. He is unspeakably precious to me. The walls of this room are precious to me – the very floor, too, on which I stand. How can I ever forget this precious place of prayer? How dear to me is this little band of brothers and sisters, who bore up my case to the throne of heavenly grace! Here mercy found me – here mercy was extended to me – here the Saviour first revealed himself to me. Oh! how precious!'

And he sat down amid the tears and the suppressed sobs of all in the room. Then a moment's pause, and they all joined in singing a hymn of joyful gratitude and praise.

Chapter 16

A Pastor's Sketch – An anxious Inquirer – Complains of a want of Feeling – Encouraged to Pray – Relapses and Returns – Instructed in the Nature of Faith – Relief not the thing to seek – Christ's Ability to save – A Glimmer of Light – The Sun of Righteousness.

There can be no doubt of the propriety and utility of introducing the following narrative. It is from a pastor's note-book, and he tells me in yielding to my request to be allowed the use of it here, that so many interesting cases have fallen in his way, that he has recorded them with a view to their publication. When his book is given to the public it will contain this and many other precious examples of the willingness of the Lord our Saviour to receive poor sinners.

'During the revival quite a number of youth visited my study for religious inquiry. Sarah —— was one of them. For several years she had been under the care of a most estimable lady, as her Sunday school teacher, and had been thoroughly taught the way of life. She came to me, therefore, with a mind already imbued with religious truth, needing little instruction in regard to the fundamental principles of the gospel. She was a young lady of excessive modesty, and could scarcely refer to herself, under any circumstances, without a blush. It was with no small difficulty, therefore, that she had decided to come to me and disclose her feelings in regard to her personal salvation.

The New York Revival of 1858

The first question which I put to her, and which ordinarily I proposed to inquirers, was, "Do you feel yourself to be a sinner?" "I do," was her reply; "but not so deeply as I ought, or as I wish I did."

"But you have not *been* a very great sinner; have you, Sarah?"

Casting her eye towards me in wonder, she said, "Oh! sir, no words can express the magnitude of my sins."

"But how so? If we were to judge by your outward conduct, it would be difficult to fix so heinous a charge upon you as you seem disposed to fix upon yourself. You have been a dutiful child; a regular attendant on religious services; amiable in all your intercourse with others – wherein have you sinned so grievously?"

"God", said she, "looketh on the heart, and where man might not condemn, my own conscience, and he who seeth not as man seeth, may. Many actions, you know, sir, which pass for good among men, if judged by the divine law, would prove the offspring of selfishness and sin. I find that conduct on which I used to pride myself is void of all virtue and goodness by reason of the vanity and self complacency which accompanied it. I see myself in a very different light now, since I began to realize my sins and short-comings. Still, I am most of all distressed by the thought that whilst my sins are so great, my sense of them is so small. Oh! sir, could I but *feel* more! This is what I want – *more feeling!*"

"But suppose you were to *have* more feeling, and as deep as you desire, what would be the effect; and what would you do?"

"Why, then, it seems to me, that I could appreciate the evil of sin better, and should be more likely to go with my burden to the Saviour."

"Perhaps so. But if God should not see fit to increase the weight of your burden, and you should see no more the evil of sin than you do now, what then would be your duty?"

[135]

THE POWER OF PRAYER

"I suppose I should have to go to the Saviour just as I am."

"Yes, you would, or not go at all. As, then, you cannot be sure of this increase of conviction, would it not be best to apply at once to him for salvation? By waiting, you may lose even what conviction you have. The world, remember, is ready to renew its temptations, and unless you are decided, and act with promptitude, may sweep you back to the point of carelessness or indifference where you once stood."

At the bare idea of this she trembled. "I hope I may never go back. But how can I go forward when my heart is so hard? Will he receive me, so guilty, yet so stupidly insensible to my condition?"

"Try him. Nothing will be lost by the experiment. I know not that any fixed standard of feeling is laid down in the Bible. It is not said – if you feel *deeply*, you may go to Christ for salvation. But if you feel your need of him at all, go and seek his mercy. He does not say, him that cometh to me under a deep sense of sin I will save; but whosoever will, let him come; and him that cometh unto me I will in no wise cast out."

"True – I see my error. But somehow an impassable barrier seems to lie between me and salvation. Look which way I will, I get no light. A dark cloud seems to envelop me. I wish I knew what to do. It seems to me I would do anything, or make any sacrifice if I could only get hold of the anchor of hope."

"Ah, my young friend, you are not willing, I fear, to do the one thing, and the only thing in your circumstances, which is required."

"What is that, I pray?"

"It is to forsake all your own doings, and cast yourself simply and solely into the hands of Christ. In one word, it is to *believe*. You think you must do something. And so, in

[136]

The New York Revival of 1858

one sense, you must. But what *is* the work required? It is not to do this and that, with a view to propitiate God, or to prepare yourself to come to Christ. 'This is the work of God; namely, that ye believe on him whom he hath sent.' Do this, and light will come."

"You are right. I see that you are, I know I must exercise faith in Christ, and that all my own righteousness is but filthy rags; and yet I can't seem to do that very simple thing. If I know my own heart, I do not depend upon my works for salvation. God knows I have no good works to lean upon. But when I think of my dull and dead state of heart, it seems as if I must pray for penitence, and exercise it, before I am in a condition to apply to the Saviour for his mercy. Is that a wrong feeling?"

"I think it is. It is a natural feeling. I meet it continually in persons under conviction of sin. They seem to think that the direct road to Christ by faith – by simply taking him at his word – is too short a one. They imagine that they must first get a certain amount of feeling: that the conviction must become so deep as to bear them like a resistless current to Christ. But mark! in this state of mind, there is evidently a leaven of self-righteousness. That deep feeling which they have not, but which they are striving after, is intended to qualify them, in a sense, for acceptance with Christ. They think he will be more likely to receive them. And at any rate that they will be much more likely to come unto him. Now the Lord Jesus receiveth sinners, sinners of all classes and descriptions; some with *more* and some with *less* conviction. If you feel yourself to be a sinner, *you* are invited to come. If you feel your *need* of him, that is the fitness he requires. What if you have a heart like a rock of ice! Still wait not for *nature* to soften it. Attempt not to soften it *yourself*. But go to Jesus, who alone can melt it into contrition. A view of him on the cross, is the surest way to convert that heart of stone

THE POWER OF PRAYER

into a heart of flesh. Is the subject any clearer? Do you understand it any better?"

"I think I do. I will try to act on your advice. And meanwhile pray for me, that I may not only feel after him, but *find* him."

Thus the interview terminated; and I confidently expected that one so intelligent as she was on points of practical religion, would at once make a surrender of her heart to the Saviour, and that the next time I should see her would be to congratulate her on the blessed change which had taken place. But I was mistaken. Her path grew darker every hour. The powers and principalities of the pit seemed to have been let loose upon her. All sorts of sceptical suggestions were thrown into her mind. Instead of making her way at once to the foot of the cross, she found the path walled up by her unbelief. Almost in sight, as it were, of the promised land, she seemed to be thrown back upon the desert to wander in weariness and despair among its solitudes. If she attempted to pray, something would whisper, "The prayers of the wicked are abomination unto the Lord." She tried to act on her pastor's advice, and go directly for help to the Lord Jesus Christ; but the *will* to move in that direction seemed to find no consenting *power*. She was like a person under the nightmare, seeking to escape some demon pursuer, and reach a point of safety, and yet incapable of moving a single step. Overwhelmed with these feelings, she seeks again the advice and prayers of her pastor.'

SECOND INTERVIEW

Who that has conferred with a sin-stricken soul, under circumstances like these, will not feel the deepest sympathy in its behalf! But along with this sympathy will come the feeling – what *can man* do? Never does a minister

The New York Revival of 1858

feel more his weakness, as well as his responsibility, than when an inquiring sinner, with a mind shrouded in the darkness of despair, comes to him for his prayers, his counsels and his sympathy. It will not do to seek relief *simply* in their behalf. The soul is in a critical state. *Relief* is not the *principal* thing. *That* will come in due time, provided the soul is enabled to exercise the feelings which the gospel requires. We are too apt, under the influence of sympathy, to apply the balm, ere yet the wound has been probed, and the morbid symptoms removed.

With a countenance wan and woeful, Sarah takes her seat and *looks* her sorrows. She cannot relate them. Her agony is too deep for *words*. She seems to think that her pastor can do something for her. 'I perceive, Sarah, that you have not yet found peace in believing.' She shook her head. 'Why is it?'

'Oh, I cannot tell. I am the most wretched of mortals. I have no faith in anything. I am tempted to doubt everything – to deny God. Yes, I tremble to think that I am almost an atheist. I try to pray; but can't. I read; but all is darkness. I fear that I am given up. I even fear, and almost believe that I have committed some sin of peculiar aggravation for the pardon of which it is unlawful to pray. There *is* such a sin; is there not?'

'There was, perhaps, in Apostolic times; and some may have been guilty of it. And I would not say positively that even *now*, a person may not commit the unpardonable sin. But I do not think *you* have. Indeed I am very sure you have *not*. In my opinion the suggestion in your case is from the evil one, with a view to discourage you from seeking pardon at the feet of Jesus. It is one of the devices of the wicked one to keep souls away from the great source of forgiveness. Your sins, however great, are pardonable. There is enough value in one drop of the Saviour's blood to atone for them all. You remember it is said, "His blood cleanseth us from *all* sin." Can you not believe this, and be comforted by it?'

'Theoretically I can. I have always believed it: but when I come to make the application to my own case, it *seems* as if there was at least *one* exception.'

'Ah, my young friend, this is unbelief. It is doing dishonor to God's word, and robbing the Saviour of his infinite merits. If that blood cannot wash *your* sins away – if its virtue is not sufficient to cancel *your* guilt, then the atonement is a failure; and God is not true when he says, "It cleanseth from *all* sin." You are treading on dangerous ground when you put your own case beyond the possibility of salvation, unless you have, by revelation, the assurance that you have actually committed the unpardonable sin.'

This view struck her forcibly. Pausing awhile, she said she thought she had done wrong to allow her mind to take a train of thought so sceptical. 'I can think of nothing more dreadful than denying Christ's ability to save. Do you think it was a temptation of Satan; and that God will not make it an insuperable barrier to my salvation?'

'I do. And now let me urge you to turn your attention more to the fullness of Christ; and dwell more on those passages of Scripture which hold up the Saviour to sinners, as able to save to the uttermost. Your view is too constantly in the direction of your own short-comings. You think only, or too exclusively on the demands of the law; and not on him who is the end of the law for righteousness to every one that believeth. The commandment has come, and slain you. But there is life in Christ. He takes the dead sinner – dead by the stroke of the law – and breathes life into him. Jesus stands between you and that broken law, and says, Come unto me and be ye saved. For every violation of that law he has paid double. The moment you accept him as the Lord your righteousness,

The New York Revival of 1858

the law has no hold upon you in the way of condemnation and penalty. It has received compensation in Jesus' blood, and the believer is free. Do you apprehend this view?'

'I think I do. There is, at least, a glimmer of light. And yet ere I reach my home, I fear it will give place to the same terrible unbelief and darkness.'

And it did. The struggle was renewed; and for weeks no light came. There was no hope, and no sign of it for a long time. What was the consequence? Did she give up in despair? *She* was not one to give up. Her mind was made up never to relinquish the subject – to *wrestle* and PRAY so long as life should last. If she died, it should be with her eyes set in the direction of the cross.

Such being her determination, after weeks of *agony*, of *weeping*, of PRAYER, traversing, as it were, the very valley and shadow of death, she at length discerned that same glimmer, as if from the cross. And this time it grew brighter as the twilight deepens into morning; and a peaceful serenity came over her – the harbinger of mercy, and the token that she had passed from death unto life.

Almost fearing to trust to this new feeling as evidence of a gracious change, she kept these things and pondered them in her heart, until, as she thought, it would be safe to reveal them to her pastor and her Christian friends. That period soon arrived. They had themselves anticipated it, in the manifest serenity, which, like a halo, encircled her countenance. Like the woman in the Gospel, who after diligent search by broom and light, had found her piece of money, and then called her friends together for their congratulations; so she, having found the pearl of great price, when assured of it, made known her joy to those who had sympathized with her, and prayed for her, and uniting with the angels of God, they gave vent to their joy and gratitude that another sinner had repented, and that another lost one had been found.

Chapter 17

A Roman Catholic Experience – Out of Employment – Reads in the 'Herald' of the Prayer-meetings – Attends – Is astonished – Power of Prayer – Contrasted with the Mass – His Deep Convictions – Fascinated – Reveals his State – Light Breaks in – His Wife follows him to Christ.

He had been in the country but a few weeks. He was born in Ireland – resided for thirteen years in England – came to this country in January last – was without friends – without employment – a stranger in a strange land. He was thirty-one years of age; was married to a wife nine years younger than himself. He was well educated – of good address – good manners – and had the appearance of a gentleman. He had been employed for some time in the London post-office as a clerk, before coming to this country. He was a competent man in almost any business, and so he thought he would try his hand in something new, and come to America. He could not have chosen a more inopportune time to come than he did – landing on these shores, and cast into this cold and heartless city when thousands of young men were thrown out of employment by the force of the money pressure – himself depending on employment for support.

In this state of things he took up the 'Herald' one day, in which the proceedings of some of the daily prayer-meetings were reported. He read them, and said to himself, 'This is a most extraordinary state of things. I

The New York Revival of 1858

have never seen or heard of anything of the kind. I will go into the Fulton street prayer-meeting this very day, and see what all this means.'

True to his resolution, at the appointed hour he made his appearance at the door of the middle lecture-room, and, as a stranger, he was invited in, and seated, as any other stranger would be. How little did the throng around know what was going on in that man's mind. A bigoted Roman Catholic – perfectly satisfied with his own religious system and belief – knowing little about it, except that the priest kept his conscience, and pardoned his sins, at stated periods, *for a consideration*, he looked over this earnest mass of human beings with wonder and amazement. He had come early, and after being seated, he watched with deep interest the filling up of the room. It became more densely crowded, till at last not another individual could be stowed away anywhere. The deep solemnity which sat upon every countenance puzzled him. He knew not the meaning of it.

The exercises began. The hymn was sung – the Scriptures were read – then followed prayer. This was such prayer as he had never heard before. All filled him with awe.

But when the requests for prayer were read, he learned something which he had never learned before. He pondered over this asking men to pray that sinners might be convicted of sin, and might be converted. His mind was perplexed. He could not understand it. After reading some of these requests, a gentleman rose up to pray. That countenance and figure bore, he thought, a striking resemblance to the celebrated Daniel O'Connell, whom he had known, and this single circumstance riveted his attention to the man and to the prayer he was now making. As the prayer proceeded, he noticed that the whole assembly seemed to be moved by one common impulse,

THE POWER OF PRAYER

and all bowed their heads in *prayer*. These *American Protestants*, he thought, had some strange ways about them. 'Was this *prayer*?' Here was no mass being *said* – here were none of the *forms* of prayer. There he sat, bolt upright, in the back part of the room, looking on. He was a simple spectator of the scene. In his own church, in *prayer*, he could be just about as much of a spectator as now. He *said* his part of the service, with not a particle of feeling in it. He had never felt the prayers he was *saying*, or the priest was saying for him. Here all seemed to pray. He knew that they *felt* – he could *feel* that they did. There was deep emotion all around him. He had seen hundreds of services performed without a single tear. But now tears flowed freely down the cheeks of him who was *waiting* at the throne of grace. Such a prayer for such objects he had never heard before. All were weeping. 'What for?'

From that hour his carnal security was broken up, never to be regained again, and leaving him to live as he had lived. The peace of his mind was destroyed. The complacency of his mind in himself – in his church – in the blind system of religious faith held life-long, was gone. He went away from that meeting in trouble. The calm, stupid serenity of his thoughtless life was an astonishment to him. He said to himself, 'These people pray for things which I never prayed for; these people make such confessions as I never made; and these people possess something which I never possessed. And if these things are suitable and proper for them, they are suitable and proper for me.'

The next day found him in the prayer-meeting – and so did the next – and so every day found him an anxious attendant there – and with the attendance upon the second or third meeting finished, he found all confidence in his church at an endless end. He wondered at himself at being so ignorant and stupid as to believe that there was any

The New York Revival of 1858

religion in it. He saw its gorgeous emptiness, its heartless pretensions, and its haughty arrogance and assumptions. His convictions from the second or third meeting were that there were no such delusions this side of the infernal pit as this church practised. Every vestige of his respect and confidence was gone forever. He was no Romanist now.

When thus shorn, almost in a day, of all spiritual strength; when all the bandages were so suddenly snatched from his eyes, was it wonderful that his mind should be roused with religious anxiety? It would have been wonderful if it had not been.

These Fulton street prayer-meetings were a means of great mental distress to him, and yet he could not stay away. The more he attended, the more he became acquainted with himself as a sinner – the more he felt his need of Christ – and the more earnestly did he desire to have a saving interest in him, and to become a true Christian.

Still his mind was very blind and dark. What it was to be a Christian he had obscurely perceived and but feebly comprehended. He walked in great and deep darkness. All this about the sins of the heart – all this about sins every day and hour – sins continually – all this about the renewal of the heart by the regenerating power of the Holy Spirit lay in a new field of moral vision. Things of awful import he saw now for the first time – and the more he learned the deeper became his distress.

At length his case became known to some of his fellow-worshippers. At first and for some time he had concealed his state of mind from every human being. He was a stranger. To whom should he apply? When his anxiety became so great that he could conceal it no longer, he made it known to those who had charge of these meetings. They conversed with him. They prayed with him. They

THE POWER OF PRAYER

induced him to pray. But still that dark cloud lay upon his heart. Not a ray of heavenly light shot through it.

Not a word was said to him about leaving his own church. Not any works of self-righteousness were suggested. Something of this kind his heart was continually seeking after. It was ready enough to run in its old ways. But he was urged simply to come to Christ, as the atoning Lamb of God, who taketh away the sins of the world. He was directed to come to Christ just as he was, and to rely on nothing except the righteousness of Christ for all his hopes of justification with God. Oh! how did his mind take in the glorious truth, 'Therefore, being justified by faith, we have peace with God through our Lord Jesus Christ.' For more than two months his mind 'wearied after a resting-place'.

He was asked: 'Is there anything that you are unwilling to give up for an interest in Christ?'

His answer was: 'I know of nothing.'

He had a Roman Catholic wife. Perhaps he was not aware of the influence this simple fact had in deterring him from coming to Christ. The struggle was a long and severe one. His mind became more and more imbued with the great and fundamental doctrines of the gospel.

At length the light broke in upon his mind and heart. The darkness disappeared. He was enabled to receive Christ, in all his offices, as his Saviour. Christ was 'formed in his heart, the hope of glory'. Oh, what a tide of joy and peace was now welling up in his soul continually. The play upon his countenance of the happy feelings within, showed how great and wonderful was the change. That expression of sadness and despair was gone, and his face was animated with the hope and joy within.

The great feature of his heart and mind now was deep humility – a deep sense of his unworthiness. It is, perhaps, very rarely that a man in his circumstances needed –

absolutely needed – so much encouragement. He was distrustful of himself to the last degree. He wished to make an open profession of religion. This he was ready and anxious to do. But to take the next step, and go to the Lord's table, and partake of the sacrament of the Lord's supper – his mind halted here – under a deep and painful sense of his great unfitness, and utter unworthiness. He seemed to be fearful of 'eating and drinking unworthily, not discerning the Lord's body'. The writer calls to mind conversations had on this subject. He seemed to be filled with a sort of dismay at the possibility of incurring the condemnation spoken of by the apostle.

When once his duty was clearly seen, and the nature of the ordinance and the qualifications of the subject were fully understood, he went forward in duty at once. He is now a worthy member of the church, and rejoices exceedingly in the 'hope set before him'. He has been discarded by all his friends of the Roman Catholic Church, and followed and pursued with all manner of petty persecutions by the minions of a priesthood as despotic and absolute as death, and of a church that never '*varies*', but is ever the same. His young wife has become so disgusted with this exhibition of the bitter malignity of those of her own faith, and so satisfied of the truth and sincerity of her husband, that she has declared her intention to go with her husband, and bear his persecutions with him. By their means he has been cut off from the little support which he would otherwise have had, and has been reduced to great hardships, which he endures without a murmur. He has confidence that the Lord, who allows him to be tried, will also provide.

Chapter 18

The Work among the Seamen – Many Languages spoken – Prayers better than Rum – An Irish Catholic – An aged Mariner – A sinking Vessel saved in the midst of prayer – 'The North Carolina' – 'The Wabash' – A Swedish Sailor at the Wheel – The awful Scene on 'The Austria', and singular coincidence – Six Sea Captains converted – Another Captain saved – His remarkable Experience.

In no sphere of influence and interest has the revival been more efficient than among the seamen of this and other ports, as well as on the 'great and wide sea'. I have never read or heard of more wonderful things connected with the power of prayer than have come to light in the communications which have been sent to me from the ships on the ocean and the meetings of sailors on shore. Some of these facts will be found in this chapter, and will be read with admiring gratitude by every one who loves the Saviour, and rejoices in hearing that 'the abundance of the sea' is given unto him.

The Rev C. C. Jones, Pastor of the Mariner's Church, who is devoted to this specific department of labor, has at my request prepared a sketch of some interesting facts, which I shall give in his own words:

The Mariner's Church may be truly called a working church. Many of its members and church officers, and gentlemen of the Port Society, are daily engaged in efforts to secure the welfare of the 'men of the sea'. The meetings

The New York Revival of 1858

for prayer, which have been sustained without ceasing, are four weekly, and three Sabbath prayer-meetings, besides the preaching morning and evening, and two adult Bible classes.

The prayer-meeting on Monday evening is set apart for Norwegians, Swedes, Danes, and Finns, and has at times been greatly blest in the conversion of the Scandinavian seamen who have been made the subject of prayer. In this and other prayer-meetings there have at times been as many languages represented as at Jerusalem on the day of Pentecost. From a record of more than four thousand names of seamen who have visited the pastor and our devoted missionary, Joseph H. Gardiner, it is found that men of seventy-six different nationalities (including the islands of the sea) are represented. Many of these men speak from two to six different languages. Not long ago a Finn called upon the pastor who spoke *ten* different languages; seven of which he could write well. He had received a university education in his own country, but is still a sailor before the mast, and is laboring actively for Christ.

On another occasion, eight men came to the pastor's study in a group, and, on inquiry, it was found that the eight together spoke twenty-six languages. There were in the company, one Norwegian, two Frenchmen, one Englishman, one Portuguese, and three Italians. The Norwegian spoke three languages; the Portuguese, three, and the Englishman, two; one of the Frenchmen spoke three, the other, two; of the three Italians, one spoke six, another four, and the other, three. The languages spoken were English, French, Spanish, Portuguese, Italian, German, Norwegian, Dutch, Arabic, Turkish, and Bengali. It will be readily seen that if the power of the Holy Ghost is but brought to bear on men possessing such facilities for communication, they will become literally

[149]

THE POWER OF PRAYER

living epistles, known and read of all men, and may be reckoned among the most efficient auxiliaries in the work of extending and building up the church of God. Among those who have given evidence of having been born again here, there have been some striking manifestations of the readiness of the Holy Spirit to answer prayer.

In all our prayer-meetings it has been our custom to give an opportunity for seamen and others who desired an interest in our prayers, to manifest that desire by rising; and it is not at all an uncommon thing for from six to sixteen to do so at a single meeting. *As a result of these prayers*, not a week has passed without one or more souls coming humbly to the foot of the cross.

One poor fellow, a sailor, who was convinced of his sins, and who flew to Christ for a refuge, was met by the missionary at his boarding-house just as he was packing his chest for sea. The landlord was quite busy filling up some jugs of liquor, which he placed in each chest for a sea stock, charging it to Jack, of course, and insisted on placing one in the chest of the inquiring sailor; but he refused, and persisted in the refusal, notwithstanding the repeated solicitations of the landlord and his wife; and, looking at the missionary, said, with much feeling: '*I would rather take your* PRAYERS *to sea with me, than all the rum in the world.*'

In another instance, a sailor was desired to abstain from intoxicating drinks, and was told that he could do nothing without prayer to God for his assistance. Determined to commence at once, he exhibited that peculiar trait of the sailor's character – impulsiveness – by dropping on his knees in the bar-room, and praying there for strength to keep his vow. That vow he has kept; and, some time afterwards, while on his rounds, Mr Gardiner was accosted, in a strong Hibernian brogue by the landlady, with '*Faith, I do believe you have converted Peter.*' So that his

The New York Revival of 1858

conduct was such that others 'took knowledge of him that he had been with Jesus'.

One, a female, the wife of a sailor, now keeping a sailor boarding-house, came to the prayer-meeting on Sabbath afternoon, was convinced of her danger as a sinner, and asked the prayers of the people of God. After a short season of deep conviction, during which she communicated her views to her husband, they agreed to put away the bar or liquor closet, and both began to seek the Lord, who, true to his promise, was found of them. She is now a member of the church, and he is a *candidate* for membership. Both are consistent Christians, and not only come to the house of God themselves, but also bring their boarders with them.

Another, an Irishman and a rigid Catholic, was induced to attend a daily prayer-meeting, held in the church for some few weeks at eleven A.M., became convinced of his sins, and rose to ask prayer for himself. After some interview with the pastor, he felt that Christ was his Saviour – he gave up the Virgin Mary and the Saints – asked prayer for his wife and child, whom he brought with him to the meeting. His wife gave herself to Christ, and he at once entered upon aggressive efforts upon the man of sin. Having obtained work at the Central Park, he armed himself with tracts and went among his former associates; and with a heart brimful of affection, read to them the tracts, and 'mightily convinced them, showing them by the Scriptures that Jesus is the Christ'. He and his wife are both consistent members of the Mariner's Church.

I will add but one more illustration out of many *answers to prayer* that present themselves to my mind at this moment, as the fruits of the present revival:

It is that of an old sailor who has spent forty-three years of his eventful life on the sea. He came at first, while slightly under the influence of liquor, to the church

THE POWER OF PRAYER

service on Sabbath evening, accompanied by his wife, and took seats near the door. The subject that evening was, 'Behold the Lamb of God that taketh away the sins of the world.' Shortly after the commencement of the sermon, the old white-headed, white-bearded sailor and his aged companion were seen making their way up the aisle towards the pulpit, and on reaching the front seat they both came to an anchor. The old man fixed his eyes on the pastor and never once took off his gaze until the sermon closed; during the address he wept much, and at the close the pastor left the pulpit and approached him, laying his hand upon his shoulder, and saying as he did so:

'Well, sir, can you look to this Lamb of God?'

He answered with much emotion: 'I don't know, sir, about that. It is not so easy.'

'But,' was the inquiry, 'do you desire to behold him as your Saviour?'

He answered: 'I wish I could.'

As the crowd were passing out, he was urged to call and see the pastor in his study on Monday morning. He promised to do so, and on Monday morning at ten o'clock in came the old sailor. Five others had come inquiring, as a result of last night's sermon. And now the old man came in leaning upon his staff, when the following dialogue ensued:

Pastor. – 'Well, sir, how is it this morning, do you still feel anxious about your soul? You are drawing near the grave and will soon step into it, and are not prepared.'

J. B. – 'No, sir, I fear not. *But do you think Christ will save* ME?' As he asked the question he looked at me with intense interest, as if he felt that everything temporal and eternal depended on the answer.

P. – 'Why do you ask that question, is there anything special in your case?'

The New York Revival of 1858

J. B. – 'Oh, sir, I have been such a great sinner; I'm afraid I've gone too far. God has been so good to me, and I have treated him shamefully. I have been at sea forty-three years before the mast and abaft it, and have been in many dangers. Out of them all the Lord has delivered me. I have been shipwrecked three times. The first time, when a boy, in the North Sea, the vessel went ashore in the breakers. I was washed overboard by a sea with two boats' paddles in my hand, that kept me afloat. I then called upon God, repeating the prayer my mother taught me; and after some hours, the men on the shore threw me a line with some lead attached to it, which I twined around the paddles and they drew me on shore. Three of us only were saved out of eleven. Once off the Falkland Islands, in a south-sea whale-ship, I was one of a boat's crew of seven who took the boat with a week's provision and deserted the ship. But we paid dearly for our desertion. We were sixty days in that open boat; twenty-six of those days not one of us had a drop of fresh water in our lips. After the week's provisions were exhausted, we lived on the flesh and blood of penguins and seals. At another time I was cast-away off Barnegat, and out of thirty-one persons, crew and passengers, only four of us were saved. I was picked up, after knocking about in the breakers on the bottom of a boat about three or four hours, during which time I prayed most fervently to God for deliverance; and he was pleased to hear my prayer. I have fallen overboard nine times, and have been 'in death oft' in various engagements and other exposures. But what kills me is that, after God had heard my prayers and promises, I should turn round and curse him as soon as I got dry clothes on.'

P. – 'Well, now, do you repent of all your sins?'

J. B. – 'Yes, sir, I do most truly.'

P. – 'Are you willing to cast away everything that offends him? To give up drinking and all other sins?'

THE POWER OF PRAYER

J. B. – 'I will, sir, with God's help, if I die by it.'

The pastor then bowed with him in prayer, and he left with full purpose of heart to live no longer to himself, but to Christ who died for him. At our next prayer-meeting he was present, and rose to ask the prayers of the people of God. Those prayers were heard and now he walks humbly before the Lord. Three months after that conversation, J. B. came before the Council of the Mariner's Church and was received into membership, on a profession of his faith in Christ, and to a seat at the table of the Lord. He is now a devout and humble follower of our Lord Jesus Christ; and there is not a more attentive hearer, or more faithful doer of the word of God in the whole congregation than that same hoary-headed, white-bearded man of the sea.

Mr Jones adds that the work is still in progress; that it appears as if the Holy Spirit has been present with us all along, so that the church has been blessed with a continuous revival; the result of which has been the reception of some three hundred and fifty persons into church membership since the month of March, 1856. On that day, we organized our church with sixty members. From that day to this, although the communion has been administered on the first Sabbath of each month, we have never sat down to the Master's table without some new trophies of divine grace to partake with us in that delightful ordinance. The members received on these separate occasions ranging from three to sixty souls, and averaging eleven each month. Of this three hundred and fifty, three hundred have been received on a profession of their faith in Christ, and one hundred and forty-six are practical seamen, many of whom are, at this writing, scattered to the four winds of heaven, and are working for Christ, as their correspondence with the pastor and the reports of foreign chaplains clearly shows.

The New York Revival of 1858

In addition to those who united with the church, there must be, at the lowest calculation, one hundred seamen who have gone to sea under deep conviction, and with the promise that they would seek Christ, or in the possession already of a flickering hope, but who could not remain on shore long enough to give to the church the necessary evidence of their entire submission to Christ. Some of these are in the mines of California. Some in Australia. Some have subsequently united with other churches, and some have been the means of presenting the saving truths of the gospel to their shipmates, and though they have gone forth weeping, bearing 'precious seed', for months, at sea, have 'come back rejoicing, bringing their sheaves with them'.

The union prayer-meetings have furnished many striking cases of interest from the same department of Christian effort. In one of these meetings, a sailor speaker rose, and said: 'I have some good news from the sea. Some time ago, a large vessel became leaky, and in a violent gale she was so strained, that she opened her seams, and leaked very badly. The captain did all he could to save his ship and his crew, but finally he gave it up in despair. He called his crew together, thirty-two in all, and said: "My men, I can keep it from you no longer. We must go down in a very short time. Are you prepared?" The captain was not a pious man. Two of the seamen stepped forward, and said: "Captain, we believe we are prepared." "Then pray for me and for your shipmates: I acknowledge I am not prepared." They all kneeled down on the deck together, and these two men prayed. They asked God to save them, if it was consistent with his will; but at all events, to prepare them to live or die. They prayed earnestly. They had discovered a large ship at a great distance from them, before they began to pray; so far off, that they did not attempt to signalize her, not supposing that they could

THE POWER OF PRAYER

attract attention. So they kept on praying, and did not attempt any means of making known their situation to the distant ship. They prayed for their lives, if it was God's will to spare them, or if not, that they might be the children of God, living or dying. While they were yet on their knees in prayer, they heard a noise, and looking over the side, there was a life-boat from the distant ship, well manned, which took them all in, and took them on board. The ship had discovered the sinking condition of the stranger, and sent her boat to their aid. The crew, thus rescued, were very much impressed that this was the hand of God, in answer to prayer. They resolved to hold a daily prayer-meeting, which they did, and when they landed at Fayal, some time afterwards, every one of these thirty-two seamen had become hopefully pious.' What power but a power divine wrought the change? How true it is, that in this great awakening, the light is breaking out everywhere, on the sea and on the land, and thousands on thousands are rejoicing in the light. The revival has, in many instances, appeared at sea, where there has been no communication with the shore.

Father Burnett has told me with tears of the glorious revival which has been in progress for some months on the 'North Carolina', a receiving ship in this port. This venerable servant of God has long been devotedly engaged in his work, especially among the seamen, but he says that he has never seen such displays of divine grace as during the present revivals. A gentleman rose at one of the Fulton street meetings and said:

'I attended divine service on this ship last Sabbath. I inquired of the preacher in charge how many had become pious since last fall. He said, not less than 150; it may be 200. Some of these are on the 'Wabash' and some on board the 'Savannah'; some go on the 'Sabine'. So these converted men are scattered abroad, some on one ship and

The New York Revival of 1858

some on another. They will let their light shine wherever they may be. There are now 350 on board the 'North Carolina'; a goodly number of these attended the service, which is an entirely voluntary one, and only those attend who choose. The exercises began with singing that beautiful hymn:

> Jesus, thou art the sinner's friend,
> As such I look to thee.

Then followed prayer and two addresses, which were listened to with deep attention and interest. A more still and solemn assembly we have not seen this many a day. Then the readiness with which many came forward after the services were over and signed the temperance pledge and took their certificates, was very gratifying. Temperance and piety go together. We were gratified to see the accomplished wife of the commander in the audience, watching the attention upon the services with great interest.'

From the U.S. steamer 'Wabash', forty-five seamen sent a request to the Port Society of New York, to be remembered in the prayers of Christians here. Later news gives us the pleasing intelligence that a daily prayer-meeting is maintained on board the 'Wabash'; that the first lieutenant has become a pious man; that he encourages these meetings, and that he often addresses them, using all his influence in their behalf. On that ship are several sailors and marines who became pious last winter and spring on board the receiving ship 'North Carolina'. What gladdening and glorious news this is from a ship of war.

A Swedish sailor, who spoke very broken English, addressed the meeting. The Holy Spirit overtook him away in mid-ocean and pursued him day and night and would give him no rest. 'I was ready to cry out,' said he,

THE POWER OF PRAYER

"Who will deliver me? who will help me?" and my heart sunk down in despair. Oh! what a miserable sinner I felt I was. My heart was sick and sore. I knew not what to do. I had no one to guide me. What was to become of me?

One night, as I was standing at the wheel, I bethought me of Christ, and my heart turned to him for help. And with my very first thoughts of him he met me at the wheel – and oh! what words of love and mercy he spoke to me there at the wheel. "Come to me, ye heavy laden; come to me: I cast none out. I am meek and lowly of heart. Learn of me; take my yoke: it is easy. Take my burden: my grace shall make it light."

There at the wheel, in the dark and solemn hour, the Saviour showed himself to me. I love him because he first loved me. I cannot speak your language well; but Christ understands me and I understand him. And ever since I met him at the wheel – poor sinner's friend – I live very close to him. I hear him tell me to hold up my sails to gales of the blessed Spirit, and he will waft me straight to heaven.'

The awful disaster at sea, the destruction by fire of the steamer 'Austria', with four hundred human beings, is fresh in the memory of every reader. It has since been ascertained that immediately after leaving port, a prayer-meeting was begun on board in which some souls were converted. At one of the Fulton street meetings this remarkable and thrilling scene occurred:

The ninety-first psalm had been read by the conductor of the meeting, and several prayers offered and remarks made, when a gentleman arose in the congregation and made some very affecting remarks on the subject of faith and trust in God under all circumstances, and by way of illustration made mention of a case on board the 'Austria'. He said that he had been informed by some one, for he had no personal knowledge of the parties, that a man whose

The New York Revival of 1858

wife and son were on board that unfortunate ship had recently been making most diligent inquiry of the rescued passengers who had arrived in our city, trying to learn, if possible, something as to the fate of his wife and son. That on describing his wife to one of the passengers that he had sought out, that passenger thought from the husband's description that he had seen such a woman on board. The husband produced a daguerreotype of his wife, and the passenger immediately exclaimed, 'That is the very woman, and God bless you, my dear sir, for it was she that organized a prayer-meeting on board, in which my soul was blessed in my conversion.' He then informed the afflicted husband that the last he saw of his wife and son they were standing as far aft as they could get away from the flames, and when at last the devouring element rushed on them with such force as to be no longer endurable, he saw the wife and mother, with a calm serene countenance, embrace the son, and then both committed themselves to a watery grave.

But the singular coincidence in connection with this we have yet to relate. When the meeting had concluded, a man who sat in the same seat with the one who addressed the meeting, and the very next man to the speaker, clasped his hands, and stood for a moment unable to utter a word, such was his emotion; but at last said: 'That woman was my wife, and I, a stranger to every one here, have come in to seek consolation, and to ask an interest in your supplications, that God would assuage my grief, and bind up my broken heart!'

The scene was deeply affecting, and never to be forgotten by those who witnessed it. This rescued passenger said, in the meeting, that when in the water, swimming, a pious friend inquired of him how he felt in view of death: I replied:

'Perfectly happy; I can now rely on Jesus, and I am

safe.' And looking up on the ship, I added, 'There stands the noble woman, with her son's hand in hers, to whom I owe all my hopes of salvation, for she it was that got up the prayer-meetings.'

What a consolation to the bereaved husband, to know that the last hours of his devoted Christian wife were spent in such acts of love to souls!

A clergyman in Philadelphia read a letter at one of the prayer-meetings, from a young man of his acquaintance who was on board the ill-fated 'Austria', in which he detailed the last interview between himself and five Christian comrades who perished beneath the waves. As soon as the destruction of the vessel was deemed inevitable, these six young men took a position between the flames and the water, with the understanding that at the last moment they would unitedly consign themselves to the sea. In the bare moment thus allowed to contemplate their fate, their hope in Christ was confidently expressed, and when, to escape the spreading fire, the leap became necessary, they grasped each other's hand, and with a parting 'farewell', and an expressed confidence that 'in a few moments they would meet in heaven', they sprang into the sea. The writer of the letter states, after sustaining himself in the water by means of a life-preserver for four hours (during which time his contemplations of a future state ripened into a joy in believing in his Saviour such as he had never before experienced), a vessel hove in sight for his release. The reading of the letter referred to elicited an outburst of feeling all over the room.

On another occasion, fifteen seamen from the ship-of-war 'Savannah' sent in their names that they might be remembered in the prayers of the Fulton street prayer-meeting. It was stated that thirteen of these were pious men, and two are anxious about their souls. They had sent a letter to the commanding officer of the ship,

The New York Revival of 1858

that they may have leave to hold a daily prayer-meeting on board, and they are pledged to sustain this, or some other prayer-meeting, as God shall give them opportunity.

A large number of sea captains have been made subjects of reviving grace, and we subjoin accounts of a few of them, taken from a sea captain's letter:

Captain S., now commanding one of the New York and Havre packets, was met in Wall street by one of his friends, who invited him to go to a noonday prayer-meeting. It being then about the hour, he, half in joke and half in good-nature, consented and went. When an opportunity was given for those who desired to lead a new life to rise, that prayer might be offered for them, he, to the surprise of his friend, rose and asked Christians to pray for him, which was done heartily and earnestly. From the meeting he went to his ship, and there locked himself in his state-room, fell on his knees, and besought God to have mercy upon him. His prayer was soon answered, and his statement, the following evening, in Mr Home's church (Brooklyn), of God's goodness to him, was listened to with deepest attention and interest. Letters have since been received from him from Havre, which bear ample testimony that the cause of Christ has in him a faithful missionary.

Captain W., of the bark B., while on a voyage from Cuba to France, met with such severe weather as to reduce his ship to nearly a wreck, in which condition, crippled in hull and spars, he succeeded in getting into New York. It was his first year as a master, and the trouble arising from his accident, added to the idea that by it he had lost the confidence of his owners, seemed to have almost broken him down. His consignee did much to comfort and reassure him, and when going to prayer-meeting was proposed by the consignee, he gladly consented; not that he cared anything for the meeting, but he was willing to do anything and everything for his friend. He went, and there the Spirit of the Lord found him, and from a rough, swearing, fighting man, he became a zealous and devoted Christian. He, too, has written home since his arrival in France, and gives good evidence of the soundness of his conversion.

Captain C., at present retired from the sea, and doing business in South street, New York, had been for some twenty years trying to become a Christian, but *in his own way*; and it was only during a Wednesday evening lecture at Plymouth Church, some few months since, that he found true peace in believing. He is now a zealous and devoted Christian. His first efforts at family prayer were met by many crosses. After he had commenced asking a blessing at his table, some friends from the East called to take tea and pass the evening. How to manage about the blessing he did not know. They did not know of his conversion, and he had not the courage to tell them. Finally, he concluded to omit the blessing *that* evening, and so, when seated at the table, he seized his knife and fork and went vigorously to work. His little daughter, some six years old, however, folded her hands and closed her eyes, and after waiting some time for the blessing, said, 'I am all ready now, father, ask the blessing.' This brought him down, and since that time he has never dodged a duty. No sooner was Captain C. converted, than his heart went out after his five unconverted brothers. He publicly asked prayers for them at the Plymouth Church prayer-meeting, and backed the request up by an earnest and faithful letter to three of them, then on shore at the East. These three were soon after converted, although one of them has since told me that to break his heart the Lord had first to break his leg!

Captain P., also retired from the sea, and doing business in South street, New York, embraced religion a few months since, and since that time few men have been more zealous

The New York Revival of 1858

and devoted in their efforts for the conversion of others. Naturally a dry joker, his old friends and associates would frequently gather about him and joke him about his present zeal. 'You can joke', said he, 'as much as you like, but if you think to joke me out of my religion, you are altogether mistaken.' It was my unpleasant task to inform him of the failure of a firm down East, by which he was likely to lose quite a sum of money. 'Poor fellows,' said he, 'I pity them, for they are fine men;' and he went on to tell me some of the incidents connected with his family worship, and did not again allude to what I had told him! After that, who can doubt *his* conversion?

Captain M., of Maine, called upon me on his way per steamer to Europe, the day before sailing. I invited him to a noonday prayer-meeting and he went. While there, he came to the conclusion that it was time he 'tacked ship', and accordingly he rose, when invitation was given, and asked Christians to pray for him, that he might receive strength to pursue a Christian life, which he was then resolved to commence. On leaving the meeting, he told us he was going to his hotel to tell his wife what he had done, and to beg her to join him. Next morning he was at the Plymouth Church prayer-meeting, and he brought his wife with him, and there, too, he arose and asked prayers for himself and wife. During the forenoon he sent for us to join him in prayer in his room at the hotel. We met there at eleven o'clock, and seldom have I witnessed a more impressive prayer-meeting than that was. He prayed fervently, and so did his wife, and both seemed humble, trusting, and joyous. At twelve o'clock that day they went to sea. What a change had been wrought in that twenty-four hours in and for him!

Captain P., of an eastern ship, attended our prayer-meeting very regularly, and with evident interest, and when questioned upon the subject, admitted his need of

THE POWER OF PRAYER

religion; but his idea was, that when the Lord intended him to have religion, he would give him such feelings as he could not resist, and so, of course, *he* had nothing to do. When at last this idea was out of his head, and he had made up his mind to use what feeling he had, and to take a step for himself, as in the case of the 'prodigal son', his Father ran and met him, and a few days afterwards he went to sea a believing and trusting Christian. A letter from him, too, from abroad, gave good evidence of the soundness of his conversion. This letter was read in Plymouth Church.

Among the many conversions in connection with the revival in B——, Mass., are several sea captains, which give the most convincing proof of the power of divine grace. One of these captains had followed the sea, and business connected with the sea, for more than forty years. He was in the Fiji Island trade twenty-six years. He had retired, and was nearly sixty years old. He was in the vigor of good health, and had the prospect before him of many years of ease and comfort. Some twenty years ago, he was the subject of serious impressions, which lasted for nearly two years, with more or less intensity.

His wife was a praying woman, and had been a professor of religion twenty-eight years. The serious impressions of this captain's mind at length wore off, and he became indifferent to the claims of religion, and regardless of his own personal interest in the salvation of the soul. Never, however, did he cease to feel a respect for religion. He had been in all parts of the world, and had escaped many perils and dangers, when by reason of shipwreck, or at the hands of cannibals, he had expected to meet death in some of its most terrific forms. For the last five or six years, since retiring from the sea-faring life, heretofore pursued, he had been going farther and farther from God, caring less and less for religious

The New York Revival of 1858

things, and was filling up the measure of his iniquity. He did not like to go to the meetings, though he went to please his wife.

When the daily prayer-meetings commenced, he did not think very favorably of them. He told his wife that they would not amount to anything, that a few would go a few days, get discouraged, see a great failure, and that would be the end of it. He seemed to regard the whole thing as a hazardous enterprise, which would end in disgrace.

His wife wanted him to go to the meetings, but he said he should not go to the lecture-room. He was a large man, and needed a larger place to sit in than *that*. He said that when they had them in the church he would go, not dreaming that they would ever be held there, as it was the largest church in the place. This he said rather out of derision than out of any expectation that he would ever be called upon to comply with the promise which he was then making. He did not suppose they would ever be held there, so he thought he was safe in making the promise.

At the end of the first week, the prayer-meetings became so thronged, that it was announced that hereafter they would be held in the church, a large building, capable of holding many hundred people. The opening of the church became a necessity. He then thought he must go, but resolved to finish up by going once or twice, simply to comply with the letter of his promise. The time drew near, and he felt ashamed to go; and to get rid of it, he told his wife, he would not go unless he could go just as he was, without changing his dress. He supposed she would object to that; but she answered: 'Go any way, only go.' He started, and felt so ashamed, that he would have denied it, if anyone had asked on the way, if he was going to the prayer-meeting.

THE POWER OF PRAYER

At this first meeting his mind was somewhat interested. But he did not intend to go again. Indeed he made up his mind that he would not. In conversing with another sea captain, he found him somewhat interested in the prayer-meetings, and they agreed to go together the next day. At this meeting of the *next* day he was more interested still. He went again the next day, and had more feeling. As his feelings deepened, he tried to keep clear of the other captain, but did not succeed. In conversing together, he found that he had similar feelings and anxieties. Still he was ashamed to be seen on his way to the prayer-meetings. In the course of a week he had deeper convictions than he had ever had before. He could not sleep and his family wondered what was the matter. He endeavored to divert attention from his case by saying it was the spring of the year, and he did not feel very well. Medicine was recommended, but he knew he needed a medicine for the soul, though he studiously avoided letting any one know that he felt religious anxiety. He would not even tell his wife – but after she was asleep he would weep and pray all night. He had not shed a tear for twenty years, and was not easily moved to tears. Oh! what a miserable, wretched man he now felt himself to be! His eyes were now literally fountains of tears.

At length he resolved to tell his faithful, praying wife just how he felt, but could not. He did, however, tell the other sea captain, and they wept together. Both of these men endeavored to get up in the meeting and ask for prayers, but both failed. They seemed to be unable to rise from their seats. As his convictions deepened, he felt that he must tell his wife. He entered his house again and again fully resolved to do so, but his courage failed. He was dumb before a praying woman. He wanted to read the Bible, but could not do so without its being known to the whole house. He started to go upstairs that he might not

The New York Revival of 1858

be seen, but was hindered by the fear that some one would follow him. So he left the house in greater distress than ever.

He went into the fields outside of the town and sat down and wept bitterly. What oppressive sorrow weighed like a mountain load upon him. A few days more and he made known his feelings to his anxious wife, who all this time was praying for him. The result was a great increase of tenderness of heart and conscience, but no relief. His eyes poured forth floods of tears. His sense of sin was perfectly overwhelming. He was so overpowered after a night of weeping that the next day he was completely exhausted. As the hour of prayer drew near he longed for the moments to fly more swiftly so that he might go – though he knew not why he should feel so. At the meeting he was greatly distressed. The meeting was nearly ended and brought no relief to his agonized spirit. He felt as if he should really die. At length the meeting was closing, when a pious sea captain – quite out of time, as it then seemed to all – begged the privilege of saying a few words. He said that the way of salvation was plain. All could make their passage straight to heaven. 'See what we have,' said he, in his earnest, blunt manner, 'see what we have! We have a book of directions; we have a compass; we have a chart; we have all the rocks and shoals laid down; we have our course laid straight to heaven. No sailor was ever half so well provided. He must be a poor sea captain that cannot get his vessel into port.' And he sat down.

Oh! what words – what words – to this poor, anxious, distressed captain. They were 'apples of gold in pictures of silver'. Blessed words sent of the Holy Spirit – the Comforter. The rays of light shot into that hitherto dark mind and heart. He thought how he had shaped and steered his course for almost every port on the face of the globe. 'I, who always knew I could get into port, felt confident I could – shall *I* give up in despair? What if I am in mid-ocean, and have been drifting about all my days – I will lay my course now – I will follow my "directions" – I will make straight for heaven.' Light gleamed into his mind. The burden on his heart was lifted up! He went home to read his Bible, and consult that book of directions which he had neglected so long that he had not read ten chapters in ten years.

As he was leaving the house, he promised that he would go home and pray with his wife that night. This promise was kept. He read the Bible, and then they kneeled down to pray. After she had prayed, he attempted to pray, and all he could say was, 'God be merciful to me a sinner.' This he repeated more than fifty times!

He could not go to sleep that night, but continued to weep and pray; hearing the clock strike and tick till near morning. Every tick of the clock seemed to say, 'Jesus lives! Jesus lives!' Suddenly he found himself walking the room in an ecstasy of delight – and, as he looked out of the window, such beauty never met his eyes before. He longed for the morning to come, so that he might tell of his Saviour, and how he had found him, and what a blessedness there was in believing in him. From that time, he had light and joy in his soul, and he shed the light all around him. He became a most active Christian, spending all his time in recommending Christ, and seeking the salvation of others.

This was an example of surprising grace. This sea captain was very generally respected, having retired from business with a competency. He makes it his business to recommend the Christian religion, in all places, on all occasions. His influence is great over men who follow the sea. His earnest voice in exhortation or prayer would be greatly missed from the daily prayer-meeting.

Another sea captain was brought to Christ under

The New York Revival of 1858

circumstances well adapted to display the grace of God and the *power of prayer*. He was over fifty years of age. He had a praying wife, who had been a member of the church about twenty-five years. He was far from being religious in his life, though, for the sake of his wife, he attended religious worship on the Sabbath.

He had retired from the sea, and settled down for the remainder of his days. At the commencement of the meetings he did not attend, though he knew that his wife greatly desired him to avail himself of the opportunity thus afforded to be in the place of prayer. During the second week of the daily prayer-meetings he began to attend, and very soon became interested, though he was backward to acknowledge that interest. He had much to overcome in becoming a Christian. He was terribly profane. So addicted was he to the use of such language, that he could hardly speak without profane words. But the Spirit of God bade him cry for mercy. He was brought to feel his sins, as of mountain-weight. For days he was a heavy-laden sinner, not knowing what to do, or which way to turn for relief. Much interest was felt for him by Christian friends. He was the subject of many ardent prayers.

At length this sea captain trusted in Christ with all his heart, and felt that all his sins were washed away. It was marvellous to all, when the report went abroad that Captain —— was converted. But the most sceptical said, 'If Captain —— can keep from swearing one week, we will believe that there is something in religion.'

He at once took a most decided stand, not half hearted – not tongue-tied – not making apologies for religion – not hiding his light under a bushel – but in his family and in the church he took the place of a devout worshipper. His voice was almost daily heard in the prayer-meeting, and he seldom prayed without using one form of prayer, or one

THE POWER OF PRAYER

expression, which his former habit of using profane language explained. That expression was, 'Set a watch upon our lips that we utter no profane word against thee.'

Some six or eight months have now passed, and he has been kept from using the first profane word. It is a convincing proof of the reality and power of religion to hear that once profane man praying from day to day in the daily prayer-meetings. The mouths of gainsayers are stopped, and scepticism is silenced. Many are led to acknowledge the power of the grace of God thus displayed. For many years this man was made the subject of earnest prayer by his wife.

In this revival, some of the worst of men have been made the subjects of renewing grace. They have been the subjects of special and earnest prayer. And instead of giving them up, and considering them as 'devoted to destruction', as has been formerly the fact in regard to such cases, there has been a rejoicing confidence and expectation that God would glorify the exceeding riches of his grace, in bringing these men to repentance. Hence, we have not been *surprised* at seeing these stout-hearted, proud men, bowed down at the foot of the cross under the weight of their sins; we are not *surprised* at the tears they shed – we are not *surprised* at the abundant joy they feel over the sense of pardon and forgiveness. Oh, that Christians would believe it, that God honors the faith of his people, and loves to fulfil his own precious assurance, when he says: 'According to your faith, so be it unto you.'

The time has come when the people of God have been made to believe, not theoretically but practically, that nothing is too hard for the Lord. There has been prayer in the sense of petition, and earnest entreaty that God would convert such men as these hardened, irreligious sea captains; but there has been no faith that he would do it.

The feeling of discouragement and almost despair would be the settled feeling of the heart. But now the animated and hopeful impression is, that God will hear and answer prayer even in regard to the chief of sinners.

Chapter 19

Influence of the Revival on Crime and Criminals – Orville Gardner – A fast Man – Labors among the Poor – The City Missionaries – Grace and Grace only – A Mother and two Children – Father and Son – The Widow's Joy – Relatives and Friends.

So dark and fearful are the records of vice in such a city as ours, so frequently is the public startled by the announcement of some terrible tragedy in New York, that it appears presumption to speak of the influence of the revival on crime and criminals. But the Lord! he is mighty. The Saviour who forgave a Mary Magdalene and a dying thief, is able to save unto the uttermost all those who come unto him. In the preceding records of this volume, it will not have escaped the reader's attention that many of those who have been brought to repentance were great sinners, hardened in sin. Of such are our criminals, as well as from the ranks of juvenile delinquents who are the offspring of profligate parents.

In all our large cities, and in this city, perhaps, more than in any other, there is a mighty multitude of men and women, who are never reached by any religious or moral influence. After all the agencies employed by the faith and charity of the church, there are whole classes scarcely touched by the spray from the ocean of Christian benevolence that seems to be rolling all around us. Our churches may be crowded, but these are not in the house of God.

The New York Revival of 1858

Our missionaries go into the lanes and lodging-houses, but they find them not. Their haunts are as far remote from the confines of Christian influence as the heathen to whom we send the gospel over sea. Some of them belong to the *rowdy* class of our population, who hide themselves in the recesses of dram-shops, or darker dens, and emerge only to make war on society, living only to make mischief, and delighting in nothing more than in scenes of riot and blood. Others, especially among the females, are regarded almost by common consent, as among the *lost*, as beyond the reach of human aid; and, in their moral pollution, from which purity shrinks as from the contagion of a plague, they are left to rot and perish. Some of them are pushed beyond the pale of human sympathy, by that inexorable law of society that forbids a fallen woman to rise again! A law enacted by woman to cut her sister from hope in this life, and sad to say, it shuts out many a poor wretch from hope of heaven hereafter. Of both sexes, there are many who are disgusted with the way of life, the way of death rather, in which they are dragging out a miserable existence here, preparing for a more wretched one hereafter, and sometimes the thought pierces the darkness and misery of their souls that they would love to retrace their steps, and seek the realms of virtue and of peace. But the thought perishes in the moment of its birth. They would stretch forth a hand if any one would take it and help them out, but, as with the wretched sailor in mid ocean, there is no friendly sail in sight, no hand reached out to help and save.

When it came to be known, as it was, through the talk of the town, and the reports of the public press, that there were daily meetings for prayer, where sinners were welcomed and prayed for, and cared for, and encouraged to turn from their evil ways and live, they took heart and began to hope. As prayer disarmed all opposition, so prayer encouraged the weak and the perishing to think that they too might come and 'get religion'. The whole city was taken by surprise, and were at first quite incredulous, when it was announced that Orville Gardner, or as he was usually nicknamed 'Awful Gardner', had come to the union prayer-meeting, and professed to desire an interest in the prayers of the people of God. He was a noted pugilist, a profligate man, whose name was familiar to the city, in the annals of violence and wrong. But he was soon seen clothed and in his right mind, sitting at the feet of Jesus. He has held on his way in the new life, a consistent, active Christian, and the prayers of many are still frequent and earnest that he may have grace to endure unto the end and win the crown.

It was often remarked, during the winter of 1857–8, that there was a diminution of vice, even under circumstances that might have been expected to increase it. The commercial revulsion threw multitudes out of employment, and crippled the resources of more. Want pressed heavily. Biting hunger urged to evil deeds. There was a time, in the autumn, when many feared that life and property here were not safe, while unemployed masses tramped the streets with banners, demanding bread. But even then the power of prayer was felt. Religious influences by personal visitation, by extraordinary efforts to relieve the distresses of the needy, and by Christian sympathy, reached the hearts and consciences of thousands, and restrained some, and lighted up hope in other breasts where was begun the reign of despair. Those who had the charge of some of our public institutions, have also assured us that they could readily detect the influence of the revival on the numbers and the character of those who came under their care. The evening meetings for prayer were resorted to by hundreds of those who had always spent their days and nights in the gates of hell. We have

The New York Revival of 1858

made no attempt to reckon the number of converts in this revival, but we have assurances from persons in situations to form accurate opinions, that several thousands of persons have forsaken the ways of crime, and are now walking in the pleasant paths of peace. Some of these reformed men are among the most ardent, active, and devoted followers of the Lord Jesus. I have been informed of one man, who but six months ago was known as 'a fast man about town', and now having been made the subject of special prayer by his acquaintances, has been brought out into the light of the gospel. He was received into the Baptist Church, and so rapid was the growth of grace in his soul, and so powerful was the operation of the Holy Spirit upon his mind, that it was soon said of him, not only, 'Behold, he prayeth!' but also, 'Behold, he preacheth!' He was set apart by the church to that work, and he now, with great acceptability and usefulness, tells what the Lord has done for his soul, and exhorts his fellow-men to turn from their evil ways and live.

We know that the flood-gates of iniquity are always open in our large cities, and when the flowing stream is dammed up in one place, it will break out in another, or cut off in one channel, it will make for itself others. Much may be done in the repression of crime, and yet it may so abound as to seem not to be diminished. And for this very reason, what the revival has done, in repressing crime, may have failed to arrest the public attention; yet that it has had a powerful influence in this direction is none the less true. The records of heaven will show that the repentance of many a poor sinner, whose steps have well-nigh slipped, and whose standing-place was only just above the fiery billows, has caused joy in the presence of the angels of God, over that poor sinner repenting. When the Saviour shall call together his 'chosen', in the judgment of the great day, oh! what throngs will come up

THE POWER OF PRAYER

before him, 'clothed with white robes, having palms in their hands', gathered up by the great revival of 1857 and 1858, out of the very purlieus of deep depravity and sin, and saved with an everlasting salvation.

Among the poor and neglected classes the revival has been greatly blessed. The missionary operations of the New York City Tract Society are more useful than almost any other agency, and the secretary, Rev Mr Orchard, has furnished me with the following, among other interesting facts, of recent occurence:

In a report presented to the board in April, a missionary remarks that persons who had lived to see their third or fourth generation had never before witnessed a religious influence so extensive, so independent of human agency, or so manifestly divine, as that which prevailed the past year; for the Holy Spirit was operating powerfully where no special human instrumentality was employed, rebuking the pride of man and plainly demonstrating the truth that 'salvation is of the Lord'. 'Often', he adds, 'we have labored and prayed a long time for the conversion of individuals – sometimes until discouraged, and sometimes until God made our efforts successful – but now we see sinners converted, and ofttimes find that something we said or did was blessed to them, although we are not conscious of that something being other than our ordinary efforts to do good; and frequently so small that we hesitate in enumerating such conversions as through our instrumentality, lest we should so speak of that which might be assigned more appropriately to some other. Thus, when passing through a street we were stopped by a woman, who said, "Oh, I am glad to see you! I wanted to see you and to let you know that I have found the Saviour." "And so have I," said her friend and neighbor, by whom she was accompanied. While they were speaking of their now happy experience, another woman came forward, saying:

The New York Revival of 1858

"I too have found the Saviour, and we were all three received into church-fellowship at the same time." We then asked what means the Lord employed in doing this great work, and one of them replied: "Do you forget what you said at my little boy's funeral? That was it. Don't you recollect that he told me to meet him in heaven, and what you said about it? We were all there and can never forget it. That was the fourth of my children whose funeral you attended, and after hearing you then I was never happy until I found the Saviour.'"

At one of our district prayer-meetings there was present a mother in whose conversion the Lord had made the tract effort effectual, who remembering that two of her children were unconverted, asked prayer for them, and when she left the meeting wrestled with God on their behalf until midnight. They knew it not, for they were living in the country; but the Lord heard and answered, and that same evening he directed their feet to a place of worship, where he opened the eyes of their understanding to see their need of a Saviour. Ere long they found peace in believing, and now they are members of a church of Christ.

A mother was a tract visitor and the father a man that feared God; but their only son was unconverted. One Sabbath evening they wished him to go to church with them; but as he was unwilling to do it, they resolved to stay at home with him and to spend the time in reading to and praying for him. This they did; but when, after pouring out the desire of their souls before God, they arose from their knees, their son was fast asleep. In bitter anguish of spirit, the mother cried aloud, 'Oh! there is nothing but the Spirit of the living God that can awaken my son.' The sound of her voice broke his repose, and the words he heard were the means of awakening in him a deep sense of his condition as a sinner. That night he

THE POWER OF PRAYER

retired to pray, and now he is a Christian rejoicing to the Lord.

To God be all the glory! How wonderful are the operations of divine grace! How powerful can the Lord make the weakest instrumentalities! A missionary having been requested to give an address at a Sabbath school, made some remarks which arrested the attention of a boy who, after he returned home, was asked by his father what he had heard? His reply was that he could not tell him all that night. He then retired to his bed, but his mind was so disturbed that he could not sleep. Early in the morning he went to his parent and said: 'Oh father – my dear father – I have not been able to sleep to-night, for I ought to have prayed with you before I went to bed and I did not; do kneel down with me and I will pray with you now.' The father was astonished, for he was not himself a praying man; but he could not resist the earnest pleading of his boy. So they knelt down and the boy prayed; the father's heart was melted; and thus commenced in that family religious anxieties which have extended to its different members, and now the father, the boy, and the boy's two brothers, having been made partakers of the grace of God, have all united with an evangelical church on profession of faith.

In some of the wards most destitute of evangelical churches, rooms have been opened for the especial accommodation of the poor, where meetings are held for singing, prayer, and religious instruction under the superintendence of the missionary of the ward, and where those who attend may feel that the attention shown them is not measured by the goodness of their apparel. These have been much blessed, and at the little meetings of the poor not a few immortal souls have been renewed by divine grace and made rich for eternity. In one report furnished by a missionary who has charge of a station, we are

The New York Revival of 1858

informed that a young female who came from the country on a visit to her friends was converted, and that such had also been the happy experience of one who had been in the House of Refuge, of another who was a papist, of two persons who were the wife and daughter of a papist, of another who was a Jew, of another who had been brought up in much ignorance, and of four persons who were compelled by needy circumstances to seek aid from 'The Association for Improving the Condition of the Poor'. One of these had been a widow six years; she had lost a small fortune by an unsuccessful speculation; she had a family to support: her first-born was a son who was living in California, where his hopes of amassing wealth had not been realized; and she was sick. Her conversion was sober, intelligent and decided, and this was evinced during her protracted illness, when for a time she heard nothing of her son. But before she died she had again the pleasure of giving him a mother's welcome. She was dying poor, and he returned home, not rich, but in such circumstances as enabled him, though then only 22 years of age, to take upon himself the care of the younger members of the family.

A man arrived in this city from England; but not succeeding in obtaining employment he went to Philadelphia, and was there equally unsuccessful. When all his money was expended and all his clothes, excepting those he wore, had been taken from him in payment for board, he walked back to New York and obtained permission to sleep at Castle Garden. When passing through Greenwich street, he noticed the Mission Hall and went in during the time of divine service. There the Lord opened his heart to receive a message from him; and the missionary conversed and prayed with him after the congregation had been dismissed. He soon became a happy convert, and without delay sought to be made useful to others. Finding a man at

THE POWER OF PRAYER

Castle Garden who had a broken limb, he conversed and prayed with him and took the missionary to visit him. Soon afterward, that man also could speak of the loving kindness of God, and wrote to a brother that lived in Ohio telling him what the Lord had done for his soul. That brother was so much affected upon reading the letter, that he came to New York to see his near kinsman, who testified that 'the Lord had broken his limb that he might break his heart'. With him, also, prayer was offered and efforts made to lead him to Christ, which the Lord condescended to bless. The afflicted one having sufficiently recovered to bear the journey, then accompanied his brother on his return to Ohio, both of them rejoicing in the Lord. The man first mentioned had left a family in his native land, all of whom were unconverted; to them he now longed to speak of the goodness of God. And as he was still without any regular employment, means were obtained for paying his passage back to England; and he left this country provided with tracts and other publications, resolved by the grace of God to use them in connection with personal effort, for the spiritual benefit of his fellow passengers. The report which contains this narrative mentions also several other persons who were converted at the same mission station; and also a man afflicted with a lingering, painful disease which will probably prove fatal. He knew not God until he had been often visited in his affliction; but now he says: 'I love my wife, I love my children; but I love my Saviour more than all of them.'

The Society that reports such interesting facts as these has recorded more than *four hundred* cases of hopeful conversions under its labors during the past year. It is the mission to the poor. It is full of the Spirit of Christ, and great will be the reward of its faithful and devoted servants.

Chapter 20

Wonderful Answers to Prayer – Two Children of a Widow – A Servant Girl – Nine Men in the Market – Seven praying Wives – Never Give Up – A German Boy – The Prayer-Meeting among the Indians – Answers to Prayer in Natchez.

At one of the daily prayer-meetings, a gentleman remarked: 'A week ago to-day I was in this meeting, and heard read a request that you would pray for the conversion of the two children of a widow – a son and daughter; I knew the family. The reading of that request was followed by the prayer of a clergyman, who was so fervent that I felt in my own soul that that prayer would be answered. When I went home, I found that daughter of the poor widow in my parlor. I invited her to go to a prayer-meeting in the evening with me, to which she readily assented.

"Where is your brother?" said I.

"I don't know," said she. "I invited him to go to the prayer-meeting with me to-night, and he refused. I do not know where he is. But I suppose in his usual haunts of pleasure."

We went to the prayer-meeting. We had been there but a few minutes before the brother came in and took his seat. He and his sister were so deeply impressed by this meeting that they resolved to come again the next night.

They did come again the next night, as proposed; and there the son of the widow resolved that he would go home

THE POWER OF PRAYER

and commence family worship, and that son and daughter are now rejoicing in the pardoning grace of God.'

Another case was mentioned by another individual. He said he had a little time ago presented the case of a Roman Catholic lady, who came into these meetings out of mere curiosity, but who heard, while here, things which she never heard before; who said she would be very thankful if you would pray for her. She was deprived of her sleep at night by reason of her great anxiety of mind – had no confidence that she was a Christian, but greatly desired to become one. Now I come to ask you to join me in thanks to God for the conversion of this Roman Catholic lady. She is rejoicing with great joy in the belief that her sins are pardoned. And when I asked in whom she relied for all her hopes of salvation, she said, 'I have no confidence in confession, no confidence in the church – I trust in Christ alone. I hope to be justified through him.'

A gentleman said: 'I was here yesterday requesting your prayers for a Roman Catholic girl living in my family. She had for some time attended family worship, read her Bible, and of late had attended prayer-meetings. She had been very much affected by the prayers made in the family, and said that sometimes she had been so overcome that it seemed to her that she would have to leave and go out, being unable to control herself. Now I am here to ask you to unite with me in giving thanks to God for hearing prayer in that girl's conversion. She now hopes she is a Christian, and her whole countenance and manner betoken the great change which has taken place in her heart.'

'As I was coming to the meeting this morning,' said the leader, 'I came through Washington market. I was told by a young man belonging to the market, and doing business there, that the revival had reached some young men there of a particular class, and pulling out a list of names, "There", said he, "is a list whom we have been praying for

The New York Revival of 1858

in different praying circles. I have carried these around to the little meetings for prayer, which we have had, and we have prayed for them one by one, and now all in this list are converted."

And then taking another list of names from his pocket, he said, "Here is another list of names," and he called my attention specially to it. There were nine on the list. "These", said he, "we are now praying for; and we pray for them one by one, and we follow them up, not only with our prayers, but with personal conversation, entreating them to become reconciled to God." Learning that I was coming to the Fulton street prayer-meeting, he begged me to ask that you would remember these nine young men in your prayers, and ask for their immediate conversion.'

A clergyman present spoke of seven praying women, all of whom had unconverted husbands. These wives met stately for prayer for the conversion of their husbands. They prayed on for ten years, and received no answers to their prayers, and then many were for giving up, discouraged and disheartened from the long delay of the blessing sought. One poor Irish woman, ignorant of the instruction of this world, but abundantly instructed in the teachings of the Holy Spirit, said, 'We must not give up our meeting. Do you not know that God is faithful to all his promises? He has never said, "Seek ye me in vain."' So they prayed on three years more, and all their children were converted, their husbands were converted, the Lord poured out his Spirit in great power, and their friends and neighbors were converted, the church received large accessions, and the Lord turned almost the whole people to himself.

'I noticed', said an aged clergyman, 'that very many of these requests, sent in here, are for the children of pious parents; many are from pious widows for their sons. I want to say', said he, 'to all such, never give up your hope

THE POWER OF PRAYER

and confidence in a covenant-keeping God. He is a faithful God, and he keeps his promise that he will be a God to his children, and to their seed after them. And now, in order to make you understand what I mean, I will relate to you what has been said of a man who had the good news sent to him that his son, who was absent, had been converted. His informant, who expected that he would be very much excited and overjoyed, was disappointed at his calmness, and supposed someone else had informed him of the conversion of his son. So he said to him:

"Who told you that your son was converted?"

He replied: "God told me. He did not tell me he had converted my son, but he told me he would convert him, and I expected it. I believe him, and I am not surprised that he has kept his word."

I would say to every one of these pious praying mothers, who send requests that we pray that their children may be converted – Don't give up your hope in God.'

Great interest has been manifested for the case of a German boy, who had desired to be prayed for in the meeting, but remained after others had gone, and begged us to go with him to some place, where we could pray with him alone.

Before prayer we endeavored to probe his mind, and find out, if possible, where his difficulties lay. We explained to him the fullness and freeness of the gospel provisions in the atonement of Christ, and exhorted him to come directly to him. He heard with patience and deep thought. He stood some time looking down at the floor, apparently absorbed in his own reflections. At length he said: 'Can I take my sins back?'

'No,' we replied, 'you cannot take your sins back. They were committed, and you cannot undo what you have done. Only through Christ can your sins be forgiven.'

The New York Revival of 1858

We then kneeled down to pray, and he kneeled too; but instead of resting his head upon the chair, he bent forward on his knees until his head touched the floor. It was very affecting to see him, and to understand how much he meant by it. He was about twenty years old, intelligent, but had grown up all uninstructed on the subject of religion. He seemed to be very anxious 'to take his sins back'. How many poor sinners would be glad to do the same! Many a man would be glad to take his sins back again, when once he is brought under conviction by the Holy Spirit. But they are gone forward to the judgment of the great day, and they will meet the sinner there, unless they are blotted out in the blood of Christ. This is the great, *great* truth which the German mind is so slow to comprehend. So this poor German boy stood in a sort of bewildered amazement, when we endeavored to teach him how a poor sinner can be saved through the 'blood of atonement', which was shed on Calvary 'for the remission of sin'. Yet he seemed most anxious to understand.

He came again the next day, and fervent prayer was made in his behalf. At the close of the services we conversed and prayed with him again. The conversation was partly in English and partly in German. We inquired what he meant when he asked the day before if he could 'take his sins back'. He answered: 'Some few days ago I thought I had suffered enough, and I told God that I did not want anything more to do with him. Now I want to take that back. I want him to forgive me. I shall have very much to do with him if he will let me take that back.' He was told – certainly he could take that back, if he felt that he had done wrong, and wanted to be forgiven, all he had to do was to go to God and tell him just how he felt about it, and ask to be forgiven through Christ, and he must be sorry for this and all his sins, and God would forgive him. He seemed to be greatly rejoiced when told that even so

[185]

THE POWER OF PRAYER

great a sin as that could be forgiven, if he was truly sorry for it, and would trust in Christ as the Saviour of sinners.

Then followed a conversation in German, a language which he could more readily understand. It was held both with him and his mother.

I inquired of him how long he was anxious about his soul's salvation? To this he answered that he had serious thoughts on this subject for some years, but that it was only within a few weeks that he felt sorely troubled on account of his guilt and danger as a sinner before God. I then asked him if he often prayed to God for relief from this trouble? He said that he had prayed for relief, but that still his burden continued. I then told him that prayer was not of itself sufficient, but that he must make an entire and immediate surrender of himself, soul, body, and spirit, to the service of God, by faith in Jesus as an all-sufficient Saviour, and thus determine in his strength to live henceforth in the love and filial fear of God; that God demanded this of him in return for that greatest of all his gifts, the gift of his only begotten and well beloved Son, to bleed and die for him on the cross of Calvary. And hence God's language is: 'Son, give me thine heart, and let thine eyes take pleasure in my ways.' I then urged him to comply without further delay, with this kind request of God as his best friend and benefactor, and which he promised that by the help of God he would endeavor to do. He then desired to be prayed for, and I offered in substance the following prayer: 'Oh God, as thou knowest the heart of this inquiring sinner before thee, we beseech thee to open the eyes of his understanding, so that he may see what hinders from an immediate surrender of his all to the Saviour, and thus find peace in believing in his all-atoning blood. For this purpose be pleased for the sake of Jesus to send thy Holy Spirit to do his beloved office work in his soul, and thus bring him into that liberty wherewith thy Son is wont

The New York Revival of 1858

to make his people free. We entreat thee, therefore, O God! to hearken to the united prayers of thy dear people, offered up in the name of Jesus in his behalf, and bid him go in peace, under a consciousness of pardoned sin, and his acceptance with God, through faith in Jesus Christ, our strength and Redeemer, Amen.'

A missionary from among the Choctaw Indians, a thousand miles up Red River, said that when this Fulton street meeting was first heard of by them, the Indians resolved that they would observe the same hour of prayer; and as they were so scattered that they could not meet together for prayer – they would set apart the hour in their own dwellings and lodges, as an hour of prayer. He said he knew the hour was faithfully observed and great had been the blessing to them, and many had been converted.

A venerable clergyman in this city writes to me: 'Early in the present year one of my sons-in-law became pastor of a church at Natchez in Mississippi, and soon afterward I received a letter stating that evil abounded there, and that about three years had elapsed since the last addition to the church upon profession of faith, and as during that time there had been removals, the number of members had decreased, so that the state of the church was discouraging, but that the hope of the pastor was in God. In my reply, I mentioned the great work the Lord was doing here, and the great honor he had conferred upon Christian union prayer-meetings, giving such particulars and suggestions as I thought might be profitable. The pastor very shortly after this announced from the pulpit, on a Sabbath day, that during the coming week he would preach every evening with particular relation to the state and duty of the church, and he did so. Ere that week had ended, other churches resolved to hold extra meetings, and but a short time elapsed before there was religious service at each of the churches every evening, and a

Christian union prayer-meeting every afternoon. For something more than a fortnight no other good result appeared than increased seriousness and more numerous attendance; but prayer was not in vain, for then four female members of my son-in-law's church arose in the same meeting, one after another, requesting prayer for the conversion of their husbands. That prayer was offered, and the Lord heard it, and those four husbands were enabled to testify their faith in Christ, and the church received them into its fellowship. From that time the work proceeded powerfully, and amongst those converted were men of high standing in the community, and notoriously irreligious, who boldly espoused the cause of Christ, and expressed their desire to use all their influence in counteracting the pernicious influence they had long exerted. How many have been converted at that place I do not know, but four months ago there had been one hundred and thirty-five received into the fellowship of his church and large accessions to other churches, and the work was then proceeding gloriously.'

Chapter 21

Prayer-meeting at Aunt Betsy's – Power of Prayer remarkably Illustrated – A Visit to the Sing-Sing Prison – The Contrast – Luther and Melanchthon – Examples of Prevailing Prayer – The Church awaking – Understanding the Subject – A Mother's Faith – A Revival predicted.

It was my first visit to the prayer-meeting in Fulton street, where God has so signally manifested his presence. The room on the first storey was full, and I made my way up to that on the second. I found a seat in the middle of the room, from which I had a good view of the persons around the pulpit, and could look out of the windows in its rear. And as I glanced upon the high brick stores in Ann street, the memories of other days rushed in upon me. Where those brick stores now rise, upwards of thirty years ago there stood some wooden buildings, of very lowly pretensions. In an upper room of one of them, there dwelt an old colored woman, then widely known as Aunt Betsy, or Sarah —— which, I now forget. She was very old and very feeble, and remarkably pious. To what church she belonged, I do not remember, nor is it necessary to my present purpose to know. She was dependent upon the hand of charity for her daily bread; nor was she neglected. Some ladies, not now unknown in the religious circles of New York, were sent to her room by their parents, on their first errands of mercy to the poor. And some young men, mostly from the Presbyterian and Methodist

[189]

churches, held a prayer-meeting in her room on each Sabbath afternoon, as she was too infirm to attend on any of the public means of grace. She lay on her lowly bed during these meetings of prayer; and as we retired, she took each of us by the hand, and gave us her parting blessing.

That meeting in the upper room of that poor disciple had passed away from my recollection, although it was in it I offered the first prayer I ever uttered in the hearing of man. But now, in a meeting for prayer, and in sight of the very place, it came up in all its freshness before me. The old buildings took the place of the lofty stores. I could go round the room of Aunt Betsy, and count its chairs, and almost talk with the young men that sat on them. I could hear them pray, and see them retire, each receiving, in his turn, the blessings of the 'aged disciple'. And as I was busy with my own thoughts, scarcely hearing the singing and praying that occupied all in the room, I was waked from my revery by a voice from behind me. It was that of a merchant exhorting his brother merchants to a deeper interest, and a warmer zeal, in the salvation of men. As the voice seemed familiar, I turned round to see who was the fervid and fluent speaker. He is now one of the princely merchants of New York, but in his youth he was one of the young men who met for prayer in the room of Aunt Betsy, and his wife was one of the little girls, who, as the ravens did to Elijah, carried to her daily food!

Those young men were not the sons of wealth; if not poor, they supplied their own resources by their daily employment, and all of them were too young to have made for themselves position or character. They were Sabbath school teachers, most of them were communicants of churches, and all of them professed to love the Bible, and the place where prayer was wont to be made. And what has become of the young men that met weekly in the room

The New York Revival of 1858

of Aunt Betsy? Of the subsequent history of some of them, I have no knowledge. It is to be hoped, that, having commenced aright, they held on the even tenor of their way – that they have finished their course with joy, or yet live to be useful. But as to others of them, my knowledge is distinct and full.

One of them rose to eminence as an accomplished writer and editor. He became an honorable politician, and for years has served his country and the cause of Protestantism, with distinction, as a minister at a foreign court.

Another of them is an ex-mayor of the city of New York, whose hand has never been withheld from any work of religion or philanthropy.

Another is the honored partner of one of the largest publishing houses of the city of his residence.

Another of them has held on the even tenor of his way; has risen to eminence as a merchant, has acquired a large fortune, and is a pillar in one of the most important congregations and one of the best known in the British Isles.

Another was the merchant behind me in the room of prayer, so affectionately addressing the audience, and now the head of one of the largest mercantile houses of the Union.

Another is also a well-known merchant of New York, who has a heart for every good work; and who has never withdrawn his hand from the plough.

Another is a useful minister in the western States, whose labors have been eminently blessed in turning many to righteousness.

Two others who gave fair promise of usefulness in the more secluded walks of life were early removed to their home in heaven. I was, myself, among the youngest of the company, and when I was first invited to join the circle in the room of Aunt Betsy, was not a communicant of the church.

On a subsequent day I made the above statement at the prayer-meeting in Fulton street, and based upon it an appeal to young men to make the religion of Christ the law and the rule of their life; and as they valued their prosperity in this life and the life to come, not to neglect the place of prayer.

When I sat down, a man rose in another part of the room, his tremulous accents showing the feelings that were within him. 'I have', said he, 'recently visited the prison at Sing-Sing. As I went from cell to cell, I met with an old man who told me a very different story from that just narrated. He said that when young he was one of a company of young men who formed an infidel club, and who met once a week for talking infidelity, gambling and drinking, not very far from the upper room of Aunt Betsy. And I was shocked as he told me of the end to which his companions came. 'One', said he, 'died by his own hand; another by the hand of violence; some in State Prison; some of *delirium tremens*; and as far as I know, I am the only one of them surviving; and here am I in the garb, and daily at the work of a felon.' And he also ended his narrative with a most striking and touching appeal to young men, to remember their Creator in the days of their youth.

The contrast which the two narratives presented was most striking. All felt it to be so. No doubt the room of Aunt Betsy, and the gambling hell, were very differently furnished. The companies that met in each were very different in character, and in their governing objects and principles. And their end was very different. Religion has the promise of the life which now is, and of that which is to come. Nor are there any youth more likely to become men, than those who first seek the kingdom of heaven and

The New York Revival of 1858

its righteousness. Even now do I feel the warm pressure of the hand of Aunt Betsy, although for thirty or more years she has been with her Lord; and it may be that the blessings which have followed those who met for prayer in her room have been in answer to her benedictions and prayers. True religion, early embraced, is a great element of success, even as to the life that now is.

On a certain occasion, a messenger was sent to Luther to inform him that Melanchthon was dying. He at once hastened to his sick-bed, and found him presenting the usual premonitory symptoms of death. He mournfully bent over him; and, sobbing, gave utterance to a sorrowful exclamation. It roused Melanchthon from his stupor; he looked into the face of Luther, and said, 'O Luther, is this you? Why don't you let me depart in peace?' 'We can't spare you yet, Philip,' was the reply. And turning round, he threw himself upon his knees, and wrestled with God for his recovery, for upwards of an hour. He went from his knees to the bed, and took his friend by the hand. Again, he said, 'Dear Luther, why don't you let me depart in peace?' 'No, no, Philip, we cannot spare you yet from the field of labor,' was the reply. He then ordered some soup, and when pressed to take it, he declined, again saying: 'Dear Luther, why will you not let me go home, and be at rest?' 'We cannot spare you yet, Philip,' was the reply. He then added: 'Philip, take this soup, or I will excommunicate you.' He took the soup, he soon commenced to grow better, he soon regained his wonted health, and labored for years afterwards, in the blessed cause of the Reformation. And when Luther returned home, he said to his wife with abounding joy: 'God gave me my brother Melanchthon back in direct answer to prayer.'

And this is but one of the multitudes of instances which prove the power of prayer. By prayer Abraham healed Abimelech – Moses prevailed in the land of Ham, and in

THE POWER OF PRAYER

the wilderness – Joshua arrested the sun – Hannah obtained Samuel – Elijah shut and opened heaven – Asa put to flight a million of Arabians – Hezekiah secured the destruction of the Assyrians – Esther saved her people from ruin – the disciples obtained the descent of the Spirit – and Paul and Silas shook the prison at Philippi. Prayer is the power that moves the hand that moves the world; and, perhaps, never in the history of the church, has this great truth been more frequently or signally illustrated than within the past year in this land. Prayer secures the baptism of the Spirit. It is the key which opens the windows of heaven. It is weakness going to Infinite Power for aid. It is emptiness going to Infinite Fullness for supply.

Perhaps never in the history of the church has there been such a call to prayer as now. 'God is now on the giving hand,' said a venerable patriarch at one of the New York prayer-meetings, during the summer, 'and now is the time to open our mouths wide.' The hopes of multitudes are excited, and they are expecting great things. China is opened, India is pacified, and these people, with trumpet tongue, are imploring us to send them the gospel. Paganism is tottering everywhere, the crescent is dying out in the sky, like the waning moon. Popery is dead at heart, however alive in its distant members. Sectarian jealousies are fast ebbing. The many things in which evangelical Christians agree are fast throwing into the shade the few things in which they differ. All are beginning to see that a simple resting on Christ by faith is of infinitely more importance than is the sectarian path in which we walk, after having professed our faith. If the sheep are only inclosed in the fold of the 'Good Shepherd', it is of little importance whether they have been led there through this or that door, or by the hand of prelate, presbyter, parent, or Sabbath school

The New York Revival of 1858

teacher. The fires of fanaticism are also rapidly burning down, and all good men are beginning to see that the wrath of man worketh not the righteousness of God. Everything seems to be tending to a greater union among good people, and especially to a greater union in prayer. Let that heroic confidence in God be ours which induced Luther to say, 'We can't spare you yet, Philip,' and what we have yet experienced will be but as 'the handful of corn in the earth upon the top of the mountains', to the harvest waving on the banks of the river of Egypt.

It is very obvious, from facts already stated, that PRAYER is rising, in the church, to the place it occupies in the Scriptures; and that it is as able to prevail with God now, as when offered by holy men of old. And, addressing ourselves to the high and lofty One, we can say now, as when Moses, and Samuel, and David, and Daniel, and Paul wrestled in supplications, 'Verily, thou art a God that hearest prayer.' I have a few things to say, very briefly, on the subject of prayer.

1. The church is beginning better to understand the nature of prayer. It is not the posture. A man may kneel until he wears the stones, and bow at the name of Jesus, until his body becomes permanently curved; he may put on sackcloth and ashes, like Ahab, and yet never pray. Nor is it the mere recitation, in solemn tones, of a neatly prepared ritual. A person may hourly repeat the Lord's Prayer, and all the suffixes and affixes that may be appended to it, and never pray. Nor is it the mere act of uniting in family, social, and public worship; as God abhors the sacrifice where the heart is not found. All these may be as the mere husk and shell without the kernel, as an altar without a sacrifice, or as a sacrifice without the heavenly fire to consume it. 'Prayer', says Hannah More, 'is the application of want to him only who can relieve it. It is the urgency of poverty; the prostration of humility;

THE POWER OF PRAYER

the fervency of penitence; the confidence of truth. It is not eloquence, but earnestness; not figures of speech, but the compunction of the soul. It is the "Lord, save, or we perish" of Peter; "the cry of faith to the ear of mercy".' And that the church is beginning better to understand the nature of prayer, is perfectly obvious from those meetings for prayer, where good men meet and mingle together, and with one heart and voice press their supplications before the throne of mercy. 'Union for the sake of the union' has become a political watchward; union in prayer for the sake of a world lying in wickedness should become the watchword of the entire church of God. When God's people are of one accord, and of one mind on this subject, we will have Pentecostal seasons, such as Jerusalem never witnessed, and as apostles never enjoyed.

The church is beginning better to understand the connection between prayer and the blessings promised. We hear not now of objections made to pray drawn from the immutability of God – that he is of one mind, and that none can turn him. That God is unchangeable, is a great truth – is the foundation of all our confidence in the divine administration. But, if prayer is useless, because it cannot change the divine purpose, then are all means to obtain any end useless. All means, without the divine blessing, can no more change the divine purpose, than can prayer. Everything in the past, present, and future, is known to God. He is beyond the reach of all contingencies. He is without variableness or shadow of turning. But his unchanging system is inclusive of the means, as of the ends – of the ploughing and sowing, as of the crop – of the rain and sunshine, as of the growth; of the asking, equally as of the giving. Were God changeable, then everything in the universe would be unsettled; but that he is immutable is the greatest possible inducement to pray, because he has

The New York Revival of 1858

immutably determined that every humble, faithful prayer shall be heard, accepted, and answered.

A warm, earnest, humble spirit of prayer, is a part of God's purpose to obtain the end prayed for. A spirit of prayer is a forerunner of coming mercies. When the prophet foretold the end of the captivity, he also predicted the prayers that would open the gates of Babylon. Jer. 29: 12. The glory of the latter days was foretold; but then the Lord must be inquired of by the house of Israel to do it for them. Ezekiel 36: 37. Divine grace kindles these ardent affections, when the blessings promised are upon the wing. Prayer is the chain which draws the soul to God, and that brings down promised mercies to us; or, like the hook which draws the boat to the shore, though the shore itself is immovable. Prayer is to the church what the breath of spring, and the sun, the rain, and dew of summer, are to the earth. Without them, the church and the earth must remain in their wintry shrouds. And all the indications are, that the church is beginning to feel, to an unwonted degree, the connection between true prayer and its true prosperity.

God is now, as in days of old, showing himself to be a God that hears prayer. The prayer of Abraham healed Abimelech; the prayers of Moses prevailed in Egypt and in the wilderness; the prayers of Daniel quelled the ferocity of the lions. 'Prayer', says Jeremy Taylor, 'can obtain everything: can open the windows of heaven and shut the gates of hell; can put a holy constraint upon God, and detain an angel till he leave a blessing; can open the treasures of rain and soften the iron ribs of rocks till they melt into a flowing river; can arrest the sun in his course, and send the winds upon our errands.' Nor is there a church, nor a true Christian, who cannot from their own history record instances of the power of prayer. A spy upon Luther followed him to a hotel, and slept in a room adjacent to that of the Reformer. He told his employer next day that Luther prayed nearly all night, and that he could never conquer a man that prayed so earnestly. Latimer prayed earnestly for three things: that he might be enabled to maintain the truth until death; that the gospel might be given to all England; that God might spare Elizabeth until the Reformation was established. And his prayers were granted.

A widowed mother who walked with God had an only son, the son of her vows and prayers. He entered college and graduated, moral and lovely, but without repentance. She ordered his furniture to a room in an adjacent theological seminary, saying that he was going to enter it at the opening of the next session. She was supposed by some to be unduly excited, and they sought to dissuade her from her purpose. But the furniture was sent as she desired, and her son went home. In a very short time a blessed revival commenced in the church of which she was a member. Her son was among the first converts; he became a communicant of it, and entered the seminary at the appointed time. That son yet lives to preach the gospel, a learned, honored, and very useful man. Here is a case like unto that of Hannah and Samuel, and there are multitudes of cases like it.

Late on a cold November night, I was retiring to rest. There was a knock at my door, and an aged member of the church, a simple, praying, warm-hearted man was introduced. After a brief silence he thus addressed me: 'My dear pastor, I have come to tell you that God is about to revive his work among us.' I asked him why he so felt? 'I went into the stable,' said he, 'to take care of my cattle two hours ago, and there the Lord has kept me in prayer until now. And I feel that we are going to be revived.' There could be no doubt as to his sincerity. And that was the commencement of the first revival under my ministry.

The New York Revival of 1858

A few years afterwards, and in another field of labor, an aged man, venerated for piety, came to my study. Though poor in this world, he was rich in faith. In prayer he seemed to converse with God. 'I have called to say to you, my dear pastor,' said he, 'that the Lord is in the midst of us, and we shall all soon see the effect of his presence.' I had observed a marked solemnity in the congregation, but nothing more. I asked the venerable man why he felt so? His reply was as follows: 'Since twelve o'clock last night the Spirit of God has been so upon me that I have been unable to do anything but pray, and to rejoice in the prospect of a blessed refreshing from the presence of the Lord.' And that was the commencement of the first revival in my present field of labor; a field which has been very often watered with the rain and dew of heaven, from the days of Whitefield until now. And many similar instances are treasured up in my memory as proofs of the glorious truth that God hears prayer now as in days of old.

And why should it not be so? Is not the same God in heaven? Prayer now is what it has ever been, and is as prevalent with God now as in the days of Abraham, and Joseph – as on the first descent of the Spirit. If only there were another pen equally inspired and eloquent, to place in the history of the church another such chapter as is the eleventh of Hebrews, where could be collected an array of holy men and women from the church of our own day, who, in the strength and triumph of faith and prayer, fall but little below the noble company of worthies placed in such glorious array by the apostle of the Gentiles. And why should it not be so? There have been years of great excitement in the church, and of high controversy, and of bold enterprise; but it is very doubtful whether in any one year since its foundations were laid, God has more signally vouchsafed himself to be a prayer-hearing God than during the year whose suns are now waning in the sky.

THE POWER OF PRAYER

Men of the highest intellect, and open in their rebellion, who mocked at religion and laughed at every earthly check, as leviathan mocks at a straw, have been brought, with the simplicity of little children, and in answer to prayer, to rest upon the atonement of Jesus Christ for salvation.

Prayer is the power of the church; and could I speak as loud as the trumpet which is to wake the dead, I would thus call upon the church in all its branches and in all lands – 'Awake, awake, put on thy strength, O Zion; put on thy beautiful garments, O Jerusalem. Arise, shine, for thy light is come, and the glory of the Lord is risen upon thee.' Patriarchs, prophets, apostles, martyrs, reformers, were mighty in prayer. It was to prayer that Henry IV of France ascribed his crown, and Gustavus his victories. Milton thought he wrote best when he prayed most. The ministers who pray most are the most successful. The churches which are most prayerful are the most useful. The heathen are to be given to Christ for an inheritance, and the uttermost parts of the earth for a possession, in answer to prayer.

Chapter 22

Means of Grace – Preaching the Word – Revival Tracts – Private Efforts – Call to Prayer by Rev J. C. Ryle – Rev Dr Guthrie of Edinburgh, On Perseverance in Prayer – Rev Dr J. W. Alexander's Tracts: 'The Revival and its Lessons', – 'Pray for the Spirit' – Power of the Press.

Often have we had occasion to say to the praise of him who is independent in power, as he is infinite in benevolence, that the revival has been carried on without the use of means that attract observation and challenge the attention of men. But it is the divine economy to work by means, and to use the servants of God to promote his purposes of grace.

The preaching of the gospel has been signally blessed, in the edification of saints and the conviction and conversion of sinners. The attendance on the sanctuary has been largely increased, and pastors have preached with energy, directness and hope, exhibiting the discriminating truths of the gospel with great clearness and fullness, declaring the whole counsel of God. And it has pleased him to put honor upon his word, making it, in thousands of instances, the acknowledged instrument of bringing lost men to the Saviour. In the early part of the year 1858, a volume was published of sermons[1] by twenty or thirty pastors in New York and Brooklyn, discourses actually preached during the present revival of religion; and it was

[1] *The New York Pulpit*, Sheldon, Blakeman & Co.

THE POWER OF PRAYER

delightful to observe that although they were by earnest men of various denominations, they taught the same doctrines, urged the same class of truths, and breathed the same blessed Spirit.

In the autumn of this same year the large hall of the Cooper Institute, seating 2,500 persons, was opened for religious worship on Sabbath evenings, with preaching by the Rev T. L. Cuyler, pastor of the Market street Church, and it was immediately filled to overflowing, and thousands were obliged to go away without the bread of life for which they came.

The Academy of Music, the largest and most splendid audience-room in the United States, was then hired at great expense for the winter season, or as long as it should be required, and pastors of the various churches cordially agreed to give their services in preaching the gospel to the vast congregations gathered every Sabbath evening within those walls, which are made vocal every night in the week with the music of the opera, and are thronged with the votaries of amusement; but rarely resound with prayer and praise.

But while these great movements command public notice and mention in this history of these times of revival, it must not be forgotten that the chief instrumentality that God has employed, is the faithful, constant and earnest preaching of the word, by his humble, diligent, unpublished pastors to their own flocks, and to those whom they are able to draw within the sound of their voices, and the reach of those holy influences that go forth from every Christian church, however limited in its range, or obscure its position. I have reason to know, and with intense pleasure state here, that some of the most remarkably favored churches have been those that are out of the great centres of attraction, in the retired or waste places of the city. And among the most efficient agencies to bring the

The New York Revival of 1858

truth directly to the hearts of men in this and other cities, has been the wide circulation of brief, pungent evangelical tracts, urging Christians to double diligence in the service of Christ, and warning the wicked to flee from the wrath to come. The societies having this as their special work bear witness to the fact that such tracts have been in demand to an extent unexampled before; and private benevolence and zeal have given still greater impetus to the same form of Christian effort. In the city of Baltimore two or three benevolent gentlemen have, at their own cost, had these little messengers of good prepared and sent forth, widely and with marked success in turning sinners from the errors of their ways.

A 'Call to Prayer' by the Rev J. C. Ryle, published by the Protestant Episcopal Society for the promotion of evangelical knowledge, has been greatly useful in rousing Christians to this duty, and in bringing the unconverted to seek the favor of God. Such words as these are as nails in a sure place.

> 'How can you expect to be saved by an "unknown" God? And how can you know God without prayer? You know nothing of men and women in this world, unless you speak with them. You cannot know God in Christ, unless you speak to him in prayer. If you wish to be with him in heaven, you must be one of his friends on earth. If you wish to be one of his friends on earth, *you must pray*.
>
> Reader, to be prayerless is to be without God – without Christ – without grace – without hope – and without heaven. It is to be in the road to hell. Now can you wonder that I ask the question – DO YOU PRAY?
>
> I have looked carefully over the lives of God's saints in the Bible. I cannot find one of whose history much is told us, from Genesis to Revelation, who was not a man of prayer. I find it mentioned as a characteristic of the godly, that "they call on the Father", that "they call on the name of the Lord Jesus Christ". I find it recorded as

a characteristic of the wicked, that they call not upon the Lord. 1 Pet. 1: 17; 1 Cor. 1: 2; Psa. 14: 4.

I have read the lives of many eminent Christians who have been on earth since the Bible days. Some of them, I see, were rich, and some poor. Some were learned, and some unlearned. Some of them were Episcopalians, and some Christians of other names. Some were Calvinists, and some Arminians. Some have loved to use a liturgy, and some to use none. But one thing, I see, they all had in common. They have all been *men of prayer*.

I study the reports of Missionary Societies in our own times. I see with joy that heathen men and women are receiving the gospel in various parts of the globe. There are conversions in Africa, in New Zealand, in Hindustan, in China. The people converted are naturally unlike one another in every respect. But one striking thing I observe in all the missionary stations. The converted people *always pray*.

Reader, I do not deny that a man may pray without heart, and without sincerity. I do not for a moment pretend to say that the mere fact of a person praying proves everything about his soul. As in every other part of religion, so also in this, there is plenty of deception and hypocrisy.

But this I do say – that not praying is a clear proof that a man is not yet a true Christian. He cannot really feel his sins. He cannot love God. He cannot feel himself a debtor to Christ. He cannot long after holiness. He cannot desire heaven. He has yet to be born again. He has yet to be made a new creature. He may boast confidently of election, grace, faith, hope, and knowledge, and deceive ignorant people. But you may rest assured it is all vain talk, *if he does not pray*.

And I say, furthermore, that of all the evidences of the real work of the Spirit, a habit of hearty private prayer, is one of the most satisfactory that can be named. A man may preach from false motives. A man may write books, and make fine speeches, and seem diligent in good works, and yet be a Judas Iscariot. But a

The New York Revival of 1858

man seldom goes into his closet, and pours out his soul before God in secret, unless he is in earnest. The Lord himself has set his stamp on prayer as the best proof of a true conversion. When he sent Ananias to Saul in Damascus, he gave him no other evidence of his change of heart than this – "*Behold he prayeth.*" (Acts 9: 11.)'

Not less effective and even more earnest in its words was the appeal to perseverance in prayer, by the Rev Dr Guthrie, of Edinburgh, which falls in so happily with the scope and aim of this work, that I transcribe a passage, characteristic of the glowing eloquence of that great light in the Free Church of Scotland.

'It is easy to know the knock of a beggar at one's door. Low, timid, hesitating, it seems to say, "I have no claim on the kindness of this house; I may be told I come too often; I may be treated as a troublesome and unworthy mendicant; the door may be flung in my face by some surly servant." How different on his return from school, the loud knocking, the bounding step, the joyous rush of the child into his father's presence, and, as he climbs on his knee, and flings his arm round his neck, the bold face and ready tongue with which he reminds his father of some promised favor? Now, why are God's people bold? Glory to God in the highest! To a father in God, to an elder brother in Christ, faith conducts our steps in prayer; therefore, in an hour of need, faith, bold of spirit, raises her suppliant hands, and cries up to God, "Oh that thou wouldst rend the heavens, and come down."

I think that I see the sneer curling on the sceptic's lips as he says, "How absurd! What presumption! as if it were not below the dignity of divinity to come at king's or peasant's, prince's or pauper's call. Should the purposes of the Eternal be shaped by your petitions? Creature of a day and of the dust! what are you, that the universe should be steered – its helm moved this or that way for your

[205]

sake?" Well, no doubt the language is bold; yet with God a Father, our Father, my Father in Christ, I feel I can be bold and confident in prayer. I know a father's heart. Have I not seen the quiver of a father's lip, the tear start into his eye, and felt his heart in the grasp of his hand, when I expressed some good hope of a fallen child? Have I not seen a mother, when her infant was tottering in the path of mettled coursers, with foam spotting their necks, and fire flying from their feet, dash like a hawk across the path, and pluck him from instant death? Have I not seen a mother, who sat at the coffin head, pale, dumb, tearless, rigid, terrible in grief, spring from her chair, seize the coffin which we were carrying away, and, with shrieks fit to pierce a heart of stone, struggle to retain her dead?

If we, that are but worms of the earth, will peril life for our children, and, when they are mouldered into dust, cannot think of our dead, nor visit their cold and lonesome grave, but our breasts are wrung, and our wounds bleed forth afresh, can we adequately conceive or measure, far less exaggerate, even with our fancy at its highest strain, the paternal love of God? Talk not of what you suppose to be the dignity of divinity. Talk not of the calm, lofty, dignified demeanor which becomes a king, who sees his child borne off on the stream that sweeps his palace wall. The king is at once sunk in the father. Divesting himself of his trappings – casting sceptre, robe of gold, and jewelled crown – he at once rushes forth to leap into the boiling flood. Lives there a father with heart so dead that he would not, at the sight of a child falling overboard, and struggling with death, back every sail, and, whatever might be the mission on which his ship was bound, or whatever the risk he ran, would not put up her helm, and pale with dread, steer for the waves where his boy was sinking?

The New York Revival of 1858

Child of God! pray on. God's people are more dear to him than our children can be to us. He regards them with more complacency than all the shining orbs of that starry firmament. They were bought at a price higher than would purchase the dead matter of ten thousand worlds. He cares more for his humblest, weakest child, than for all the crowned heads and great ones of earth, and takes a deeper interest in the daily fortunes of a pious cottager, than in the fall and rise of kingdoms.

Child of God! pray on. By prayer thy hand can touch the stars, thy arm stretch up to heaven. Nor let thy holy boldness be dashed by the thought that prayer has no power to bend these skies, and bring down thy God. When I pull on the rope which fastens my frail and little boat to a distant and mighty ship, if my strength cannot draw its vast bulk to me, I draw myself to it, to ride in safety under the protection of its guns, to enjoy in want the fullness of its stores. And it equally serves my purpose, and supplies my needs, that prayer, although it were powerless to move God to me, moves me to God. If he does not descend to earth, I, as it were, ascend to heaven.

Child of God! pray on! Were it indispensable for thy safety that God should rend these heavens, it should be done. I dare believe *that*; and "I am not mad, most noble Festus". Have not these heavens been already rent? Eighteen hundred years ago, robed in humanity, God himself came down. These blue skies, where larks sing and eagles sail, were cleft with the wings, and filled with the songs of his angel train. Among the ancient orbs of that very firmament, a stranger star appeared travelling the heavens, and blazing on the banner borne before the King, as he descended on this dark and distant world. On Canaan's dewy ground – the lowly bed he had left, the eye of morning shone on the shape and form of the Son of God; and dusty roads, and winter snows, and desert

[207]

sands, and the shores and very waves of Galilee, were impressed with the footprints of the Creator. By this manger, where the babe lies cradled – beside the cross, upon whose ignominious arms the glory of the universe is hung – by this silent sepulchre, where wrapped in bloody shroud, the body is stretched out on its bed of spices, while Roman sentinels walk their moonlit round – and Death, a bound captive, sits within, so soon as the sleeper wakes, to be disarmed, uncrowned, and in himself have death put to death – faith can believe all that God has revealed, and hope for all that God has promised. She reads on that manger, on that cross, deeply lettered, on that rocky sepulchre, these glorious words, "He that spared not his own Son, but delivered him up for us all, how shall he not with him also, freely give us all things?" And there, lifting an eagle eye to heaven, she rises to the boldest flights, and soars aloft on the broad wings of prayer.

> Faith, bold faith, the promise sees,
>   And trusts to that alone,
> Laughs at impossibilities,
>   And says, It shall be done.'

But more efficient and directly useful still were the little tracts written by the Rev James W. Alexander, D. D., of this city, and now gathered into a volume.[1] They were very brief, but distinguished by the author's eminently practical tact, adapting them to the tastes and needs of the masses, while they are clothed with a gracefulness of manner, and cogency of reasoning, that make and leave an impression on the most cultivated minds. One of these tracts by Dr Alexander, "To FIREMEN', was through the liberality of a single individual printed, and circulated in

[1] *The Revival and its Lessons*, Randolph, New York, 1859.

The New York Revival of 1858

sufficient numbers in every fire-engine house in this city and Brooklyn. Others in this series, bear such titles as, 'Seek to save Souls'; 'The Unawakened'; 'Oh! for more Feeling'; 'Compel them to come in'; 'Looking unto Jesus', and 'Pray for the Spirit'. In this last-named appeal, Dr Alexander says:

> 'In order to mighty and unexampled revival, what we especially need is for the whole church to be down on its knees before God. Past redemptions should make our cravings great. "I am the Lord thy God, which brought thee out of the land of Egypt; open thy mouth wide, and I will fill it." Thousands have already been seen gathered in one place for prayer, but when "the Spirit of grace and of supplications" is poured out on the great body of Christians, touched with pity for the desolations of the spiritual Jerusalem, that word will come true: "Thou shalt arise and have mercy upon Zion, for the time to favor her, yea, the set time is come; for thy servants take pleasure in her stones, and favor the dust thereof." Oh, that God's people were awake to the privilege of crying aloud for his great gift!
>
> Open your mind, believing reader, to the extraordinary truth, that God has an infinite willingness to bestow in answer to prayer that which, since the sending of his Son, is the greatest of all his possible gifts. "If ye then, being evil, know how to give good gifts unto your children, how much more shall your Heavenly Father give THE HOLY SPIRIT to them that ask him?" O parent! ponder on this blessed verse; there is that within thy heart which will reveal its meaning! And what is it that God is so ready to give? It is that which secures and applies all the benefits of Christ's mediation; that which makes revivals here, and heaven hereafter, it is THE HOLY SPIRIT! Ought not all disciples, all over the world, to be prostrate before the throne of grace, beseeching God for Christ's sake to communicate this all-comprehensive boon? To him

THE POWER OF PRAYER

only do we look, because with him is "the residue of the Spirit". But we ask in the name of CHRIST, for the very name means *anointed*, and the anointing, which flows from him as head, to all the members, is this very gift, the Holy Ghost, "for God giveth not the Spirit by measure unto him". He hath it immeasurably, and for his church, and they draw for it in his name by prayer. Occupy a few moments on this great gift; it will aid your prayers.

1. *There is such a thing as the pouring out of the Holy Ghost.* As Moses "poured of the anointing oil on Aaron's head", so God pours the unction of his Spirit on the head of our Great High Priest. And as the ceremonial fragrance flowed down to "the skirts of his garments", so the gift of the Spirit comes on all believers. "The anointing which ye have received of him", says the Apostle John, "abideth in you." But the effusion is sometimes uncommonly great, even to outpouring. Some have found fault with the term, which nevertheless is intensely biblical, and consecrated in the church. Among promises to Israel in the latter day, the Lord says: "Neither will I hide my face any more from them; for I have poured out my Spirit upon the house of Israel," saith the Lord God. Apostolic comment applies to New Testament times the words of another prophet: "I will pour out my Spirit upon all flesh." So in another place: "Behold, I will pour out my Spirit unto you." The idea necessarily presented is that of bountiful effusion. Let us ask for it. The Lord Jesus comforted his sorrowing disciples by the promise of this gift, as the result of his ascension. "If I depart, I will send him unto you." This Comforter he *did* send, oh! how graciously and gloriously, at the first Christian Pentecost. "Having received of the Father *the promise of the Holy Ghost*," saith the Apostle Peter, "he hath shed forth this which ye now see and hear." There had just been suddenly a sound from heaven, as of a rushing mighty wind, filling all the house where they were sitting; "and they were all filled with the Holy Ghost." Do not fail to observe that

believers had been in union of prayer for this very gift, thus complying with the Lord's injunction that they should "wait for the promise of the Father". The gift was continued, under early preaching; and "the Holy Ghost fell on them that heard the word". The same apostle, many years afterwards, refers to the known fact of "the Holy Ghost sent down from heaven". Every great awakening and plentiful harvest of souls has proceeded from the same Spirit, sought by the same importunity of beseeching prayer. Therefore, pray for the Spirit!

2. *The influence of the Holy Spirit of God is exceedingly powerful.* We ask something mighty and revolutionizing. It is Omnipotence that we are praying for. A wicked city, a wicked world, will yield to no inferior strength. What an encouragement that "with the Lord Jehovah is everlasting strength"! It is as applicable to revival of the church as to the rebuilding of the temple. "Not by might, nor by power, but by my Spirit, saith the Lord of hosts." Let Christians no longer despair of the conversion of high-handed sinners, even the vilest of the vile, in our filthiest and bloodiest dens; as if we expected in answer to our prayers only some weak, half-way operation. "Our gospel", says the Apostle of the Gentiles, "came not unto you in word only, but also *in power, and in the Holy Ghost,* and in much assurance." This is our ground of hope when the ministers of the word proclaim the glad tidings; that the preaching may be "in demonstration of the Spirit and of power". God grant us deliverance from our unbelief, as to the power of the Holy Spirit in giving efficacy to the truth!

3. *The Spirit whom we seek is the author of Regeneration and Sanctification.* If God vouchsafe us these, in wide extent, our revival will be indeed complete. "That which is born of the Spirit is spirit." All believers shout the same praise: "According to his mercy he saved us, by the washing of regeneration, and renewing of the Holy Ghost." Look at thousands, utterly blind as to spiritual realities, and say, what can we ask of them so

THE POWER OF PRAYER

indispensably important, as that SPIRIT OF TRUTH, who will "reprove", or convince "the world of sin, and of righteousness, and of judgment"? He is just as able to convert the ruffian, or the fallen woman, as the church-going Pharisee; just as able to renew a thousand as one. Who is sufficiently awake to the necessity of imploring God to convert a multitude of sinners?

All revival of the church is increased sanctification; and all reclaiming of the impenitent is sanctification begun. For both we need the gift of the Spirit; and we need it now. We need it to break the power of sin in professing Christians, and to nail their lusts to the cross; for it is by this influence that we "do mortify the deeds of the body". Some of the primitive believers had been atrocious sinners; "but", says the Apostle Paul, "ye are washed, but ye are sanctified, but ye are justified, in the name of the Lord Jesus, and by the Spirit of our God." Hope, Joy, Love, and consequent activity and success, are fruits of the same Spirit. In a word, the Spirit of God is the spirit of revival. Earnest, daily, united prayer of the people of Christ for this high gift puts honor upon God in a remarkable degree; and we already have cause to note how signally he blesses endeavors which were openly begun in prayer. Beloved brethren, let us not mistake the token, nor fail to go in the path pointed out by Providence and the Spirit.

4. *The Holy Spirit sends those gifts which are necessary for successful work*. When miraculous gifts were necessary, they were not withheld. All inspiration, wisdom, and ministry are from the same source. So also are the common qualifications for service demanded in the daily walk of an earnest Christian, who seeks to save souls. "There are diversities of operations, but it is the same God which worketh all in all; but the manifestation of the Spirit is given to every man to profit withal." The Lord promised that the Spirit should prompt his disciples when arraigned. Equally does the blessed Monitor fill their hearts and lips for common service. Apostles themselves sought for "utterance" by means of

prayer; and a praying church will have a ministry and members, bold and loving in owning and recommending their Lord. The supplications, which bring down such influences, are themselves wrought of God, when believers, keeping themselves in the love of God, are at the same time "praying in the Holy Ghost". See thus how completely dependent we are for all upon the Holy Spirit of God. Grace manifestly began the work; grace keeps it alive; grace must carry it on and give it extension.

'Brethren, we must pray as we have never yet prayed. Our want of success is due to our coldness of desire and niggardliness of request. We are not straitened in God, but in our own low, slender conceptions and hopes. We have not, because we ask not. If we were under a deep and solemn impression of the divine power, bounty, and faithfulness, "how should one chase a thousand, and two put ten thousand to flight"! The lesson which the revival should teach us is the duty of being instant in supplication for the larger and more glorious effusion of the Holy Spirit. Acting on this, we shall behold new marvels of love in the place of prayer.'

With such missives as these side-arms Christians supplied themselves, and freely gave them to their friends and acquaintances in the store, shop, market, on 'change, or in the street. They went everywhere preaching the word. These and other leaflets, with spiritual songs, or striking passages of holy writ, or piercing thoughts from the works of good men, were used as covers to letters, and sent in envelopes in the ordinary business or social correspondence of the people, so that the mails were constantly busy in this noiseless but personal and effective distribution of the good seed by the side of all waters. And when to this we add the agency of the press, religious and secular, partaking so largely of the revival spirit as to give unusual prominence to reports of sermons, remarkable conversions, and revival intelligence, it is safe to say that in no former period has the power of the printed word been more marked, never has God so honored the instrumentality of tracts and newspapers as in the present blessed awakening.

Chapter 23

Prayers for our Children sure to be Answered – Rev H. W. Smuller's Thoughts – The Promises of God – The Vials with Prayers of the Saints – Visions of John – Experience of Daniel – Long Delay – The Old Ladies' Meeting – Mrs F. and her Soldier Boy – Have Faith in God.

In the most interesting prayer-meeting that it has been my joy to have a part, the prayers of Christians were again and again requested in behalf of the children. The meeting was held at Jamaica, Long Island, during the sessions of the Synod of New York; but it was on the evening of the union prayer-meeting of the village, and ministers and people of various names thronged the large church. A power from above fell on the assembly. The children of the Sabbath school had unitedly signified their desire to be made the special subject of prayer. One venerable pastor rose and requested his brethren to pray for his unconverted children. As one after another prayed or offered a word of exhortation, the Rev Mr Smuller indulged in a strain of thought so encouraging to parental hope and prayer, that I asked him to permit me to use his remarks in this connection. In no other aspect do we contemplate this revival with more satisfaction than in the evidence it affords that God will answer prayer, and we know that there is no prayer more ardent, importunate and persevering than that which goes up from yearning yet believing hearts of pious parents. 'How often', said Mr Smuller,

[215]

THE POWER OF PRAYER

'during this period of glorious revival, do we hear parents asking the prayers of God's people for their children. "A mother requests prayers for an only daughter absent from home pursuing her education, that she may be brought to the knowledge of the Saviour." "A widowed mother requests prayers for her two sons, now in a distant western State, that God may grant them repentance unto life." "A father requests prayers for two children. God hath graciously given five of his seven children to his prayers, and he is exceedingly anxious that the remaining two may be brought to a saving acquaintance with the dear Saviour." Nothing can be more interesting to ministers of the gospel and other pious persons who have themselves in infancy been given to the Lord in covenant, and who realize the beauty, value and propriety of covenant relations, than such requests as these.

'Many of us, at the age of thirty, forty, fifty, look back to former years, to the prayers, instructions and example of a godly mother, and the holy life and triumphant death of a sweet younger sister perhaps and confess that all the spiritual good we have received in this world has come to us mainly through these beautiful and sacred ministries. And yet we often fear, when we hear these requests, that there may be failure and disappointment; not because the covenant is not broad, deep, divine and precious enough, but because the faith and hope of the parents may depend too much upon *instrumentalities*; and because they may become impatient of results; and because there is no immediate or sudden answer, relax their effort and fall back into indifference, if not into despondency. The danger is, that we may trust too much to the *prayers* and not enough to the promises and covenant engagements of the blessed God.

'Our prayers, in themselves considered, are poor, and weak, and wretched, and sinful enough – a very insult to the infinite holiness of the Being to whom they are addressed.

The New York Revival of 1858

And yet everything in regard to the spiritual and eternal welfare of the inhabitants of this world is promised to prayer. "Ask and ye *shall* receive" is the motto upon the altar.

'There is nothing so certain in the vast universe as that God will hear and answer prayer for the blessings contained in his covenants. "He keepeth covenant and mercy to a thousand generations;" nay, to assure the faith of his people, he pledges his existence and honor to the fulfillment of his covenant engagements. "My covenant will I not break, nor alter the thing that is gone out of my lips. Once have I sworn by my holiness that I will not lie unto David. His seed shall endure forever and his throne as the sun before me. It shall be established forever as the moon and as a faithful witness in heaven;" Ps. 89: 34-37. There is a solemn and awful grandeur in this passage, a kind and infinite condescension. That the God of truth, who cannot lie, should permit us to stand upon the immovable foundation of his promise and urge *that* as our argument in prayer would surely seem sufficient to satisfy the demands of every reasonable mind, especially when we consider that his promises are but the expression of his purposes, that run back through the entire eternity of his being, whereof the memory of the oldest archangel runneth not to the contrary, and come down to us freighted with all the wealth of the divine veracity, mercy, goodness, wisdom and power, and invested with all the sanctity of the divine consistency. We plead not only the truth of the promise, but the precedent of the divine conduct forever. This charter of rights and privileges is certainly full enough and strong enough to sustain our faith in prayer for all the blessings of that "godliness which is profitable unto all things, and which hath the promise of this life and of that which is to come." But in addition to this, we have the oath of God, based upon his holiness, which is comprehensive of all his attributes – of his very being – as if he had said, If I redeem not the promises and pledges made to David – which is Christ – let me cease to be. How, then, in pleading for the blessings of life and salvation – the blessings secured to Christ in the covenant of the Father, and to us through Christ in answer to prayer – our feet are permitted to take hold of the beams of his habitation which are laid "in deep waters", the deep, unfathomed sea of his infinite and eternal nature – the deep and troubled sea of his inscrutable providence.

'But the immense, the infinite, the eternal purity and claim of the divine being, and all his attributes, are sustained and honored in the atonement of his dear, co-equal, co-eternal Son, the *Immanuel*, the *God manifest in the flesh*; the declaration of the divine justice – the manifestation of the divine love and mercy in the forgiveness of sin, he who, upon the might and merit of his obedience and suffering in our stead, is exalted to the right hand of majesty and power in the heavens; and whom our faith is permitted to see, a Lamb as it had been slain in the midst of the throne of God; the king-priest upon the throne; nay, the king, the priest, and the sacrifice all in one, upon the throne, as our advocate, and intercessor, who presents our prayers to the Father; made precious and efficient by being invested with the might, the merit, and the mercy of the intercessor. And, shall they not prevail? Nay, shall not *he* prevail? With what confidence, courage, and cheerfulness may not the Saviour, the mighty intercessor, say to his suffering, struggling people, "Whatsoever ye shall ask in my name, that will I do, that the Father may be glorified in the Son. If ye shall ask anything in my name, I will do it"? And, with what cheerful confidence may not our faith grasp such promises as these in prayer, especially when we ask the regeneration and salvation of our covenant children?

"Ah!" saith that anxious parent, "all this is true. I believe it all, and yet my child is not converted."

Anxious, weeping soul, the promise is to Abraham, that in his seed, which is Christ, shall all the families of the earth be blessed. This promise is still the glorious inheritance of the church. It must, it will be fulfilled.

"What has become of all the prayers that have been offered to God for the salvation of this world?" What has become of them? Why, all that have been offered in faith have been received in heaven, and accepted in the name of the great intercessor. Some of them have been already answered, and many of them wait only the times and the seasons which the Father hath put in his own power; but not one of them is lost, or shall remain unanswered. The prayers of Abraham, and Isaac, and Jacob, and Moses, and Elias, and David, and the prophets, and apostles and martyrs, and the godly of all ages, all that vast column of prayer that has travelled along down the pathway of the covenant, from the first accepted sacrifice at the gates of the lost Eden, all are in heaven and all will be answered. The prayers of your ancestors, the pious and covenant-keeping Huguenots, Hollanders, Scotch-Irish and Puritans; the pioneers of the American church; the strong crying and tears that they offered to God for their descendants and for their country, are all in heaven, and will all be answered. *Your* prayers, dear child of God, are not all answered; but they are accepted, if offered in faith, in the name of Christ, and for the blessings of the covenant, and shall be answered – some of them, perhaps, during your lifetime on earth, and all of them, certainly, during your lifetime in heaven.

Turn, for a moment, to the visions of the beloved disciple in the "Isle that is called Patmos", Rev. 5: 8: "And when he (the Lamb) had taken the book, the four beasts, and the four and twenty elders fell down before the Lamb,

THE POWER OF PRAYER

having every one of them harps, and golden vials full of odors, which are the prayers of the saints." The *prayers of the saints* – something so very precious that is fragrance even in heaven. Commentators will tell you that the word rendered beasts means living ones, and that they are the symbols of the divine government, or providence. The face of a lion, an ox, a man, and a flying eagle, will then bring before you the dominion, the stability, the intelligence, and celerity of the divine providence, and your prayers are committed to the keeping of this government, thus symbolized. The divine providence holds the golden censers containing the accepted, but unanswered prayers of the saints, and surely we may, with confidence and cheerfulness, commit our prayers to such keeping. But this is not the whole of the celestial vision with regard to the prayers of the saints. Turn to Rev. 8: 3–5: "And another angel came, and stood at the altar, having a golden censer, and there was given him much incense, that he should offer it (add it) with the prayers of all the saints upon the golden altar which was before the throne. And the smoke of the incense which came with the prayers of the saints, ascended up before God out of the angel's hands. And the angel took the censer, and filled it with fire of the altar, and cast it into the earth. And there were voices, and thunderings, and lightnings, and an earthquake." The fragrance belongs not originally to the prayers, but it was given to the angel to add to the prayers of *all the saints*. That sacred and heavenly perfume is the merit of the high priest and the advocate. The angel is not the intercessor, but the angelic minister, charged to carry the answers to our prayers. We are let somewhat into the secret of this arrangement in the history of the Prophet Daniel, 9: 23: "At the *beginning* of thy supplication the commandment came forth, and I," Gabriel, mentioned in the previous verse, "am come to show thee." The Lord

The New York Revival of 1858

must not wait until Daniel had finished his prayer, before he could determine the nature, or the extent of his request. Nay, at the "*beginning* of thy supplication, the commandment came forth". Your prayers are heard, accepted, and the commandment issued for their answer; and yet, much time may elapse before the answer is received. In Daniel 9 we have an account of the prophet's mourning, and fasting, and prayer, for three full weeks; and after the one and twenty days of bitterness and prayer, "Behold, a hand touched me, which set me upon my knees, and upon the palms of my hands. And he said unto me, O Daniel, a man greatly beloved, understand the words that I speak unto thee, and stand upright, for unto thee am I now sent. And when he had spoken this word unto me, I stood trembling. Then said he unto me, Fear not, Daniel, for from the *first day* that thou didst set thine heart to understand, and to chasten thyself before thy God, thy words were heard, and I am come for thy words. But the prince of the kingdom of Persia withstood me one and twenty days. But lo, Michael, one of the chief princes, came to help me, and I remained there with the kings of Persia." This scene is laid between heaven and earth, the territories traversed by our prayers and the returning answers. What conflicts occur in this field between the ministering angels, who are charged with the answers to our prayers, and the fallen spirits, who hate God and oppose our holiness and his cause on the earth, we know not. In this instance, in the history of Daniel, the patron demon of Persia opposed the angel of God one and twenty days, and would, no doubt, from his intense hatred of God and his people, have continued his opposition for an indefinite period, had not the Almighty commanded the Archangel Michael to go to the relief of the faithful messenger. Aye, while Daniel held on in prayer, not only would Michael, but all the glittering host that wait the bidding of their eternal King, have come forth to minister to the praying saint. Oh, it is precious to know, that all the bright, benevolent, and holy ones around the throne on high, are employed about the affairs of the saints on earth. "Are they not all ministering spirits, *sent* forth to minister for those that shall be heirs of salvation?" But if, in the case of Daniel, there was required a delay of "one and twenty days", so in the case of our prayers for ourselves, our children, and the world, the high proprieties of the divine government may demand a delay of not only one and twenty days, but of one and twenty years, or one and twenty centuries, for that matter; yet are we assured, that the prayer of faith offered in the name of the Mighty Advocate, for the blessings of the covenant, is heard, accepted, and the commandment for its answer sent forth; while the faith of the praying saints, and the efforts of the ministering angel, await only the times and the seasons which the Father hath put in his own power. In the meantime, those prayers, as sweet perfumes, are kept in the vials and censers of the holy ones in heaven; and at the appropriate times, the fires of the divine rectitude and love from the golden altar will be kindled upon them, and the angel will cast them upon the earth. And then shall follow those great revivals, those mighty moral and spiritual revolutions, fitly symbolized by "voices, thunderings, lightnings, and an earthquake". What are our revivals now, but a few of those fragrant drops poured out upon the earth; but the time cometh, as the church approaches the culminating period of this dispensation, when God will hasten his work, and the thousands and millions of earth, in answer to the prayers of all the saints, shall flock to the cross, and go forth for ages the washed, redeemed, and joyous millennial church on earth. Still the cry is, "O Lord, how long?"

The New York Revival of 1858

'My native village, years before I was born, was blessed with the prayers of some pious Scotch-Irish, and Helvetians. But when I was a little boy, the praying people of that village were a little company of pious ladies, almost all of them widows. My godly mother used to take me by the hand and lead me to those places of prayer, and my young eyes were sometimes employed to read the holy Scriptures for them. How well I remember the deep solicitude expressed by that godly company for their children, and the agonizing prayers for their salvation. About the time of the holidays, when passion ran riot, and Sabbath-breaking, drunkenness, profanity, and every evil thing made the days and the nights hideous, how did those dear ladies mourn! What will become of the honor of God? what will become of our children? On one such painful occasion, I remember that Mother F——, a very intelligent and godly Irish Christian, a poor asthmatic, at whose house the prayer-meeting was held, sat bolstered up in her cushioned easy-chair; and as her sisters were uttering their complaints, with the tears and smiles mingling on her face, she turned and whispered: "My dear sisters, God is not dead, the covenant is not broken. Why, I should not be surprised, if in less than five years, God should so revive his work here, that the place would become too strait, and we should be compelled to adjourn to Squire S——'s woods to find room. I may not live to see it. I am a poor, frail, broken reed; but you may – yes, you may." But she did live to see it. Before the five years had elapsed, God did pour out his Spirit on that place. Many were converted, and the noise of it travelling, as it did, throughout the country, called many persons from a distance to witness the strange scene. The little clap-boarded church became too small, and during the pleasant summer weather, we did adjourn to Squire S——'s woods, erected booths and a stand for the preachers, and

THE POWER OF PRAYER

hundreds flocked to hear the precious words of salvation, so mightily grew the word of the Lord.

One beautiful Sabbath morning, I saw that godly Irish Christian lady seated at the root of a beautiful tree; her eyes were closed, and her hands clasped, and again the smiles and the tears were mingled upon that face, now radiant in the rays of the sun, as they crept down through the massive foliage and rested upon those dear features; and still more radiant with the glow of joy and gratitude that came up upon them from a heart basking in the beams of the sun of righteousness. And what is the result? The vast majority of the children, and many of the older persons for whom those pious ladies prayed during weary years, were brought to the Saviour. Many of the fathers and mothers have gone to their reward, but the boys of that period are now the men of position, fortune and influence, and the whole character of the village has been changed. "This is glorious." Yea, verily, so it is; but remember, praying mothers, it was not the achievement of a day, or a week, or a year, but the mighty effort of persevering prayer for many years.

Let not your faith fail you. It may be compelled to meet many and sore trials while it waits at the throne and bides the time of the Father. You may be called away from earth before that gay daughter, or that wild, wandering son of yours, given to the Lord in covenant infancy, is effectually called and saved; but in death, oh, grasp the horns of the altar, and stay your soul in the covenant promise and oath of your God. Your prayers of faith are in the censer held in the hand of the angel; and perhaps when you are there too, that wandering boy may bend at the little mound that covers your poor remains, and the better thoughts of the boy chase away the sinful thoughts of the man, and a fragrant drop from the heavenly censer be poured upon him there, that shall send him away a renewed one! And

The New York Revival of 1858

how know you, but that you yourself may be the angel that shall be commissioned to bear the answer to your own prayers for the salvation of your boy. "HAVE FAITH IN GOD."

'But, your wandering boy may be called to the eternal world before you, and you may have no certain evidence that he had met with a change of heart. What then? why then stay your soul on the living God. Mrs F., the wife of Judge F., of western New York, was a member of the church in which I commenced my ministry; she was a woman of rare intelligence, and as rare simplicity of character – a woman of true devotion and of unwavering faith in the covenants. Her children had all been given to the Lord in faith in their early infancy, and all save one, as they arrived at maturity, were hopefully converted. Willie, the remaining one, was my school-mate in the academy. He was a frank, noble, generous boy, a firm believer in the Scriptures, in which he had been carefully instructed. Willie revered his mother, but was so full of life and mischief that he could not think seriously with regard to his spiritual interest. He could not think of being a Christian until he had "sowed his wild oats". So Willie went to Canada to teach school, and during the Patriot war had an opportunity to sow some of his fatal crop. Still, Willie was the same frank, generous, joyous, moral Willie. Texas afforded a better field, and Willie tried his fortune there, passed through some terrible scenes during the wars of that infant state; still his correspondence with his mother and myself exhibited the same frank, generous, joyous Willie, with no evidence that his moral principles had suffered any serious abrasion; and still that godly mother held on in prayer for her boy. During the Santa Fé expedition she wrote me to inquire if I had heard anything of Willie. I, too, had been on the same search, and found Willie in company B. of that ill-starred

THE POWER OF PRAYER

adventure. He, with the rest, was taken prisoner, was carried on that weary journey of a thousand miles to the city of Mexico, and returned in safety to Texas. Still his correspondence, though somewhat subdued in tone, exhibited the same frank, noble, generous Willie. And still that mother, in tears, pleaded the covenant, day after day, for the salvation of her son. She began to give up the hope of seeing him again in this world, and her faith reached across to the other, while she continued to pray that God would save her child. The Mexican war came on, and poor Willie was so much involved with the military movements of Texas, that now he found it almost impossible to extricate himself. He was with the Texan cavalry in that war, and one day, while engaged in pistol practice on horseback, with his company, by some mysterious casualty in the wheeling of his horse, he was shot with his own pistol, and poor Willie was buried by his companions in the soil of Mexico. I received the intelligence, and immediately went to see that godly praying mother. Poor woman! how should I break the fatal news to her? As I approached her, she saw a paper in my hand, and asked:

"Have you news from my poor Willie?"

"Yes, my dear friend, terrible news. The Lord, in whom you trust, give you strength to read," and I handed her the paper. I watched her face as she read. Her chin quivered. The big tears rolled down her cheeks. A deep, deep sigh, but one, came up from her broken heart. She turned to me and said:

"And what now of the covenant?"

I replied, "It is unbroken, my dear friend."

"Yes," she replied, "it is unbroken. What has become of my dear boy I know not. What God, the blessed Spirit, could have done for the saving of his soul, I know not. But this I know, it was right for me to give my boy to the Lord in covenant. It was right for me to pray for his salvation; it is right for me to believe that those prayers have been heard and accepted through the merits of the Saviour, and that they will, in some way, in accordance with the divine wisdom and faithfulness be answered. *How*, I know not, and because I know not, I will possess my soul in patience, and wait in hope, the time when the good Father shall explain all; and I shall be able to bear the explanation."

Glorious, triumphant faith! Sorely wast thou tried, dear, precious mother! and signally hast thou triumphed too!

"Have faith in God." There is no parallax in the Father of Light. There is no peradventure in the covenants. "For all the promises of God in Christ are yea, and in him amen, unto the glory of God by us."'

Chapter 24

The Book of Requests – Written with Tears – Desire – Affection – Conviction of Sin – Sorrow – Faith – Conversations with the Drawer – The Converted gathered into the Kingdom.

In the upper room of the house in which the Fulton street prayer-meetings are held, is a large folio volume, prepared for the purpose, in which are placed the requests for prayer that come in from day to day. What a record this is! What a volume of the heart's experience! What a story of the whole country, and almost the whole world's experience is here! From all parts of our own land, from many lands beyond the sea, from all classes and conditions of men, from saints and sinners, old and young, from the dying and those who are watched by the dying, these requests have come. The names of the persons sending them are not recorded, but the requests speak for themselves with the tenderest eloquence of that sincerity, anxiety and faith which take hold on the arm of almighty strength and prevail with God.

Anxious desire for others marks most of these petitions. For years and years some have been looking for fruit, and finding none, have been ready to faint and despair. But far above all other wishes, the desire is irrepressible that these friends may be brought to the Saviour. They have now sought help in the prayers of God's people in the great city, and with speechless anxiety, wait and watch to see

The New York Revival of 1858

what God the Lord will do. There is much that is beautiful and sublime in this posture of the soul. It longs for the answer; it summons others to its aid, and looks away to the heavenly hills, from which alone help can come. Such prayer will prevail.

Tender affection breathes in every line of these uncounted requests. Perhaps this feature is the most patent and impressive by which they are marked. A fond wife pleads that her husband may be led to love the Saviour. And here and there a husband asks that the wife of his love may be also one with him in Christ. And oh! how many parents – page after page is full of them – begging that their children may be converted. Some go on to speak of the promises on which they have trusted, and which are yet the anchor of their hopes, and now they would blend their own prayers with those of Christians at this meeting, that their offspring may be saved. And children, too, have sent up their requests that unbelieving parents may be brought to Christ! Brothers and sisters plead for each other; friends for friends; all bound by ties of tenderest love, and all believing that the love of God surpasseth all other love, and makes the love of earth a foretaste of the love of heaven.

On some of these petitions is written a deep sense of conviction of sin. Poor sinners, some almost despairing, many long seeking, now venture to call upon Christians to implore mercy in their behalf. A few of these are so surcharged with a sense of guilt and desert of punishment, that no one can read them without commiserating sympathy. The prayers of David in the fifty-first Psalm are not more painfully filled with the anguish of a broken heart, than some of these written petitions.

And many of these requests come up from the sons and daughters of sorrow. 'To the mercy seat' 'come the disconsolate.' 'A father begs the prayers of the people of

THE POWER OF PRAYER

God for his prodigal son.' 'Parents implore God's mercy on their daughter who has gone astray.' The bereaved ask that their affliction may be sanctified. The sick that they may be prepared to die. What volumes of grief would be written, if the private history to which each little note is an index, were drawn out! Some of them seem to bleed, so keen are the pains, so deep the wounds. Families that for months or years have been hiding a bitter grief, wearing a smile before the world while the secret anguish was gnawing at their hearts, have now come to the prayer-meeting with their petition that the God of mercy would have compassion on them in their distress, and bring help in time of trouble. All these requests are written in tears; the tears of parental, conjugal, fraternal love: such tears as no sorrow brings but the waywardness of one loved and lost.

And these requests are prayers of faith. As we turned over the pages and read them, one after another, a person standing by, remarked, '*These* are the prayers that get the answer.' These are prayers that go out from earnest, loving, trusting hearts, and when they are repeated here, it is impossible they should call out the same emotions that their petitioners feel. But when a soul is moved to send up such a request as this, it comes with faith and strong desire, and that request is heard in heaven. And the answer comes. It is followed up by more prayer than was offered before, and the spirit of the Syro-Phenician woman, the spirit of faithful importunity has power with God and prevails.

There is a drawer in a table in the upper lecture-room, that contains the envelopes of all these requests for prayer which have been sent in. A thousand thoughts rush in upon the mind every time we see this drawer. We went up to this room the other day, and sitting down by the table in which this drawer is, and drawing it out, we began to run

The New York Revival of 1858

our eyes over these envelopes, and their contents as lately contained in these precious folds, till we were all absorbed in a *conversation* with the *contents*.

Each envelope seemed to come up before us to tell us its own story. They came to tell of what they had seen and heard – away and away – when those messages which they contained were written. Some of them told us of the bitter tears they had seen shed – some of them of the fervent prayers they had heard made – some of the strong hopes they had heard expressed – some of sinking fears. Oh, what histories did they rehearse to us, so affecting as often to compel tears!

We were invited to take wing with them, and fly to the places where they were written, and to look into this chamber and that parlor, and this humble cottage and that splendid mansion, and up and down in the highways and by-ways, and to find the actors in these scenes; and then, too, we were taken to churchyards, and bidden to look a moment and see where beneath those little hillocks of earth at our feet, these gentle sleepers slept. 'Oh, is it possible, said we, that since this prayer-meeting was begun, only a little more than one year ago, some of these have fallen asleep?'

'Yes,' they answered. 'Some are sleeping the sleep that knows no waking.'

'And how asleep?' we inquired.

'Asleep in Jesus, some of them,' they answered, and then they asked if I did not remember a lovely one, who, from one of the upper streets of the city, sent down a request, or her father for her, that we would remember her in our prayers; a lovely one, then feeble, lacking only the one thing needful, but in every respect most lovely in all the natural attributes of her character. She was prayed for here. She came to Jesus, the sinner's friend; she humbly trusted in him; she cordially received him. The

THE POWER OF PRAYER

loveliness of her character after this shone out more lustrously than ever. All those sweet affections which took hold on her friends with such a strong, tender grasp in her unconverted state, seemed stronger and more tender than ever. She went with her friends into the country to spend the summer, she was smitten more deeply; she sunk rapidly; all was done to save her, all however in vain; heaven was to be made richer. One voice more was to join the everlasting song. She slept. In just three months from the day that the request was put up for prayer on her behalf by the Fulton street meeting, she slept in Jesus.

'Do you not remember?'

We did remember.

And again, the profligate young man, the prodigal, spending his father's substance with riotous living – an only son – was prayed for – was converted – was received into one of our city churches – attended one communion – went South – was accidentally killed – was brought back – is under one of these little hillocks – sleeps in Jesus.

'Do you not remember?'

Again we did remember.

So the contents of the drawer continued to talk to us, and to tell of the dead. They talked too of the living.

'Look down once more,' said they, and looking down, we saw one looking up to us, which said,

'I am from Marietta, Ohio; I told you only yesterday of the message I brought you; a request from a widowed mother for the conversion of her children.'

I bent my ear down to the drawer again, and it said – read what it said:

'Your prayers are requested for the widow and the fatherless. The father after planting a church in the far West, and preaching near a score of years, lay down to *rest*. But nature was exhausted, and he called his children and his wife around him; and after bidding them an affection-

The New York Revival of 1858

ate and tender farewell and commending them to the care of the Friend of the unprotected, he crossed his weary hands upon his breast; and with a shout of triumph – saying heaven was presented to his view – entered his everlasting rest. One of his children is a great sufferer. Now, Christian friends, will you pray that a covenant-keeping God will remember his promise and gather these little ones into his fold, now in this day of mercy, that the widow may be sustained and her faith strengthened, etc?'

Oh! shall that faith ever waver? Shall the great and good Shepherd be doubted? Will he not gather the lambs in his arms and carry them in his bosom? Christians have earnestly prayed that he would and he will.

Again the drawer spoke to us, and asked us 'to remember the 5th of November to pray for Gouverneur, St Lawrence Co., N.Y., that the people of God there may enjoy a season of refreshing from the presence of the Lord.' We did remember, and for several other places the same day. Some in one State, some in another – East, West, North and South.

Again the drawer speaks: 'My husband is not a Christian though often thoughtful. I have prayed for his conversion every day since our marriage – nine years. May I ask an interest in your prayers that my husband may seek *now* an interest in Christ, and that we may both become devoted, earnest, Bible-Christians.'

How many praying wives make just such errands as this to the Fulton street prayer-meeting! God bless these praying wives.

What voice is this that comes out of the drawer? Listen! 'The prayers of the Fulton street meeting are earnestly requested for a Bible Class of twenty-two young ladies, connected with one of the Dutch Reformed churches in this vicinity, some of whom appear to be anxious for their souls.'

[233]

THE POWER OF PRAYER

What a world of interests are bound up in that one appeal. How many hearts would rejoice if they all should be converted!

But we will not prolong the conversation. This book of requests, and the drawer in which these envelopes are preserved, will be memorials of the faith and earnestness of the saints; and the answers shall be recorded also to the praise of infinite grace.

Chapter 25

A Year of Prayer – Review of the Meetings – Anniversary of Fulton street Meeting – Extraordinary Case of Awakening at that Meeting – Murder and Suicide prevented – The Sinner saved.

In bringing the sketches of these meetings to a close, it would be a grateful work to review the ground we have gone over, and admire the wonders of redeeming grace and love that have been disclosed. I am sensible of the imperfection of the history, in that it makes no distinct mention of many meetings and series of meetings in this city and in other places, of which I should love to speak. The year 1858 will be memorable in the city of New York for these union prayer-meetings. Among the most profitable was the one that for many weeks was held in the Ninth street Reformed Dutch Church (Dr Van Zandt's), and afterwards was held in rotation in various churches of different denominations, in the upper part of the city, daily at noon. In these meetings, pastors and people assembled in great numbers; and on Saturdays such children were encouraged to come, as were of years to understand the truth, and for them prayer was specially made, and words of instruction addressed to them with tenderness and power. At one of these meetings held in the First Presbyterian Church (Dr Phillips') we saw pastors of nearly every evangelical denomination present, Rev Dr Gillette, of the Baptist Church, presiding, while a spirit of love and prayer pervaded the great assembly, filling the entire house at the middle of the day. Other series of meetings held in rotation, were sustained until the heat of the summer required the usual migration of families into the country.

The Rev Dr Peck (Methodist) held a series of services for six successive evenings in his church. The gospel was preached by ministers of six different denominations, all pervaded with the same spirit, and exhibiting the same great truth, salvation by the Lord Jesus Christ.

And the same spirit of union seems to have prevailed all over the land. If the revival has been more marked in some parts of the country than in others, it cannot be said of any large portion that it has been exempt. This fact has been abundantly developed in the reports made at the meetings of which we have given accounts in preceding pages. No classes of persons have been left unaffected by the power of the Holy Ghost. The rich capitalist in the city, and the hard-working laborer, the merchant shipper and the sailor, the master and the slave, the pioneers of civilization in the far West, and the dwellers among the institutions of the gospel in New England, have shared in the blessings and power of this work of grace. So far as human observation goes, the Lord has been no respecter of persons in this outpouring of his Spirit, but has sent the rain upon the good and the evil, the just and the unjust, gaining praise for himself in the edification of his saints and the conversion of sinners.

It was very becoming that the day on which the prayer-meeting in Fulton street was established should be commemorated on the return of its anniversary. Previous notice having been given that the church adjoining the lecture-room would be thrown open on that day (Thursday, September 23, 1858), at noon, it was crowded to overflowing. The congregation was one of the most

The New York Revival of 1858

interesting and deeply interested that we have ever seen gathered together. Its most striking feature was the cordial and affectionate union of ministers and private Christians of so many different denominations in celebrating the sacred occasion. It was a scene of hallowed, heavenly enjoyment, never to be forgotten by those who participated in it.

The Rev Dr De Witt, Senior Minister of the Collegiate Dutch Churches, appropriately presided. He opened the exercises by some remarks, in which he gave a brief history of the origin and progress of the daily prayer-meeting held in the lecture-room of the church. After the congregation had joined in singing the psalm –

> I love thy kingdom, Lord,
> The house of thine abode, etc.,

Rev Dr Leland, of South Carolina, read the 62d chapter of Isaiah. Rev Dr McCarrell, Presbyterian, of Newburgh, N.Y., led the assembly in prayer. Rev Dr Krebs, of the Old School Presbyterian Church, made an address contrasting the present religious aspect of the city, and the position and prospects of the churches, with what they were when he first entered the city about thirty years since, and when he came to this church on his first Sabbath in the city to hear the Rev Dr De Witt preach. He said that a few years ago it seemed almost as if this portion of the city was to be given up to mammon, the churches were so generally moving up town. But in view of the wonderful results of the past year, in which at the busiest hour of the day, and in the midst of the marts of trade and of business of every kind, each day in the year, crowds had been gathered together for prayer – in which so many souls have been converted to God and so many hearts quickened and cheered, we are all compelled to exclaim, 'What hath God wrought!'

THE POWER OF PRAYER

The venerable Dr Bangs, of the Methodist Episcopal Church, said that this was the first successful attempt at Christian union which had been made. For a great part of his ministerial life he had battled with other denominations, but of late he had been preaching on Love, and he was going to preach more on this theme until he should be called to rest from his labors. His remarks, uttered in a spirit of warm affection toward all who love Christ, and coming from a veteran minister of the gospel who has not long to remain, produced a deep impression.

After prayer by Rev Dr Bangs, Rev Dr Gillette, of the Baptist Church, spoke, and touched many a tender chord in the hearts of his hearers. He referred to the scenes of triumph which had attended the labors of God's people during the past year, and in the estimate of its great results, carried his hearers up to those courts above where saints and angels, in sympathy with ransomed souls on earth, were harping with their harps, praising God for the displays of his grace made to perishing sinners.

Rev Dr Van Pelt, of the Reformed Dutch Church, made a few remarks, and Rev Dr Asa D. Smith, of the New School Presbyterian Church, led in prayer, when Rev Dr Adams, of the same church, made an address, recounting many of the great mercies which had descended upon our land and upon the world as the fruits of the great revival; the souls that had been saved; the Christian hearts that had been cheered; the homes that had been blessed; the family altars that had been erected; the number that had been added to the ministry, and the great addition which had been made to the working power of the church. He referred to other lands which had caught the influence; he spoke of the remarkable movement going on in the established church of England, in giving the gospel to the poor and persuading them to listen to it, and said he had just received a letter from a distinguished

The New York Revival of 1858

servant of Christ, at Geneva, Switzerland, making inquiry about this revival, and giving information which showed that they have the same thing going on in the old world, if they do not give it the same name.

A stranger then rose and related some incidents illustrating the power of the work, and exhorted Christians to persevere, sowing the seed beside all waters, and waiting on God in believing prayer for his blessing.

Dr De Witt said he had received letters from two Episcopal clergymen of the city, expressing their regrets that they could not attend, owing to engagements.

Rev Dr Spring made the concluding address; Rev Mr Cuyler led in prayer, and Rev Dr Bangs pronounced the benediction.

While this glorious meeting was in progress – a meeting of thanksgiving and praise – how little did any one in that great congregation imagine the emotions of one poor sinner who was standing among the crowd within the doors; yet then and there, while the people were praising God for what he had done, the Spirit was in power upon one who had been meditating horrible crime, restraining him from sin and bringing him to repentance. Seeing the crowd pressing into the church as he was passing, he turned in with them, reckless of himself and only anxious to see what was going on. He succeeded in getting a standing place within the door, and soon heard words that arrested his attention. He was even then resolving murder in his own mind, but the word of God, which is sharper than any two-edged sword, pierced him to the heart.

This was September 23. About nine days afterwards, October 2, a man came running into the upper lecture-room, in Fulton street, and said he 'wanted to write a request for prayer'. We sat, at the time, at a table, writing out the report of the previous meeting. So we handed a pen and paper, and said to him, 'Sit down, and write what you please.' He wrote as follows, and handed it to us to present for him to the meeting, which was to commence in ten or twelve minutes:

> 'The prayers of this meeting are respectfully requested for G—— B——, who has lived all his life in wickedness, and only a week ago contemplated suicide and the great crime of murder, in hope of ending his misery.
>
> G——B——'

He signed this request with his own proper name. We looked at him with incredulity and amazement.

'You did not really intend to commit murder and suicide?' we said.

'Yes I did,' he answered, with great promptness and decision. 'I really meant it, and should have done it, if it had not been for the prayer-meeting held in the church.'

We were still incredulous, and surprised to hear him talk so. We stood up together at the table. We looked at him calmly and steadily in the eye for a minute or two. We could see no murder there.

'It is not possible,' we remarked.

'It is possible,' he said. 'It was truly so, and I and another would have been in eternity before now if it had not been for the prayer-meeting in the church.'

This was said with so much calmness and firmness, that we began to believe him, and inquired,

'Whom did you intend to murder?'

'A woman.'

'What for?'

'She had most outrageously wronged me.'

'Have you any murder in your heart now?'

'Not a particle.'

'Have you ever committed any heinous crime?' we asked him, looking down and reading over the request,

The New York Revival of 1858

and thinking that some of his expressions might refer to crimes he had committed in past life.

'Never,' said he, with great firmness.

'Have you been in prison?'

'I never was imprisoned in my life.'

'Of what country are you?'

'I am an Englishman, but have been several years in America.'

'Had you a pious mother?'

The tears stood in his eyes, blinding him by their flow.

'I had a praying mother, sir, and I really believe her prayers for me prevented my hand on that day.'

'How so?'

'I had the deadly knife in my bosom, and the poison in my pocket. I intended to meet my victim on the street, and to stab her on the instant, and take the poison on the spot and put an end to my troubles. But I hope that God prevented me in answer to my mother's prayers.'

'Do you really desire to be a Christian?'

'I do.'

'Are you really sorry for the awful crimes you have contemplated?'

'I am, sir – I am sorry. I am a great sinner.'

'The Lord Jesus is a great Saviour. He prayed for forgiveness for his own murderers, when he was dying, and he can forgive you.'

At this time the singing had commenced in the room below, and we went down together. We edged him in, and found a seat for him in the crowded assembly, and then sent up his request. It went from hand to hand, till it reached the leader's desk. We saw him read it with evident surprise, and as an opportunity offered, he rose, and read it to the audience.

Fervent prayers were offered, and this poor miserable man was remembered. Notwithstanding all his crimes,

THE POWER OF PRAYER

there was something in the prayers which seemed to say: 'We believe that this man's sins, which are many, will be forgiven him.' The chief of sinners can be forgiven.

The agony of his mind seemed to become more and more intense from day to day. Often did a little band of Christians retire into a small upper room, and when the doors were shut, converse and pray with him. He could get no relief. He was sometimes questioned, to see if there was any disposition to commit suicide, lurking in his heart but he seemed to shudder at the thoughts of the crimes which he had resolved upon, and was fully aware of the great enormity and awful wickedness of his heart, in that it could entertain for a moment such murderous intentions. He was always present in the daily prayer-meetings, and was cast down under his burden of sorrow. Remorse gnawed terribly at his heart, and it was not mere sorrow, but it was agony of spirit. He was also present at the evening meetings, and no opportunity for mingling with Christians, who met for prayer, escaped him.

His countenance bore the plain hand-writing of the suffering which was endured within. His prevailing feeling was that of despair. He felt that he had sinned so long, and had sinned so grievously, that it was useless to expect that his sins could be forgiven.

He was one evening at a prayer-meeting. It was a Sabbath evening, and the room was full. In about the middle of the house his voice was heard. He was found kneeling by his seat, and crying aloud for mercy. The congregation was standing, and singing a hymn. It was the hymn

> Rock of ages cleft for me,
> Let me hide myself in thee.

His language was: 'Oh, what shall I do! – what shall I do – what can I do to be saved?' He kept uttering short

The New York Revival of 1858

expressions of prayer, begging for mercy and forgiveness through Jesus Christ. The singing proceeded to the end, and when the hymn was closed, no notice being taken of the interruption, prayer was at once commenced, making him the one and only object of supplication. When the voice of prayer was heard, his own voice was hushed, and all hearts united in one solemn, earnest cry for mercy on this poor sinner. Prayer followed after prayer, till the hour was closed, and his case was the burden of all the supplications offered. The meeting closed, and this man was almost the last to leave the room, so reluctant was he to go.

The next day, at noon, he was at the prayer-meeting. But oh! what a change in his countenance. It wore a quiet, placid smile. That look of sadness and despair was gone, and *gone forever*. He was rejoicing in Christ as a Saviour – as his Saviour – with exceeding joy. His faith strengthens daily, and he gives abundant evidence that he is a 'new creature in Christ Jesus'.

Chapter 26

PRAYER SHOWN TO BE EFFICACIOUS

BY THE REV WM. S. PLUMER, D.D., LL.D.

I have been requested by the author of this volume to write something on prayer, particularly on the relation between the prayer and the answer, illustrated by facts ancient or modern.

There is not on earth any form of religion that does not include prayer. It may be corrupt in doctrine, morals and worship, but it cannot be a religion and dispense with prayer.

It is not possible to over-estimate the value of prayer. For more than thirty-five years I have had much intercourse with dying saints and sinners of various ages and conditions. In all that time I have not heard one express regret that he had spent too much time in prayer; I have heard many mourn that they had so seldom visited a throne of grace.

There can be no true piety without a devotional spirit. He whose soul does not thirst after God, and seek fellowship with him, is an entire stranger to vital godliness.

Prayer is efficacious. It has power with God. It averts sore judgments. It brings great blessings. Nothing that men can do has so vast an influence. This can be proven in many ways.

The New York Revival of 1858

The Scriptures expressly say so. 'Call upon me in the day of trouble: I will deliver thee, and thou shalt glorify me;' 'Every one that asketh receiveth; and he that seeketh findeth; and to him that knocketh it shall be opened;' 'The effectual, fervent prayer of a righteous man availeth much.' Often does God's word say as much.

It also records very clear and remarkable answers to prayer in the cases of Abraham, of Jacob, of Joseph, of Moses, of Joshua, of Hannah, of David, of Asa, of Elijah, of Elisha, of Isaiah, of Hezekiah, of Mordecai, of Nehemiah, of Paul and Silas, and of many others.

And God's honor is as much involved in answering the prayers indited by his Spirit, as it is in his continuing to rule the world. When we ask him to hear the right, we ask him to maintain his own glory, and to support his own throne.

Nor is anything that concerns us too minute to claim God's notice. Nearly a century ago a man settled in Western Pennsylvania. He owned a tract of land with some improvements and stock. But he was far from market, and money was scarce. His family being large, he fell in arrears. He owed his merchant some ten or more dollars. His taxes were also due. He promised the money as soon as he could get it. He offered some of his stock and grain, but no purchaser could be had. At length he was urged to fix a day when the money should be paid with certainty. He went to his home and was much afflicted. Early in the autumn a neighbor and himself built a fish-basket. Each was to have the fruits of it every other morning. The time for paying the money was rapidly approaching. A failure involved the honor of religion. The good man got nothing considerable from his basket, the fish not descending the river. At length he spent most of a day in prayer. Towards evening it grew cool. He continued in prayer. He slept none all night. After midnight he

[245]

THE POWER OF PRAYER

went to the river, and found the fish coming down. He prayed on, and at daylight he had a canoe well filled with fishes. He descended the river rapidly, found ready market for his fishes in Pittsburg, paid all his debts and taxes, procured some needed comforts for his family, and returned home to give thanks to God. That fish-basket stood near the place where the first lock now is on the Youghiogheny River. Many of the descendants of that man still live. I have the story from their own lips.

God hears and answers the prayers of little children. In 1835, when my health threatened to fail, I travelled through New England and made many pleasant acquaintances. At the house of an eminent Christian, I found a little boy supporting himself by making himself useful in any way he could in the intervals of school. I became interested in him. I got his confidence. He told me his plans and his practice. He was aiming at a professional education. He did not profess to have a new heart; but he prayed often every day, and said he knew God would hear and help him. I encouraged him to persevere in prayer. I suppose he did. For years I lost sight of him, till I learned that my little friend was an ornament to the bar in —— in the north-west.

'What do you do without a mother to tell all your troubles to?' said a child who had a mother to one whose mother was dead.

'Mother told me whom to go to before she died,' answered the little orphan. 'I go to the Lord Jesus; he was mother's friend, and he is mine.'

The other replied: 'Jesus Christ is up in the sky; he is away off, and has a great many things to attend to in heaven. It is not likely he can stop to mind you.'

'I do not know about that,' said the orphan; 'all I know is, *he says he will, and that is enough for me.*'

The orphan was right. God's ear is as open to babes and sucklings as it is to divines and senators.

The New York Revival of 1858

Oh, that all the children were told as much, and believed it.

In May, 1858, I attended the Fulton street prayer-meeting in New York. A plain man, who had but recently indulged a hope in Christ, arose and told of the mercy of God in his own salvation. He said he had formerly asked the prayers of the meeting for his pious but insane mother, that she might be restored to reason, so as to be filled with joy and receive his thanks for her fidelity to him in the days of his wickedness. Said he: 'That prayer is already so far answered that she has ceased to rave, and is rapidly improving. I shall soon see my mother well.' His statement reminds me of a case that occurred in the seventeenth century. 'Richard Cook, a pious man, during Mr Baxter's residence at Kidderminster, went to live in the next house to him. After some time he was seized with melancholy, which ended in madness. The most skillful help was obtained, but all in vain. While he was in this state, some pious persons wished to meet, to fast and pray in behalf of the sufferer; but Mr Baxter, in this instance, dissuaded them from it, as he apprehended the case to be hopeless, and thought they would expose prayer to contempt in the eyes of worldly persons, when they saw it unsuccessful. When ten or a dozen years of affliction had passed over Richard Cook, some of the pious men referred to would no longer be dissuaded, but fasted and prayed at his house. They continued this practice once a fortnight for several months; at length the sufferer began to amend, his health and reason returned, and', adds Mr Baxter, 'he is now as well almost as he ever was, and so hath continued for a considerable time.' Have you not read in the Gospels? *'This kind goeth not out but by prayer and fasting.'* And, *'This kind can come forth by nothing, but by prayer and fasting.'* – Matt. 17: 21; Mark 9: 29. What mean these Scriptures?

[247]

THE POWER OF PRAYER

As we need God's Spirit in all things, so he is freely given in answer to prayer, to guide our minds in right channels. Rev Dr Wm Nevins, of Baltimore, prayed for years that he might be able to write one good tract. In his last days he did not doubt that God had answered his prayer, nor can any good man, who has read his tracts and books, doubt that God heard his cry. He asked for little and he got much.

God can answer prayer for anything agreeable to his will. John Welsh, the son-in-law of John Knox, and ancestor of Rev James Paine, of Somerville, Tenn., and of Rev H. H. Paine, of Holly Springs, Miss., used to say: 'I wonder how a Christian could lie in a bed all night, and not rise to pray.' This wonderful man, when banished for the word of God, mastered the French language in fourteen weeks, that he was able to preach in it so acceptably that several churches in France called him. If we did study less like atheists and more like Christians, we should make more progress. Philip Henry made this entry on a day set apart for study: 'I forgot when I began, explicitly and expressly to crave help from God, and the chariot wheels drove *accordingly*. Lord, forgive my omission, and keep me in the way of duty.' It was once said to a useful minister: 'Sir, if you did not *plough* in your closet, you would not *reap* in your pulpit.' I know two men in one of the middle States, who say, that if they ever got aid from God in anything in answer to prayer, it was in their studies. Good old Thomas Boston, in his autobiography, tells us the secret of his success in study, when he spread out the Hebrew Bible and prayed to the Lord to have mercy on him, and to give him wakefulness, for he had lately lost much sleep. And long before him David had prayed: 'Teach me thy statutes;' 'Open thou mine eyes that I may behold wondrous things out of thy law.' The history of Solomon shows that it was chiefly a blessing on

The New York Revival of 1858

his studies that he sought when he prayed for wisdom. Let students pray.

The instances in which, in answer to prayer, God has sent remarkable deliverances to a people, are numerous and striking. In the days of Queen Elizabeth the terrible Spanish Armada was scattered or destroyed in answer to fervent prayers offered by the people of God in England. In 1746, the French armament of forty ships, prepared under the Duke d'Anville against the American colonies, was, in answer to prayer, totally ruined by a tempest. The leaders of the expedition were so overwhelmed at the suddenness and completeness of their disaster, that both of them committed suicide.

But God can save his beleaguered people without destroying their foes. LeClerc tells us that when, in 1672, the Dutch were expecting an attack from their enemies by sea, 'public prayers were ordered for deliverance. It came to pass that when their enemies waited only for the tide, in order to land, the tide was retarded, contrary to its usual course, for twelve hours, so that their enemies were obliged to defer the attempt to another opportunity, which they never found, because a storm arose afterwards, and drove them from the coast'.

How wonderfully God has answered prayer in behalf of good institutions founded to alleviate human misery. Of this we have a striking instance in the Orphan House, at Halle, founded by Francke. His school was unendowed. In 1696 he had not money to support the school a week longer. When the last morsel was about to be consumed, a thousand crowns were received from an unknown source. At other times of distress he received, in answer to special prayer, twenty, thirty, and fifty crowns. He says: 'Another time all our provision was spent, but in addressing myself to the Lord, I found myself deeply affected with the fourth petition of the Lord's prayer, "Give us this day

[249]

our daily bread," and my thoughts were fixed in a more especial manner on the words "this day", because on the very same day we had great occasion for it. While I was yet praying, a friend of mine came before my door in a coach, and brought the sum of four hundred crowns!'

And who needs prayer more than a preacher of the gospel? Chalmers was right: 'A minister has no ground to hope for fruits from his exertions until in himself he has no hope; but he has learned to put no faith in the point and energy of sentences, until he feels that a man may be mighty to compel attention, and mighty to regale the imagination, and mighty to silence the gainsayer, and yet not mighty to the pulling down of strongholds.' The apostles felt at liberty to devolve the distribution of the church's alms on others chosen for the purpose. But they did not dare to quit praying and preaching. Nay, they did not dare to do anything to diminish their attention to both these duties. They say, 'We will give ourselves continually to prayer, and to the ministry of the word.' – Acts 6: 4. A preacher without prayer is dreadfully weak as well as miserable.

I have known one preacher who would not exhort *sinners* to pray. His own child sustained an injury, and while the kind surgeon was doing his best to give effectual relief, the little boy was venting his wicked passions in oaths and curses. This made one of the neighbors say, 'When children are not encouraged to pray, they may be expected to blaspheme.'

It is very true, indeed, that we ought to exhort men to pray sincerely, and not hypocritically – in faith, and not in unbelief. But he who will not pray until, on good grounds, he is sure that he has all right affections and graces, will go to hell before his prayer begins. It is also true that the promises of the covenant of grace are to the believer, and that to any soul of man 'unbelief is the annihilation of the

The New York Revival of 1858

promises' of salvation. Yet who can show, by any truth of natural or revealed religion, that God will never hear the cry of distress of any of his creatures on earth? Are not his tender mercies over all his works here below? Does he not hear the cry of the young raven and the young lion? And is not a man better than many birds and beasts? Does the Lord not invite men everywhere to come to him? Nay, more: in Psalm 107 he has twice recorded his goodness in answering the prayers of two classes of men notorious for their wickedness. One is a class of men who, for their destructive vices and indulgences, are called *fools*. 'Fools, because of their transgression, and because of their iniquities, are afflicted. Their soul abhorreth all manner of meat, and they draw near unto the gates of death. Then they cry unto the Lord in their trouble, *and* he saveth them out of their distresses. He sent his word and healed them, and delivered *them* from their destructions. Oh that *men* would praise the Lord *for* his goodness, and *for* his wonderful works to the children of men!' (Verses 17–21.)

The other class is that of sailors, who, in nearly all ages, have been quite irreligious and profane. 'They that go down to the sea in ships, that do business in great waters; they see the works of the Lord, and his wonders in the deep. For he commandeth and raiseth the stormy wind, which lifteth up the waves thereof. They mount up to the heaven, they go down again to the depths: their soul is melted because of trouble. They reel to and fro, and stagger like a drunken man, and are at their wits' end. Then they cry unto the Lord in their trouble, and he bringeth them out of their distresses. He maketh the storm a calm, so that the waves thereof are still. Then are they glad because of the quiet; so he bringeth them unto their desired haven. Oh that *men* would praise the Lord *for* his goodness, and *for* his wonderful works to the children of men!' (Verses 23–31.)

THE POWER OF PRAYER

Surely if God will hear the cry of such men in their distresses, he may hear the cry of any other poor sinner on earth who needs his friendship. On the first of these passages Scott says: 'Loss of strength and of appetite are attended with excessive pain, and death presents itself before their affrighted minds; then the most profane will sometimes cry unto the Lord, and though their prayer is often the mere instinctive voice of distress, yet he frequently hears them, and unexpectedly restores their health and strength.'

That God can and will hear the earnest prayer of one in distress, I have been assured by many. I will state one case. More than a quarter of a century ago, I went by invitation to bury an old lady on a Virginia plantation. Riding in front of the hearse towards the family burying-ground, I came to a place where, in the stubble-field, it was necessary I should have a guide. Accordingly, the son-in-law of the deceased came forward, and rode with me. From him and others then and afterwards I learned that he had been born of respectable parents, had had a good business education, had been made a teller in a bank, had fallen into habits of intemperance, which greatly grieved all around him, that his ruin had proceeded so far, that when awaking on a Monday morning from a revelry of thirty-six hours, he has seen all nature look fair and gay, and it overwhelmed him with sadness; but that when a thunderstorm has arisen, he felt it so in unison with his horrible state of mind, that he said he could have shouted and clapped his hands, had he seen the earth wrapped in a sheet of fire. Nay more; he promised, in the most solemn way, that he would reform, but he broke his word. He even took a solemn oath that he would desist from his vice, but he forswore himself. He was now so far gone, that he had to drink a pint of brandy before he could write up his books in the bank. At length he attempted suicide, but his stomach was so diseased, that it rejected the laudanum. He now felt himself disgraced, resigned his office, went on a vessel to the West Indies, hoping to be cured of his drunkenness. But after some months, he returned home not a bit improved. All this time he had lived without prayer. At last, walking alone in the field, it occurred to him that there was a kind and strong God, who could hear the cry of distress, and help him. He then began to pray often every day just to be kept from the power of strong drink. He asked for nothing else. For nine months he thus prayed, and during all that time he yielded not once to his appetite. In this state I found him, and told him of the wickedness of his heart, of the need of more than mere sobriety, of the new birth, of the forgiveness of sins, of the blood of Christ and of the Holy Ghost. These truths surprised him. I urged him to pray on, and to include the blessings of the gospel in his prayers. He said he thought he would. I soon visited him, and spent many hours with him. He prayed against drunkenness more than ever, but he prayed for salvation also. In a few weeks, hope in Christ began to cheer him. He regained comfortable health, became a decided Christian, having very much of the temper of John Newton, got a good appointment as a bank officer, was a blessing to his family, for more than twelve years walked in great tenderness and much humility before God, and then died a blessed death. Hundreds of excellent people, among whom are three eminent ministers of the gospel, of whom one lives in New York, one in Philadelphia, and one in St Louis, will know that I have sketched the history of John Ennes, of the Brick House, near Petersburg, Va. Years ago I had the permission of his excellent widow, since passed into glory, to make any use of these facts, which I supposed could commend prayer and the grace of God to my fellow-men.

THE POWER OF PRAYER

Remarkable outpourings of God's Spirit have always been granted in answer to extraordinary prayer, and in no other way. The great revival in Ezra's time, when he and others preached from morning until midday, to a congregation of *fifty thousand* people before the water-gate of Jerusalem, was preceded by that extraordinary season of devotion mentioned in the 9th chapter of Daniel, where he says, 'I set my face unto the LORD my God, to seek by prayer and supplications, with fasting, and sackcloth, and ashes.' Before he had ceased, Gabriel flew swiftly and told him that God had granted his request 'at the beginning of his supplications'. By the same means that great revival was promoted, as we particularly learn from Ezra's own account of it.

The great revival on the day of Pentecost was preceded by a prayer-meeting of the whole church, lasting ten days – Acts 1: 4–14; Acts 2: 1. By the same and similar means that work was continued – Acts 2: 41–47. But these things are well known and need not now be dwelt upon.

One of the best preachers that Scotland ever produced was John Livingston, the ancestor of the family of Livingston in the United States. Since the days of the apostles, perhaps no man has ever preached with more power or more success, at least on one occasion. He says, 'Earnest faith and prayer, a single aime at the glory of God and good of people, a sanctified heart and carriage, shall availl much for right preaching. There is sometimes somewhat in preaching that cannot be ascribed either to the matter or expression, and cannot be described what it is, or from whence it cometh, but with a sweet violence it pierceth into the heart and affections, and comes immediately from the Lord. But if there be any way to attaine to such a thing, it is by a heavenly disposition of the speaker.' Again he said: 'I never preached ane sermon which I would be earnest to see again in wryte but two: the one was

The New York Revival of 1858

on ane Munday after *the communion at Shotts*, and the other on ane Munday after *the communion at Holywood*; and both these times I had spent the whole night before in conference and prayer with some Christians, without any more than ordinary preparation; otherwayes, my gift was rather suited to simple common people, than to learned and judicious auditors.' John Brown, of Haddington, says that five hundred souls were converted under that one sermon at Shotts.

The revival which began at Enfield, Mass., on the 8th of July, 1741, under a sermon preached by the elder President Edwards, on the words, *'Their feet shall slide in due time,'* has long been regarded as one of the most powerful on record. The impression of eternal things was awful and overwhelming. Many, knowing nothing of the history of that work, are surprised at so great effects from one sermon. But the fact is, that some Christians in that vicinity had become alarmed lest God should in anger pass by that church, and had spent the whole of the preceding night in prayer.

The great revival of 1857–8, in the United States, began and has been wonderfully continued in answer to prayer. In September, 1857, one of the western synods invited three others to meet it in a convention for prayer and conference respecting the revival of the work of God. That convention was held, and such a meeting had not been seen in the western country. It was followed by others of a like nature. Daily prayer-meetings in cities, towns and villages were established about the same time all over the land. Thousands and scores of thousands of business men drop all employment at a given hour and go to the house of prayer. So the work has gone on, and so it will go on, until these meetings are forsaken, or become formal, or vain, or self-righteous, or theatres of display.

That God has many a time put special honor on the

[255]

THE POWER OF PRAYER

prayers of even one of his servants for the reviving of his work, is proven by many incontestable facts. About twenty-five years ago a plain, aged elder, whose name is purposely omitted, lived in a retired congregation. His mind was overwhelmed with a sense of the value of souls, and of the dangers to which sinners were exposed. He prayed much. His church was without a pastor or any preaching for some time. When a servant of Christ visited him, he said, 'It makes me glad to see you. I have been praying much for your coming, and for a blessing on your labors. At times it has seemed as if it would kill me, if God's Spirit was not soon poured out upon us.' That very week a wonderful revival, which produced lasting good fruits, made its appearance. That minister still lives to tell that story and to preach Christ.

Another case is no less worthy of note. I personally knew the facts. They occurred when I was about twenty years of age. Capt James McClung married the sister of Dr Samuel Campbell, who married the eldest sister of Rev Dr Archibald Alexander. When I knew Capt McClung he lived on the South River, in Rockbridge County, Va., about three miles from Fairfield. He often told me that he believed that he had in early life been called to the ministry, and had sinned in not obeying the call. My impressions on this subject are the same as his. He was a man of remarkable gifts in prayer. He seemed to have also, to an unusual degree, the spirit of prayer. In 1822, God began to pour out his Spirit on some of the churches in Rockbridge County. But as yet the united churches of Timber-ridge and Fairfield seemed to be passed by. I was invited by some kind friends to visit Fairfield at its approaching communion season. I went down on Saturday, heard some good preaching, but saw no unusual seriousness, except in Capt McClung and one or two others. Saturday night there was a prayer-meeting with-

The New York Revival of 1858

out unusual evidences of God's presence. The meeting over, most retired to sleep. But Capt McClung started on foot for his home. Much of the road was through forest. When the sun rose he had not entered his own door. He had spent the whole night in prayer. The answer came that day. I never heard the same minister preach so before, and but once or twice since. I never saw the work of God advance so gloriously in one day in so small a congregation. The face of the preacher did shine 'as it had been the face of an angel', and his voice, usually not very powerful, might have been heard to a great distance, pronouncing in awful solemnity and with glorious distinctness and amazing penetration the urgent claims of God on men's souls for time and eternity. I believe the impression was general that the great blessings of that day descended in answer to the prayers that had been offered the previous night, especially the prayers of Capt James McClung, whose name must still be precious in all that favored portion of our country.

In Dr Elliott's life of the Rev Elisha Macurdy, there is frequent mention made of a man in western Pennsylvania, whose name was Philip Jackson, *the praying elder*. This man was rude and untutored, not even knowing how to read, until God's Spirit remarkably renewed his heart and gave him a thirst for divine knowledge. One of the last addresses father Macurdy ever made contained this statement: 'My dear brethren, I am not able to say much. There is a single point to which I shall confine myself. It is one with which the prosperity of the church is connected. It is the piety of the church. Forty years ago, the piety of the church was of a most vigilant and active kind. Those who were leaders made it a business on all favorable opportunities, to converse with those who were yet out of the church. This was not confined to the pastors, but was attended to particularly by the elders. I have in my mind

THE POWER OF PRAYER

one, who, when brought into the church, could not read the Bible; yet that man did more for the cause of Christ than many ministers. He lay, I think, at the foundation of the great revival which took place forty years ago. He addressed himself to sinners on all occasions. He was a wrestling Jacob, who poured out his soul to God. A hundred times have I knelt with him in a solitary thicket, and implored God to pour out his Spirit upon the whole church. My meaning, then, is, that elders and others should do as this man did, if they would have God to pour out his Spirit. BRETHREN, WAKE UP! Talk to sinners kindly, affectionately, frequently, and God will pour out his Spirit. I have no doubt but God is ready to pour out his Spirit, if we will do our duty.' One man may be a blessing to a whole commonwealth. One Philip Jackson in every county would fill the land with joy.

'On their way to Buffalo, to attend a meeting, Mr Macurdy and Philip Jackson, a ruling elder in the church of Cross Roads, became acquainted. Happening to fall in together, they proceeded in company, conversing familiarly on the subject of religion. They were men of like spirit, and had drunk at the same fountain. Their intercourse soon became free and unrestrained. Philip had a son who was wild and irreligious, for whose salvation he was deeply concerned. He made known the particulars of his case to Mr Macurdy, and desired him to turn aside with him into the woods, that they might unite in prayer for his conversion. His request was complied with, and in a grove near the road, with the aged elder kneeling at his side, Mr Macurdy poured out his soul to God on behalf of this ungodly youth. Not long after this, young Jackson became seriously impressed, and hopefully converted. Philip ever afterwards connected this happy result with Mr Macurdy's prayer in the woods, and on this account was very strongly attached to him.' The time referred to

The New York Revival of 1858

was that of the great revivals about the beginning of this century.

A living useful pastor relates the following: 'A Christian mother in my congregation, whose husband was a dissipated man, had a son in a military academy in the East. He was wayward, and seemed bent upon quitting it to seek his fortune at sea. The mother prayed earnestly for the boy, that he might be controlled by God for his salvation. One night she wrestled till day-dawn for her son, not having heard recently from him, and fearing the worst. As it afterwards proved, he had the day previous quit the school, and engaged himself with a shipmaster in New York for a voyage, to set sail the next day. But that night he could not sleep. He was disturbed, and knew not why. He felt an indescribable drawing towards his home. He could not get over it. He must get home. He could not help it, and so he went early the next morning to the shipmaster, and broke off his engagement, and started home. He arrived there greatly to his poor mother's surprise, and he found the whole community engaged in the daily prayer-meetings. But he hated the very mention of them. A few days passed by, he meanwhile absenting himself from these services. At length he came knocking at the door of the pastor, asking, with tears, What must I do to be saved? The pastor directed him to Christ. That night he arose at midnight sleepless, and knocked at his father's chamber door, begging him to pray for him. The father grew angry at his importunity, began to threaten him, if he did not cease, and told his mother if she did not take him away or silence him, he would lay violent hands upon him. But he could not desist from his earnest inquiries for salvation until he found Christ. And as the facts all came to light, it proved that the very night that mother was wrestling till day-dawn in her closet, 500 miles away from her son, that son was kept sleepless and

THE POWER OF PRAYER

troubled on his bed, so that he must break his rash engagement to go to sea, and must seek the face of his injured mother, and then the face of his injured God.'

A prominent pastor recently related, at a prayer-meeting of the Synod of Pittsburg, the following:

'At the time of my ordinaton and installation, and just after the exercises were concluded, one of the elders of the church over which I was installed pastor, came up to me, took me earnestly by the hand, and said: "Do you remember a few years ago, you were stopping for the night in the town of ——, and lodged at the hotel? You came into the room and retired, when an old man, lying in an adjacent bed, remarked to you, that he observed you got into bed without offering prayer, and added a few words of address to you on the subject. I am that old man. I turned my face around from you and prayed earnestly to God that he might convert you to himself, and make you a minister of Christ. *And* here," said he, "*God has heard my prayer, and I take you by the hand to-day as my pastor.*"'

IT IS GOD'S MEMORIAL THAT IN EVERY GENERATION HE HEARETH PRAYER.

Index of Names and Subjects

Academy of Music
  –preaching meetings, 202
Adams, Dr William, New School Presbyterian Church, 238
Alexander, James W. (1804–59), 7
  –*Pray for the Spirit*, 209–13
  –*The Revival and its Lessons*, 208–9
American Temperance Union, 75
Anville, N. de la R., Duke d', commander of French fleet sent to Louisburg 1746, 249
Association for Improving the Condition of the Poor, 179
Aunt Betsy
  –influence for good, 189–93
Austria, steamship
  –fire, 158–60

Baltimore, 203
  –prayer meeting, 25
Bangs, Dr Nathan, Methodist Episcopal Church, 238, 239
Baxter, Richard, 247
Beman, Dr Nathan S. S., First Prebyterian Church, Troy, 51
Betsy, Aunt *see* Aunt Betsy
Bingham, L. G., xii, 126

Black churches *see* Colored churches
Boston, Thomas, 248
Broadway prayer meeting, 22–3
Broome Street Church
  –prayer meeting, 10–11
Brown, John, of Haddington, 255
Buchanan, President James, 43–4
Burnett, Father, worker among seamen, 156
Burton's Old Theatre
  –used for prayer, 22
Businessmen, 16, 119–25
  see also Merchants

Castle Garden, New York, 179, 180
Catskill Mountains, 92–3
Chalmers, Thomas, 250
Children
  –prayers for, 215–227
  –work among, 109–18
Choctaw Indians
  –prayer meeting, 187
Christian union, 69; *see also* Prayer meetings – non-denominational character
Cincinnati
  –convention on revivals, 38
  –prayer meeting, 25

[261]

Collegiate Dutch Churches, 237
Colored churches, 43
Columbus, Ohio, 113–14
Conversion and Regeneration, 69
Cook, Richard, of Kidderminster, 247
Cooper Institute
 –preaching meetings, 202
Criminals
 –work among, 172–6
Cuyler, T. L., Market Street Church, 202, 239

De Witt, Dr, Collegiate Dutch Churches, 237, 239

Edwards, Jonathan, 26, 68, 255
Elizabeth I, of England, 198, 249
Elliott, Dr Charles, 257
England, movement of the Spirit, 238
Ennes, John, Petersburg, Va., 253
Enthusiasm, 31

Fasting, 37: *see also* Prayer
Feelings, 164
 –want of, 134–41
Financial Panic (1857), 1–2, 35
 see also Unemployment
Finney, Charles
 –*Lectures on Revivals*, 51
First Presbyterian Church
 –prayer meeting, 235
Francke, Auguste H., 249
Fulton Street prayer meeting, 8–10
 – anniversary of first meeting, 236–9
 –Book of Requests, 228–34

 –Choctaw Indians, 187
 –cause of mental distress, 145
 –early sermons, 13–15
 –influence of Aunt Betsy, 189–92
 –outline of typical meeting, 40–8
 –references to seamen, 156–60
 –suicide and murder averted, 239–43
 –other references, 21, 22, 35, 73
 see also North Dutch Church

Gardiner, Joseph H., Mariner's Church missionary, 149, 150
Gardner, Orville, pugilist, 174
Geneva, Ohio, 114–15
Geneva, Switzerland, 239
German boy
 –conviction of sin, 184–7
Gillette, Dr, Baptist Church, 235, 238
Globe Hotel
 –prayer meeting, 60, 78, 87, 88
Great Awakening
 –compared to 1858 revival, 26–7
Great Commission, pursued by all, 100–8
Greene Street Methodist Episcopal prayer meeting, 50–60 *passim*
Greenwich Street, Mission Hall, 179
Gustavus II, of Sweden
 –and prayer, 200
Guthrie, Dr Thomas, Edinburgh
 –tract, 205–8

Halle, orphan house, 249

[262]

Hell Corner, NH., 76–8
Henry IV, of France
 –and prayer, 200
Henry, Philip, 248
Holy Spirit
 –and prayer, 209–13
Home's Church, Brooklyn, 161

Jackson, Philip, the praying elder, 257–8
Jamaica, Long Island
 –prayer meeting, 215
Jaynes Hall, Philadelphia
 –prayer meeting, 24–5, 45
Jesus Christ
 –Divinity of, 68
John Street Methodist Church
 –prayer meeting, 21–2, 47
Jones, C. C., Mariner's Church, 148, 154
Justification by Faith, 68

Kalamazoo, Mich., 91
Knox, John, 248
Krebs, Dr, Old School Presbyterian Church, 237

Lamphier, Jeremiah Calvin, 6–7
 –journal, 7–8, 8–10, 13
Latimer, Hugh, 198
Laymen
 –role in meetings, 33–4
Leland, Dr, South Carolina, 237
Livingston, John, 254
Luther, Martin, 68, 193, 195, 197–8

McCarrell, Dr, Newburgh, N.Y., 237
McClung, Capt. James, Rockbridge County, Va., 256–7

McIlvaine, Bishop Charles P., 25
Macurdy, Elisha, 257, 258
Magdalen Asylum, 63
Mariner's Church, 148, 151, 154
Market Street Church, 202
Melanchthon, Philip, 193
Merchants, 22, 61–3, 190, 191
 see also Businessmen
Milton, John, 200
More, Hannah, 195
Murray, Dr James O., xii

Natchez, Miss, 187–8
Nevins, Dr William, Baltimore, 248
New York City Tract Society, 176
New York Pulpit, The, 201–2
Newton, John, 253
'North Carolina', U.S. Ship, 156, 157
North Dutch Church, 5, 7, 32, 40, 87, 89 *see also* Fulton Street prayer meeting

Old School Presbyterian Church, 237
Orchard, Rev., New York City Tract Society, 176
Orphan house, Halle, 249

Paine, H. H., Holly Springs, Mass., 248
Paine, Jas., Somerville, Tenn., 248
Peck, Dr J. T., Greene Street Methodist Episcopal Church, 50, 236
Pennsylvania, 82–3, 99
Pentecost, 68, 254

Philadelphia *see* Jaynes Hall
Phillips, Dr, First Presbyterian Church, New York, 235
Pittsburgh, 246
 –convention on revivals, 36–8
 –prayer meeting, 25
 –Synod, 260
Plumer, Dr W. S., xii, 244
Plymouth Church, Brooklyn
 –prayer meeting, 11, 162, 163, 164
Poorer classes
 –work among, 176–80
 see also Randall's Island
Port Society of New York, 148, 157
Prayer
 –and fasting, 37
 –and God's immutability, 196–7
 –and the Holy Spirit, 209–13
 –biblical examples, 69–70, 193–4, 195, 197, 245, 248, 254
 –efficacious, 244–60
 –for children, 215–27
 –for deliverance of American Colonies, 249
 –for deliverance of Holland, 249
 –of the saints, 219–23
 –perseverance, 205–8
Prayer meetings
 –non-denominational character, 19, 22, 32, 91, 235
 –reviewed, 235–43
 –Scandinavian seamen, 149
 –seamen's, 155, 156
 –venues, New York City, 23–4
 –venues, other cities, 25
Preaching, blessed, 201–2

Press reports
 –religious, 10, 20, 43, 82, 213
 –secular, 17–18, 142, 213
Profanity, conquered, 169

Randall's Island reformatory, 109
Reformed Dutch Church
 –denomination, 32, 68
 –Ninth Street, prayer meeting, 235
Revival (1857–8)
 –at sea, 36
 see also Prayer meetings – seamen's; Seamen – work among
 –compared to revivals of 1830 and 1832, 30
 –compared to the Great Awakening, 26–7
 –early marks, 11–12
 –in Pennsylvania, 82–3, 99
 –its extent, 236
Roman Catholics
 –testimonies, 142–7, 151, 182
Ryle, J. C.
 –*Call to Prayer*, 203–5

'Sabine', U.S. Ship, 156
St Louis, Mo., 42–3
'Savannah', U.S. Ship, 156, 160
Sea Captains, 161–70
Seamen
 –work among, 148–71
 see also Revival – at sea
Ships, 156, 157, 158–60
Sing Sing prison, 192
Smith, Dr Asa D., New School Presbyterian Church, 238
Smuller, H. W., 215

Spanish Armada
 –and prayer, 249
Spring, Dr Gardiner, 239
Sunday Schools
 –visitation, 38–9
Synod
 –New York, 215
 –Pittsburgh, 260

Taylor, Jeremy, 197
Temperance pledge, 75, 87, 102–3
Tennent, Gilbert and William, 27, 68
Testimonies
 –lawyer, 49–60, 102
 –man of pleasure, 126–33
 –merchant, 61–3
 –Roman Catholic, 142–7, 151, 182
 –sailor, 65–7
Toledo, Ohio, 114
Tracts
 –distribution, 17, 38, 96, 151, 176–80, 203–14, 248
Tyng, Dudley A., 25

Underprivileged *see* Poorer classes
Unemployment, 142
 see also Financial Panic (1857)
Unity *see* Christian union

Van Pelt, Dr, Reformed Dutch Church, 238
Van Zandt, Dr, Ninth Street Reformed Dutch Church, New York, 235
Vice
 –diminution, 174

'Wabash', U.S. Ship, 156, 157
Washington Market, New York City, 182
Welsh, John, son-in-law to John Knox, 248
Wesley, John, 26
Whitefield, George, 26, 68